DISSOLUTE
CHARACTERS

DISSOLUTE CHARACTERS

Irish literary history through Balzac, Sheridan Le Fanu, Yeats and Bowen

W. J. Mc Cormack

Manchester University Press

Manchester and New York

distributed exclusively in the USA and Canada by St. Martin's Press

Copyright © W. J. Mc Cormack 1993

Published by Manchester University Press
Oxford Road, Manchester M13 9PL, UK
and Room 400, 175 Fifth Avenue, New York, NY 10010, USA

Distributed exclusively in the USA and Canada
by St. Martin's Press, Inc., 175 Fifth Avenue, New York, NY 10010, USA

British Library Cataloguing-in-Publication Data
A catalogue record for this book is available from the British Library

Library of Congress Cataloging-in-Publication Data
McCormack, W. J.
    Dissolute characters : Irish literary history through Balzac, Sheridan Le
Fanu, Yeats, and Bowen / W. J. McCormack
      p.   c.m.
    Includes index.
    ISBN 0-7190-3962-2
    1. English literature—Irish authors—History and criticism. 2. Le Fanu,
Joseph Sheridan, 1814-1873—Criticism and interpretation. 3 Yeats, W. B.
(William Butler), 1865-1939—Criticism and interpretation 4. Bowen,
Elizabeth, 1899-1973—Criticism and interpretation 5. Balzac, Honoré de,
1799-1850—Influence. 6 Characters and characteristics in literature. 7. Gothic
revival (Literature)—Ireland. 8 Ireland in literature.
    I. Title.
    PR8711.M335   1993
    820.9'9415—dc20   92-37200

ISBN 0 7190 3962 2 *hardback*

Set in Dante and Tiffany Demi
by Koinonia Ltd, Manchester
Printed in Great Britain
by Biddles Limited, Guildford and Kings's Lynn

Contents

Contents

Foreword

The twentieth century has seen an exponential growth in the production and consumption of fiction and (simultaneously) a great diversity of assaults upon a central feature of traditional fiction – character. This paradox, or even conflict, has been thought symptomatic of a modern condition. But suspicion, amounting at times to hostility and even outright rejection, of fictional character, was manifest in the work of novelists and short-story writers (consider D. H. Lawrence and James Joyce) long before the more abstract pronouncements of Roland Barthes. Behind the literary and critical exchanges lay the broader inquiries of psychologists, sociologists and political theorists whose sole common ground perhaps was their debunking of the supposedly autonomous human subject.

The history of literature has inevitably come under revisionist and deconstructive scrutiny in the light of these developments. Radical discontinuities and strategic contradictions have been discovered where earlier readers had presumed to identify Moll Flanders or Lemuel Gulliver. Yet the extensive and detailed examination of a body of fiction openly parading such features is rarely attempted, except of course where recent fiction indebted to such theories obliges with a practical conformity to them.

One area or period where the extra-literary dimensions of such an examination become immediately evident is Victorian Ireland, the forcing ground not only of Joyce (1882–1941) but also of Oscar Wilde (1854–1900), G. B. Shaw (1856–1950), W. B. Yeats (1865–1939), and other notable contributors to Anglophone modernism. (To these is added here that last-minute Irish Victorian, Elizabeth Bowen (1899–1973), for whom the 'happy autumn fields' of mid-nineteenth-century Ireland provided an agonising contrast to the anaestheticised decay of wartime and post-war England.) The period – and even the term – is still a newcomer in intellectual history, though I have previously explored it in a biography (*Sheridan Le Fanu and Victorian Ireland*, Oxford, 1980, revised edition Dublin, 1991) to which the present work acts as a critical and reflective counterpart.

Rejection of social norms had characterised much English romantic thinking about the relationships linking politics to cultural production. Such rebellion might be read in the broader context of the late-eighteenth-century revolutions, successful in America and France, manifestly unsuccessful in Ireland. But the mid-nineteenth-century emphasis on the artist as criminal and criminal as artist (familiar to readers of French literature) is a quite different matter, one which does not fully emerge in Anglophone literature before Wilde. It is, however, intriguingly implicit throughout the extensive and discontinuous career of a less well known Irish writer. As Sheridan Le Fanu (1814–73) set most of his stories and novels in England (and as his names declared both Gaelic and French Huguenot orgins), even his identity as English novelist becomes questionable.

For these reasons, Le Fanu plays a large part in the argument which follows. However, his uncertain place in what is uncertainly called an 'Irish gothic tradition' unexpectedly implicates the fiction of Honoré de Balzac and the quasi-mysticism of Emanuel Swedenborg. The mediated presence of all three of these (Le Fanu included) in the work of Yeats brings to a head political questions of the utmost gravity, the most notable being Yeats's engagement with fascism. In the 1930s and after, the ethical, political and cultural crisis which fascism posed for Yeats and many of his contemporaries was interrogated by Elizabeth Bowen. A practitioner of the ghost story and an admirer of Le Fanu's nervous literary style, Bowen produced during and immediately after the Second World War a body of fiction which serves to give coherence and depth to seemingly minor and finicking issues – Le Fanu's interest in Dutch painting, his use of historically evocative proper names.

It is true that the visual arts pervade nineteenth-century fiction in English. Landscape is everywhere, and much attention is devoted to the 'portrayal' of character. Yet Le Fanu's case is both curious and instructive. In his treatment of painting he might be placed equidistant from Charles Lever and George Eliot. In *The Martins of*

Foreword

Cro' Martin (1856), the popular Irish novelist includes a historico-satirical painter who in turn might be placed midway between James Barry and Gully Jimson. In *Adam Bede* (1859), Eliot breaks off her realistic narrative to discourse lightly on the merits of Dutch art. Le Fanu is neither as heavy-handed as Lever nor as well-bred as Eliot. It is notable that she approves one little-known artist, Gerard Dou, whom Le Fanu had treated in an early story. And it should be said on Le Fanu's part that he seems to have grasped instinctively something of the moral duplicity, the coded ambiguity and vestigial emblemism which latter-day art historians have rediscovered in *genre* painting.

The structure of the present essay might be represented by a straight line with two cross bars – a croix de Lorraine – in which the main trajectory attends to questions of fictional character and representation, while the two other lines follow out implications in relation to the invocation of visual imagery and to strategies of character-naming. This latter aspect implicates a good deal of Irish history, dissolved and distributed through fragmentary allusion and subversions of nominal authority. Naturally, any such structure has a crucial point of intersection, and this I would identify as the political domain, with specific reference to Yeats's authoritarianism.

It is a central, if discretely placed, thesis that nineteenth-century Ireland went through a series of traumatic processes of modernisation which have been denied and repressed in their aftermath. In Bowen's work a political transformation, by which the land of her birth changes from metropolitan colony to semi-independent nation-state, is acutely apprehended in the operations of fictional character. Notions of character, generally based on assumptions of male bourgeois rectitude and power, inevitably implicate notions of participatory citizenship which in turn raise questions about the ideological nature of the state and the operations of civil society.

The title of the present essay can be read literally in relation to the murderers, forgers, seducers, traitors and other ne'er-do-wells of Le Fanu and Bowen's plots. But it should also be taken to characterise the underlying theme – of character itself being a process of dissolving, of being disjointed or disunited. And this at both the psychic and political levels.

I am conscious of proceeding much of the time without overt reference to the work of other critics and historians concerned with the authors, texts and themes which I examine. To a great extent, this feature of the book derives from my wish to keep close to the texts and, when theorising (or vaporising), to keep within my own intellectual experience. I readily agree that all thought about literature – or anything else – implicates theoretical questions, and personally acknowledge debts to the school of critical theory.

Frankfurt, however, is now distanced from us, not least by the unspeakable horrors of which it tried prophetically to speak. One must work from one's actual locus and not some universalised ideal professional vantage point. I have had stimulating and helpful recourse to some work by American-based thinkers, especially Fredric Jameson, but also Jerome McGann who (like Edward Said) combines theoretical acuity with massive learning of a more traditional kind. (If other names appear very infrequently, it is because I have become suspicious of Weetabix Theory, incredibly dense and regular in structure, but lighter than its box.) It follows, regretfully, I am less convinced than the participants that recent theoretical debates in and about Irish culture have maintained any degree of self-critical and dialectical awareness. Too often they seem occasions when comrades either engage in violent agreement with each other, or pour the milk of human unkindness over 'the other'.

In the lesser matter of references and 'the secondary literature', I also hope that I have not borrowed except where I have acknowledged a debt; beyond that I am reluctant to swell the body of notes with matter destined only for the citation indexes. It was intended that a list of names should follow here, acknowledging personal gratitude to many for the stimulation which their publications and conversations provided during a ten-year period when I dislocated myself from the academic world. But the list is too long, and I shall simply name Ciaran Brady in Dublin and Ferenc Takács in Budapest as two patient friends to whom I have talked at length when I should have listened more, and finally a third such, Seamus Deane, with whom it has been a valuable pleasure to dissent for nearly a quarter of the century.

More recently, I have benefited from the professional advice of Robert Towers, also Anita Roy, my editor in Manchester University Press, and the anonymous reader to whom she sent my original typescript. To these, to many unlisted friends and to my patient wife and son, a hearty word of thanks.

Lastly, may I record once more a sincere and warm debt of

Foreword

gratitude to William Le Fanu of Chelmsford, still answering queries after twenty years of my interrogating him, and also to his daughter Nicola whose music now adds further laurels to the name she bears?

PART ONE

On literary history

1

Cashiering
the gothic tradition

Irish literary history is thriving – if one were to judge by the number of literary histories published in recent years. Yet even the most sophisticated of these retains a doggedly chronological method, and declines to take up challenges posed by the diverse approaches evident in – say – the long-running American journal *New Literary History*. Irish literary history, it is assumed, poses few problems whether of method, definition, or material. It amounts to nothing more or less than the history of Irish literature over the centuries. To be sure, there are difficulties about a change of language (Gaelic to English), and about who is wholly Irish and who is acceptably Irish. But the task in hand is to simplify, even at the risk of refusing to clarify.[1]

Of course, a great deal of scholarship, research, critical inquiry and exposition has gone ahead side by side with these simplifying chronicles. As a consequence, the Jonathan Swift whom editors know is scarcely recognisable as the figure of similar name recurring as a patriot in the literary histories. (Perhaps, from this point forward, these should be characterised as chronicles, with the term 'history' etc. reserved for the kind of thing attempted here.) Problems of readership immediately disclose themselves, as the editors are branded academic specialists and the chroniclers continue to hear a response (though diminishing) from those sectors of the Irish public who cling to a familiar view of the past. The chroniclers inhabit a last ditch of cultural nationalism.

Literary history proper is unlikely to inherit the earth when these retreating veterans are finally dislodged. The military metaphor suggests a conflict, and guarantees no unambiguous victory for one view over another. Cultural nationalism, in certain quarters at least, has already sent out emissaries to parley (or rather *parler*, for French is becoming compulsory in the academy as Gaelic becomes extinct in the community) with post-modernism. There is an undeniable excitement generated by the recent operations of the Field Day Company and its directors – Seamus Deane, Brian Friel, Seamus Heaney and the others – but this may have obscured the irony of their apparent endorsement of a Terry Eagletonian quick-change ideological chat-show. What the two parties believe they have in common is an intermittent, shared distaste for radical modernism, for what they see as an expansive, even imperialist ambition in modernism.[2]

Quite distinct from these attitudes, there has grown up a small but significant body of work which has drawn its material from the accepted canon of Irish literature and its methodology from the historical sciences. No anthologies or illustrated manifestos have emerged from this quarter, though individual articles and books testify to its vigour over the years. The accepted canon has been quietly challenged and modified, even if the notion of a canon as such continues to hold sway. Some exercises in comparative criticism have been published but these have been restricted for the most part to the consideration of individual authors, even of individual poems. An Irish literary history which attempts comparative work at length is as yet inconceivable.[3]

The present essay, however, aims at something modest along these lines. By focusing mainly on Sheridan Le Fanu it deals with a Victorian novelist of Irish birth and French background who utilised English, Welsh and Irish settings in his fiction. Le Fanu has been persistently aligned with a so-called Irish gothic tradition, inaugurated by Charles Robert Maturin (another Dublin Huguenot) and rendered notorious by Bram Stoker whose *Dracula* successfully transferred to the twentieth century and the snuff movie. Quite enough has been written about gothicism as such; the objective now is to observe the historical forces inscribed in Le Fanu's distinctive non-affiliation to this doubtful tradition.[4]

The first stage of the exercise involves a French response to Maturin's *Melmoth the Wanderer* (1820), followed by discussion of a triangular pattern linking Balzac, Le Fanu and Yeats. The stages which follow, dealt with in Chapters 4 to 10, may give the appearance of concentrating their attention within the texts of Le Fanu's novels and tales, with only a due regard for the historical setting of *The House by the Church-yard* (1861). The next three chapters (11 to 13) should make it clear that the earlier concentration on textual

[3]

minutiae can bear fruit in terms of a renewed awareness of historical consciousness in Le Fanu's most prolific period – the 1860s. This is not so much a matter of the novelist's individual consciousness, as of the historical quality of Irish culture in those years. Yeats is naturally to the fore in this argument, but in the final three chapters (15 to 17) a detailed examination of Elizabeth Bowen's *The Heat of the Day* (1948) serves to reopen questions of fixity of character, national identity and historical reflexivity.

Melmoth the Wanderer is a highly complex network of interlocking tales which take the reader from seventeenth-century London madhouses to islands in the Indian Ocean. The opening sentence however is remarkably plain in its presentation of a few circumstances: 'In the autumn of 1816, John Melmoth, a student in Trinity College, Dublin, quitted it to attend a dying uncle on whom his hopes for independence chiefly rested.'[5] This seems straightforward enough, especially as the dying uncle's residence lay in the neighbouring county of Wicklow, perhaps no more than fifteen or twenty miles away. But there are wrinkles in the plain texture even within this one sentence. In the phrase 'a student in Trinity College', the college is treated as an institution rather than as a place. Thus to quit the college would imply taking oneself off the books, resigning, or whatever the idiom of the day was. We learn soon enough, however, that John Melmoth has not done any such thing; he has merely departed from the college premises in order to travel to Wicklow. On his uncle's death he is urged to return immediately to his studies. However he delays, ostensibly to pay his respects but in fact to have the opportunity to read an old and discoloured manuscript which has come into his possession in the old man's house. Through this document, the series of interlocking tales gradually unfolds, and by its intervention the question of young Melmoth's return to Trinity is totally obscured and forgotten.

Place, in the opening sentence, has been imperfectly stabilised in the phrase 'a student in Trinity College'. The scenes in Bedlam, in the Spain of Inquisition days, in Mortimer Castle in Shropshire, in the Indian Ocean are of course mediated initially through the gappy pages of the manuscript which the young man has begun to read in a ruined County Wicklow mansion. But the part-dissolving of fixity of *place* in the phrase quoted, so that it merges to a degree with the less tangible *institution*, has contributed to the fluidity with which locations are treated in the narrative. (Melmoth can be a student in Trinity while he is in Wicklow.) In turn, fixity in time is slackened to a degree also, at least in so far as the narrative is free to sift and shift through the documentary accounts of earlier incidents. Yet one iron chronology remains in place: the original John Melmoth is condemned to walk the earth century after century in search of someone sufficiently desperate to take over the terms of a Satanic pact which he contracted in the era of Cromwell and Charles I. As of autumn 1816 he has failed to find any wretch willing to escape even the Inquisition at the price of his immortal soul.

The locations in which the Wanderer is discovered are forms of exotic distance, of course, but the twelfth chapter of the third volume suddenly alters the perspective to concentrate on very closely focused objects within the persepctive of a very large and dispersed body of observers. It does so by means of several footnotes, which drastically shift attention from the Spanish Inquisition to Irish politics of the 1790s and the years immediately following. The first of these relates to a fire in a house on St Stephen's Green, Dublin, in which sixteen people are alleged to have been burnt alive – 'the writer of this heard the screams of sufferers whom it was impossible to save, for an hour and a half.'[6] As the incident is said to have occurred in 1816, it is very immediate to the date cited in the opening paragraph of the novel – some several hundred pages back. The second relevant footnote relates the circumstances of the death of the Reverend Dr William Hamilton (1755–97) who was killed in County Donegal by agrarian assassins. In the fictional scene a crowd had torn apart one unfortunate man whose body could not be identified when troops eventually came to his rescue. 'The officer who headed the troop dashed his horse's hoofs into a bloody formless mass, and demanded, "Where was the victim?" He was answered "Beneath your horse's feet;" and they departed.' The footnote to this (keyed nicely to the word 'feet') tells us punctiliously that 'this circumstance occurred in Ireland 1797, after the murder of the unfortunate Dr Hamilton. The officer was answered, on inquiring what was that heap of mud at his horse's feet, – "the man you came for."'[7]

But it is the third note which deserves quotation in full:

In the year 1803, when Emmett's insurrection broke out in Dublin – (*the fact* from which this account is drawn was related to me by an eye witness) – Lord Kilwarden, in passing through Thomas Street, was dragged from his carriage, and murdered in the most horrid manner. Pike after pike was thrust through his body, till at last he was *nailed to a door*, and called out to his murderers to 'put him out of his pain.' At this moment, a shoemaker, who lodged in the garret of an opposite house, was drawn to the window by the horrible cries he heard. He stood at the window, gasping with horror, his wife attempting vainly to drag him away. He saw the last blow struck – he heard the last groan uttered, as the sufferer cried, 'put me out of pain,' while sixty pikes were thrusting at him. The man stood at his window as if nailed to it; and when dragged from it, became – *an idiot for life.*[8]

Here, immediacy of both time and place has replaced the exotic and antique. Moreover, the psychological trait which Maturin is seeking to examine is itself founded on a kind of permanent immediacy – the shoemaker remains transfixed or (as the Freudians might say) fixated by the brief scene he once witnessed. Maturin renders this trait in the very stuff of his writing – Lord Kilwarden is dragged from a carriage and nailed (as it were) to a door; the watching shoemaker is twice dragged at, and he 'stood at the window as if nailed to it'. These precise verbal repetitions enact a kind of identification between victim and witness which is at the heart of Maturin's novel. Ideally, it aims at a virtual abolition of the reader.

This aesthetic of terror is given a kind of plausibility in a preface where Maturin quotes (without blushing) a passage from his own *Sermons* published the previous year:

At this moment is there one of us present, however we may have departed from the Lord, disobeyed his will, and disregarded his word – is there one of us who would, at this moment, accept all that man could bestow, or earth afford, to resign the hope of his salvation? – No, there is not one – not such a fool on earth, were the enemy of mankind to traverse it with the offer![9]

Two tightly engaged and fiercely conflicting timetables are active here. The spiritual consequences of resigning one's salvation are spiked on the psychological immediacy – repeated – of 'this moment'. Eternity and the instantaneous are brought into melodramatic collision, with the effect of obscuring any less absolute concept of time. Narrative in *Melmoth the Wanderer* constants seeks to manipulate and neutralise history, with the footnotes instanced above giving testimony to the immense strain which this endeavour involves.

One could readily find less theologically coloured epigraphs for Maturin's romance. In the second edition of the *Essay on the Sublime and Beautiful*, Edmund Burke drew into his argument the recent experiences of Robert Francis Damiens who was horribly tortured and executed for an attempt on the life of Louis XV:

> I am in great doubt, whether any man could be found who would earn a life of the most perfect satisfaction, at the price of ending it in the torments, which justice inflicted in a few hours on the late unfortunate regicide in France ... there are very few pains, however exquisite, which are not preferred to death; nay, what generally makes pain, if I may say so, more painful, is, that it is considered as an emissary of this king of terrors.[10]

Where Burke considers the perfect mortal life unacceptable to anyone at the price of a relatively brief but measurable period of dreadful torment, Maturin exponentially inflates the terms of the comparison to render torment eternal and life momentary. Between the young aesthetician and the ageing novelist there intervened of course the great Revolution in France. Burke, who had written on the occasion quoted that 'whatever is ... analogous to terror ... is a source of the *sublime*', came to denounce terrorism (in the Jacobins) as an offence virtually against God. Regicide, rather loosely charged against Damiens in 1757, became actual in the death of Louis XVI in 1793.[11] In Burke's political writing there is a constant reference to history wherever he invokes precedent, tradition, the venerable past. But there is also a marked endorsement in the late writings of a trans-historical world existing beyond time and embodying eternal verities. Burke may have been a non-enthusiastic Christian, he may even have acknowledged that faith in its conventional formulations was no longer possible, but in the revolutionary age he accepted a providential interpretation of reality which was ultimately a metaphysics.

We have reached an intermediary point in our initial exercise of liberating Le Fanu from the claims of a gothic tradition. Ironically, it has taken the form of tracing, in connection with his famous precursor, a debt to the aesthetics of the young Edmund Burke. This is not in itself new, though the connection has been less than fully acknowledged by students of Maturin. What is more significant is the shift in Burke, or rather the double valuation, whereby terror is first endorsed as an aesthetic category and then denounced as an instrument of revolutionary politics. Burke never recanted his earlier philosophical opinions, and the force of this lies neither in a meritorious consistency nor in an admirable refusal to engage in public confession. Burke's aesthetics and politics are co-temporary in literary history, they are not stages in a process of development within which early views are obliterated by later ones.

The conflict of traditional religious belief and revolutionary politics threw up some curious hybrid theories of which Balzac was a zealous student. Of these we might note two apparently contrasting instances – the *Fêtes de la raison* inaugurated in Nôtre-Dame cathedral in November 1793 and the doctrines of Emanuel Swedenborg (1688–1772). Of course Swedenborgianism predated the Revolution, but its appeal to William Blake, J. W. von Goethe and Balzac signals its renewed prominence in the ideological turmoil of the revolutionary decades. If the cult of reason sought to replace God with Rousseau, the engineer-mystic Swedenborg provided a comprehensive system according to which nature in all its proliferating and newly classified detail could be read as symbolic of spiritual values. In each case, a compact between an infinite and unchanging realm and the tangible here-and-now was attempted.

Honoré de Balzac (1799–1850) is celebrated as the supreme novelist of French society in the years of the consulate, the empire, the restoration and the July monarchy – in other words, of France from the year of his birth to 1830. No series of novels compares with Balzac's *Comédie humaine* in the sustained and vigorous analysis of a society. Individual psychology, legal system, financial manoeuvre, political nuance, metaphysical implication – all are equally subject to his mastery. Balzac's official yearnings for the *ancien régime* – in some interpretations at least – positively enhanced his understanding of the successive new dispensations in which money took the place of inherited status. Thus he became the anti-laureate *en prose* of French capitalism and bourgeois society. Yet for all his passionate engagement in the political ramifications of the individual character's behaviour, he maintained a steady and intelligent interest in science and astrology, art history, religion, mysticism and the occult. All of these preoccupations find a place in the tripartite *Comédie* of 'études de moeurs, études philosophiques, études analytiques'. Nothing better illustrates the syncretism of his imagination than the story he published in 1835 as a sequel to Maturin's *Melmoth the Wanderer*.

Maturin was much translated into French in the 1820s, and Balzac was among his enthusiastic readers. But in *Melmoth reconcilé*, a pact with the devil is not so much an eternal covenant as it is a transferrable contract. Set at the time of the Bourbon restoration,

Cashiering the gothic tradition

Balzac's story is an essentially cynical one in which the devil's victim does the obvious thing and takes his problem to the banks and money markets of Paris. In turn a cashier-cum-forger and a bankrupt stockbroker demonstrate the negotiability of Satanic bonds as a means of remedying their financial difficulties. In turn a notary, a building contractor and an iron merchant take up and pass on the bond and, as a consequence, Melmoth dies an edifying death quite in tune with the religious hypocrisy of the day. 'We all hold shares in the great Speculation of Eternity.'[12]

Yet Balzac's tale is more than a *riposte* to the weighty involutions of Maturin's original novel. When Castinier, the forger, initially complains of the dreadful deal he has struck with Melmoth, he uses a contrast of secular and theological terms which underlines the terror of residual belief in an age of increasing secularism – 'He has taken my *self*, and given me his soul in exchange.'[13] Prior to this unequal deal, he may have been fooled by his mistress, Aquilina, but he quickly finds the stockbroker, Claparon, to whom he sells the Satanic compact. If house-painters and contractors subsequently take up the deal and demonstate how assets circulate, the benefit devolves to the reader. In Maturin's original novel, the endless pattern of a non-transferrable and yet intolerable bond threatened the formal existence of the reader in its amalgamation of the eternal and the instantaneous. But on the Paris bourse a specific fate (that of being bound for ultimate and eternal damnation) can be rolled from one participant on to another, with each playing a limited and formally contracted part in a series of exchanges which need never come to an end. By implication, the commercial law of limited liability has been applied to spiritual values, and that of prescription imposed even on the eternal punishment of Hell.

Balzac's *Comédie humaine* mimics this fundamental principle of finance, as the characters are transferred from novel to novel in demonstration of the pervasive and totalising power of capital in society. When Raphael de Valentin, in *Le Peau de chagrin* (1831), declares that 'an income of a hundred thousand francs ... gives us wonderful help for putting a stock-exchange valuation on moral principles', he is unconsciously synopsising *Melmoth reconcilé*.[14] The reappearance of Aquilina in the novel extends the serial relationship between the elements in the *Comédie*. A courtesan, whose sexuality is (so to speak) serialised, she derives her name from a character in Thomas Otway's *Venice Preserved* (1682), and thus exists in a further serial pattern of transferred identity. The historical basis of Balzac's work is identified by György Lukács when he describes *Illusions perdues* (1837–43) as an analysis of 'the transformation of literature into a commodity ... the capitalization of literature'.[15] In Vautrin (alias Jacques Collin, alias the abbé Carlos Herrera, alias Saint-Estève, etc.) Balzac perfects the serial character who, in keeping with the nature of his society, is successively a master criminal and a policeman. In Le Fanu's recurrent character, Richard Marston, there is perhaps a nervous impersonation of Vautrin.

Known in English as *The Wild Ass's Skin*, the 1831 novel engages uncannily with Le Fanu's story 'Borrhomeo the Astrologer' (1862): both revolve round the infernal powers of a magical piece of skin which endows its possessor wonderfully – but at a price. Most remarkable of the several resemblances between the two fictions, however, is the emphasis in each on *possession* of the skin, possession in the formal sense of a regular, contracted acquisition of the object. (This is no genie's lamp to be rubbed by anyone chancing to pick it up.) Raphael acquires the fatal skin in an old curiosity shop, for which Balzac provides a veritable catalogue in which the names of artists are prominent – among them the Dutch *genre* painter Gerard Dou, who features in Le Fanu also. The dealer refers to 'a mysterious conformity between the destiny and the wishes' of the skin's possessor.[16] The anonymous so-called editor of Le Fanu's anonymous 'Borrhomeo' tells how portraits induced on the magical skin 'establish a sympathy between the originals and their possessor which secures discipline and silence'.[17]

Considered in relation to Irish literary history, then, Balzac can also be seen as an intervention. The conventional view that Maturin is succeeded by Le Fanu and Le Fanu and by Stoker has been aggrandised to the status of a veritable tradition. Yet twenty-five years elapse between the publication of *Melmoth* and that of Le Fanu's first novel, *The Cock and Anchor* (1845), which is in any case closer to Walter Scott than to the gothic masters. A further nineteen years elapse before the appearance of *Uncle Silas* (1864), the novel of Le Fanu's most frequently cited as exemplifying the Irish gothic tradition in its mid-Victorian phase. *Melmoth reconcilé* (1835), on the other hand, is published during the years when Le Fanu was composing his early anonymous stories. Le Fanu's relation to his distinguished French contemporary raises far more engaging problems than those of a merely convenient tradition of Irish gothicism.

Cashiering the gothic tradition

Notes

1 These chronicles notably include Roger Mc Hugh and Maurice Harmon *Short History of Anglo-Irish Literature from its Origins to the Present Day* Dublin: Wolfhound Press, 1982. A. Norman Jeffares *Anglo-Irish Literature* London: Macmillan, 1982. Alan Warner *A Guide to Anglo-Irish Literature* Dublin: Gill and Macmillan, 1981. In a different category one can place Seamus Deane's more reflective *A Short History of Irish Literature* London: Hutchinson, 1987.

2 See for example Thomas Docherty *After Theory: Postmodernism/Postmarxism* London: Routledge, 1990. However, a review by David Brett in *Circa* no. 49 (Jan./Feb. 1990) of Steven Connor's *Post-Modern Culture* rightly brings out the consumerist/imperialist nature of post-modernism itself.

3 I have in mind here pioneering work by a number of people whose training or professional practice has been based on the historical sciences – Louis Cullen, Liam de Paor, Oliver MacDonagh. To these should be added the name of Terence Brown, a professor of English and author of the influential *Ireland, a Social and Cultural History 1922–1985* London: Fontana: 1985.

4 Introducing a section of *The Field Day Anthology of Irish Writing* (ed. Seamus Deane. London: Faber 1991), I have discussed at greater length the difficulties involved in this notion of an Irish gothic tradition – see vol. 2 pp. 831–949. Differences of opinion between myself and Field Day on this and other issues should not obscure the great debt which we all owe to the anthology and its satellite projects.

5 Charles Robert Maturin *Melmoth the Wanderer* (ed. Douglas Grant) London: Oxford University Press, 1968 p. [7].

6 Ibid. p. 251n.

7 Ibid. p. 256n.

8 Ibid. p. 257n.

9 Ibid. p. [5].

10 Edmund Burke *A Philosophical Enquiry into the Origin of our Ideas of the Sublime and Beautiful* (ed. James T. Boulton) Oxford: Blackwell, 1987 pp. 39–40. Damiens remained a point of literary reference; see Honoré de Balzac *The Wild Ass's Skin* (trans. H. J. Hunt) Harmondsworth: Penguin, 1977 pp. 89–90.

11 See W. J. Mc Cormack 'The Aesthetics of Terror' *Studies* (1990).

12 Honoré de Balzac *The Unknown Masterpiece and Other Stories* (trans. Ellen Marriage) London: Dent, 1896 p. 103.

13 Ibid. p. 87.

14 *The Wild Ass's Skin* p. 63.

15 György Lukács *Studies in European Realism* London: Merlin Press, 1972 pp. 51, 53.

16 *The Wild's Ass's Skin* p. 55.

17 Joseph Sheridan Le Fanu *Borrhomeo the Astrologer; a Monkish Tale* Edinburgh: Tragara Press, 1985 pp. 28–9. The story is discussed at length in Chapter 5.

2

Between
Balzac and Yeats

In *Reveries over Childhood & Youth* (1914) – the first volume of his autobiography – W. B. Yeats slyly informs us that he has read all of Balzac's novels. Twenty years later he is writing an essay on *Louis Lambert* (1832) in which he relates certain elements in that tale and in *Séraphita* (1834–5) to George Berkeley's idealist philosophy. In turn, he relates Berkeley to Emanuel Swedenborg. Little of the essay constitutes philosophical argument as such; it is an arrangement of names in suggestive close proximity to each other. Nevertheless, we find in Yeats's attitude to Balzac an anxiety to find a means of drawing Berkeley into some demonstrable tradition, a continuity of influences to which Yeats himself will provide the crowning glory.[1] Yet as he acknowledges, Balzac did not personally hold to any of these mystical or anti-materialist views.

The influence of the French novelist on the Irish poet has been recognised by critics from F. A. C. Wilson to Warwick Gould.[2] Wilson argued at length that the play *The Herne's Egg* systematically transcribes the essentials of *Séraphita* into an Irish dramatic scene, and he laid particular emphasis on certain Swedenborgian doctrines about sexuality as he traced them in the play. This is in line with Carl Benson's even earlier suggestion that Balzac was 'the first writer to suggest to Yeats that he might be able to retain the order of a world-view which grew out of his occult study ... a view which enabled him to encompass the experiences of "actual men and women"'.[3] This desire to retain the actual and the visionary is expressed by Yeats in a passage of his Louis Lambert essay where he likens the *Comédie humaine* to a *theatrum mundi*: 'Balzac leaves us when the book is closed amid the crowd that fills the boxes and the galleries of grand opera; even after hearing Séraphita amid her snows, we return to that crowd which is always right because there is so much history in its veins ... '⁴ The tribute is a little ornate, perhaps because it is also a shade reluctant. Nevertheless, even a reader of Balzac so hungry for confirmation of the transcendental as Yeats is locates the mystical marriage of Séraphita and God in a context explicable in concretely historical and social terms. Yeats's own historical context at that moment was deeply conditioned by his interest in three topics – in contemporary politics of the authoritarian kind, in the Irish eighteenth century, and in the Victorian Charles Stewart Parnell as a mediator between these two phases. Not only *The Herne's Egg* but also, among the plays, *The Words Upon the Window-pane* (1934), *Purgatory* (1938) and *The Death of Cuchulain* (1939) draw on the same occult sources which Yeats found in Balzac, notably Swedenborgian sources. As for the poetry, the Cuala volume *The King of the Great Clock Tower* (1934) performs a massive exercise of concentration and synthesis, drawing drama, poetry and commentary together around the memory of the long dead Parnell. In that volume, Parnell's presence strongly resembles that of the Swedenborgian spirit-in-judgement.

This is not yet an occasion on which to reconsider the vexed question of Yeats's politics in the 1930s. Nevertheless, the contribution of such diverse heroes as Balzac and Parnell underlines the importance of the nineteenth century both in Yeats's construction of an ideal eighteenth century and in his judgement on the filthy modern tide. In an earlier essay, 'Swedenborg, Mediums, and the Desolate Places' (1914), he gave oblique evidence of further links with a Victorian application or version of Swedenborg – 'stories to make one's hair stand up.'⁴ Here is no reference to the sublime ecstasies of Balzac's *études philosophiques*. The stories in question – I have argued elsewhere – are Le Fanu's collection of 1872, *In a Glass Darkly*, treated at length in Chapter 11 below. In that later stage of his career, when Yeats was preoccupied less with the spiritualism of folklore and more with the politics of the dead, Le Fanu's *Uncle Silas* featured in Yeats's early drafts of the play about Jonathan Swift's post-mortem existence.⁵ All three of these Irish texts – the collection of stories, the novel, the play – draw on the doctrines of Emanuel Swedenborg whose family and relatives feature in Balzac's amazing tale of Norwegian villagers and hermaphrodite angels, *Séraphita*.

A striking feature of the story is its insistence on a personalised timetable in which even the most sublime spiritual experiences can be synchronised to the seasons of the year and the dawning of a new century. The action occurs in the last spring of the eighteenth century in the village of Jarvis at the head of a frozen fjord. This is also the first spring (1800) in Balzac's life (born 1799) though the authorial parallel remains unstated. Close to the village, in the Swedish Castle, lives Séraphita, child of Baron Séraphitus, the beloved cousin of Emanuel Swedenborg. On the day in 1783 when the child was born, Swedenborg (died 1772) appeared to the parents in Jarvis and declared the unique spiritual status of the new-born infant who thereafter was never seen naked by any human eye. Nine years later, the parents both died at the same instant and without pain, leaving Séraphita in the care of a servant, Old David. Various superstitions grow up concerning this prodigy. The local pastor, a man both scholarly and sceptical, studies Jean Wier's *Treatise on Sorcery* to learn something of this 'fantastic creature'.

Jarvis itself maintains village life in the most ordinary provincial manner. The story opens with the pastor's daughter Minna accompanying Séraphita across dangerous ice at the head of the fjord. Minna is full of admiration – and more – for her companion. So too is the visitor Wilfrid, a much travelled man, who has also fallen under Séraphita's spell. To Minna, the inhabitant of the Castle is unquestionably male whereas, to Wilfrid, Séraphita is a beautiful woman. After much expounding of Swedenborgian doctrine, the story concludes with Séraphita's death (or union with God) and the decision of Minna and Wilfrid (now lovers) to seek God in some similar fashion. Throughout most of the text the linguistic registration of the seraph's sex is sustained in the use of both feminine and masculine genders, without any reference to the inconsistency of this. Only when Séraphita's account of the spiritual world has been accepted by the young mortals does the text comment on the dual gender previously employed: 'Wilfrid and Minna now understood some of the mysterious words of the being who on earth had appeared.to them under the form which was intelligible to each – Seraphitus to one, Seraphita to the other – seeing that here all was homogeneous.'[6]

Readers of the fiction are perhaps expected to react similarly: to those whose spiritual eye has not been opened to the truth of Swedenborg's further revelation of the divine, *Séraphita* is a village tale climaxing in an incident of local superstition in which two young people dedicate themselves to a mission imposed by a deluded stranger; to believers of course, the village itself is a mere parable or set of symbolic correspondences through which truth is broadcast to the relatively uninitiated. Yet there is a pattern which accommodates both readings. The geographical settings – fjord, mountain pass, castle – are all precipitous and readily interpreted as being 'on the edge of the abyss'. In due course Ibsen will ransack these metaphorical possibilities in the Norwegian landscape, but for the moment Balzac is content to exploit simply the vertical axis as a graph of spiritual activity. As the story moves into its explicitly allegorical vein, and leaves behind the empirical world, the stages of Minna and Wilfrid's transformation are precisely charted: 'The life on whose brink they stood, trembling and dazzled in a close embrace, as two children take refuge side by side to gaze at a conflagration – that Life gave no hold to the senses.'[7] And a moment later:

> They fell into the abyss, into the dust of the lower worlds, and suddenly saw the earth as it were a crypt, of which the prospect was made clear to them by the light they brought back in their souls, for it still wrapped them in a halo, and through it they still vaguely heard the vanishing harmonies of heaven.[8]

Séraphita then is a parable of the apocalypse. It is at once a revelation of the future which is yet to come, an inauguration of that future, and a decoding of those mysteries which have hidden the future from us. Prior to his initiation by Séraphita, Wilfrid had nurtured dreams of world conquest, of training a small race of northern people to dominate Europe 'shouting to these "Liberty!" to those "Plunder!" to some "Glory!" to others "Pleasure!"' because Europe 'is now at a period when she looks for the coming of the new Messiah'.[9] He has yet to learn that this Bonapartism of the soul is not what Séraphita has in mind for him, but the outburst serves to correlate the contemporary history of revolutionary France within a spiritual timetable. Events in the political domain can be translated into stages of a spiritual illumination which gradually draw the initiate away from the lower world and towards the higher. But with this ambiguous difference – that a *downward* plunge into the abyss may be the assigned route towards what is conventionally called 'the higher world'.

Before attempting to link this strange fable to Le Fanu's fiction, we may be advised to relate it to some more central figure in Irish literary history. The apocalypse, of course, preoccupied W. B. Yeats, not only as an aspect of his theosophical system but also as a metaphor in the political domain. 'The Second Coming' links Lenin and

Bethlehem in a pattern which retains something of Balzac's sardonic irony. Less emphatically, Yeats also employs a series of phrases deriving from apocalyptic thought to the condition of the dead John Synge. An unusually formal entry in the poet's *Journal* at the beginning of April 1909 works through some of the implications of this imagery. Headed 'Celebrations' it consists of four propositions:

i

He was one of those unmoving souls in whom there is a perpetual 'Last Day', a perpetual trumpeting and coming to judgment.

ii

He did not speak to men and women, asking judgment of them as lesser writers do; but, knowing himself a part of judgment, he was silent.

iii

We pity the living and not such dead as he. He has gone upward out of his ailing body into the heroical fountains. We are parched by time.

iv

He had no need of our sympathies and so kept hid from all but all the knowledge of his soon-coming death, and was cheerful to the very end, even joking a little some few hours before he died. It was though we and the things about us died away from him and not he from us.[10]

This image of Synge owes much to Yeats's preoccupation with the apocalypse, regarded both as a vision of one's personal extinction (or translation to another order of reality) and as a metaphor for drastic change in the outer world. In the *Journal*, Synge's death is associated with the triumph of logic and democracy – with the defeat, that is, of what Yeats regarded as civilisation. An epoch died in the man, and he died with a civility and courtesy now lost to all. In the very circumscribed conventions of Balzac's Norwegian village, the same interdependence of death and life is evidenced in Séraphita's influence over her servant David, but with – so to speak – the terms reversed. In Balzac the central figure acts upon the near-dead so as to render them in a state of constant resurrection:

> When David was alone you would have thought him a corpse; if Seraphita appeared, or spoke, or was spoken of, the dead rose from the grave and recovered motion and speech.
> Never were the dry bones that the breath of God shall revive in the valley of Jehoshaphat – never was that Apocalyptic parable more vividly

realised than in this Lazarus perennially called forth from the sepulchre by the voice of this young girl.[11]

David, then, is not just the conventional family retainer asleep amid his whiskers; as his name, with the allusion to the Book of Joel, suggests he is the old dispensation, the history of those kings and prophets in whose line Christ will come with a redeeming power. Joel, for all that he was a minor prophet, spoke of apocalyptic war in which Israel would be re-established among the nations of the earth. As against the peaceable kingdom foretold by Isaiah, Joel urges the faithful into the final battle: 'Beat your plowshares into swords, and your pruning hooks into spears: let the weak say, I am strong' (Joel 3: 10). Yeats himself occasionally looked for, even called for, a final battle. In 'Poety and Tradition' (1907) he recalled the time when 'we were to forge in Ireland a new sword on our old traditional anvil for that great battle that must in the end re-establish the old, confident, joyous world'. The mood is wistful, the opportunity never having presented itself. A degree of self-mockery colours the sentence so that one cannot clearly distinguish between an abandoned insurrection of the Fenian kind and a War in Heaven of the Miltonic. Yet at the end of his career, Yeats revamped the project in 'Under Ben Bulben', turning for support to those 'that Mitchel's prayer have heard, / "Send war in our time, O Lord!"'[12] Exactly a year later, Hitler obliged.

There is an apocalyptic sense in which parables of spiritual conflict converge with the mundane actualities of barricades, bombs, and millions of dead bodies. One trajectory can be followed through the romantic cult of violence in European literature generally from – say – the *Sturm und Drang* movement to the fiction of Ernst Jünger. The German references are comforting, of course, at least to Anglophones. In the late nineteenth century, however, Yeats was associated with a series of subversive movements in which violent politics, irrationalist philosophy and sexual irregularity overlapped. When English literary history terms this Decadence it characteristically misses the political engagement of, say, Yeats in the Irish Republican Brotherhood and Maud Gonne in the anti-Drefusard cause. Like Balzac with regard to Swedenborg, Yeats was perhaps never fully convinced of, or committed to, the doctrines he espoused from time to time; nevertheless, the name of Aleister Crowley will serve as an adequate shorthand for some of his activities. In French literature, a line could be traced back from Verlaine and Rimbaud through Baudelaire to Balzac. Somewhere along the line, Balzac's irony had become a heady amalgam of damnation and delinquency. Yeats's own life-long search for a transcendentalist belief, interacting with and interrupted by his engagements in politics, may be read as a personal interrogation of that tradition, an interrogation complicated by the linguistic and social distances between Paris and Dublin, Balzac and Yeats's own uncertain Irish precursors.

Instead then of the familiar traditions – of Irish gothicism from Maturin to Stoker, and of Irish idealism from Berkeley to Yeats – literary historians will look at the interventions, the discontinuities and the unacknowledged transactions taking place in less brightly lit areas of academic discussion. If *Melmoth reconcilé* jeopardises any easy declaration of Le Fanu as heir to Maturin, and so requires one to consider more closely why Le Fanu wrote as he did, then *Séraphita* sheds an equally unexpected light on links between Le Fanu and Yeats. Yet what was it in Swedenborg's doctrines which attracted Yeats? Ernst Curtius, writing of Emerson, sees the Swede as one of the principal intermediaries in the transmission of 'The Theory of the Unity of All'. Asiatic in origin, and magical in essence, the theory runs through the thought of antiquity, is active in neoplatonism, hermeticism, the cabbala, the development of certain physical sciences (via alchemy) in the Renaissance. 'Traces of it are detectible in the seventeenth century in Leibniz and heterodox mysticism, in the eighteenth century in the natural philosophers, the social reformers and the preachers of esoteric doctrines ... it penetrates the intellectual syncretism of the nineteenth century.'[13] Respectable Yeatsians will recognise here something close to their hero's Unity of Being; others may detect ideological support for his indulgence of totalitarian politics.

What occurs to this elusive yet influential body of ideas in its transmission from Balzac to Yeats? How is one to explain a succession which commences with the great exposer of capitalist society and concludes with a part-time apologist for fascism? One answer doubtless involves Balzacian irony, both in the immediate textual sense of the novelist's comic attitude towards his characters and their follies, and in the larger sense (articulated by Lukács) that the fervent royalist makes a radical appraisal of bourgeois regimes. Another lies precisely in the relatively early state of French capitalist development under scrutiny in the *Comédie humaine*. The bankers of

Balzac's fiction are still experimenting, testing one technique against another, using his heroes as guinea-pigs. The system is little more than half in place, and its awkwardness as much as its energy derives from this condition. Remnants of the *ancien régime* are still discernible, pathetic perhaps but capable of showing up the new arrangements for what they are. By Yeats's day, especially by 1934 when he was so concerned with Swedenborg and related matters, capitalism had survived its greatest crises – the war among Great Britain, France and Germany, the revolutions of 1917–21 in Russia, Germany, and Hungary, and the economic depression of the late 1920s. To be sure a sense of crisis pervaded the intellectual climate, but this produced precisely the indulgence of 'strong measures' against Bolshevism advocated by the Nazis and their allies in defence (ultimately) of the capitalist world order.

Much of this sounds abstract and cliché-ridden, and the shorthand is regrettable. There *are*, however, specific areas of social development occurring in the mid nineteenth century where the gradual transformation of 'the theory of the unity of all' from an arcane doctrine of final redemption into an instrument of imminent repression can be traced. Sheridan Le Fanu's novels and tales give access to one highly significant such area – the altered relation between citizen and *polis* inscribed in the problematic condition of the individual fictional character and his inherited milieu. Even more conveniently, Le Fanu explicitly employs a Swedenborgian symbolism (in *Uncle Silas*) to demonstrate the drastic isolation of character and the threat posed to character by various modes of imitation or duplication. Curtius's account of the theory summarises many of its inherent instabilities: where it makes itself known

> it always avails itself of the same language. It has its own vocabulary of concepts and signs, which is self-consistent and always recurs. Since it conceives of the All as One ... it is a kind of Monism ... But as the unity is divided into energy and appearance, inner and outer, cause and effect, this monism simultaneously becomes a dualism ... In this way it arrives at the concepts of polarization, antagonism, and compensation.[14]

In Balzac and Emerson, the theory can be absorbed as a means of charting an unknown or still emergent society. In Le Fanu, on the other hand, things are all too clear, and even the cloudy rhetoric of Swedenborg fails to conceal the mutual ruination of past and present, the implosion of character into vacuity, and the undirected automatism of language itself.

On literary history

Notes

1 W. B. Yeats *Autobiographies* London: Macmillan, 1955 p. 48; the essay on *Louis Lambert* is published in W. B. Yeats *Essays and Introductions* London: Macmillan, 1961 pp. 438–47.
2 See F. A. C. Wilson *W. B. Yeats and Tradition* London: Gollancz, 1958 pp. 104–10; Warwick Gould 'A Crowded Theatre: Yeats and Balzac' in A. Norman Jeffares (ed.) *Yeats the European* Gerrards Cross: Smythe, 1989 pp. 69–90.
3 Carl Benson 'Yeats and Balzac's *Louis Lambert*' *Modern Philology* vol. 49 (1952) p. 247.
4 W. B. Yeats *Explorations* London: Macmillan, 1962 p. 32.
5 See W. J. Mc Cormack *Ascendancy and Tradition in Anglo-Irish Literary History from 1789 to 1939* Oxford: Clarendon Press, 1985 pp. 364–6.
6 Honoré de Balzac *Séraphita [and other tales]* (trans. Clara Bell) Sawtry, Cambs.: Dedalus, 1989 p. 151.
7 Ibid. p. 147.
8 Ibid. p. 155.
9 Ibid. pp. 129–30.
10 W. B. Yeats *Memoirs* (ed. Denis Donoghue) London: Macmillan, 1972 p. 205.
11 *Séraphita [and other tales]* pp. 83–4.
12 W. B. Yeats *Collected Poems* London: Macmillan, 1950 p. 398.
13 E. R. Curtius *Essays on European Literature* (trans. Michael Kowal) Princeton: Princeton University Press, 1973 pp. 213–14.
14 Ibid. p. 213.

3

Swedenborg's
ghost

It would be wrong to give the impression that Yeats venerated Swedenborg. On the contrary, *A Vision* is distinctly unsympathetic in describing 'a mind incredibly dry and arid, hard, tangible and cold'. In that strange psycho-philosophical system, Swedenborg is classified under the twenty-second phase of the moon where his companions are all nineteenth-century figures. As is frequent in these lists of Yeats's, the names constitute an odd group – 'Flaubert, Herbert Spencer, Swedenborg, Dostoieffsky, Darwin.'[1] Quite how the author of *Crime and Punishment* fits in among the otherwise plodding exemplars of the phase is hard to tell. Yet Swedenborg's association exclusively with mid-nineteenth-century figures may indirectly confirm the view that Le Fanu (and not Blake) was, for Yeats, an important mediator in the process.

Dry, perhaps, and arid, Swedenborg was no less useful to the system-building poet. His patchwork quotation and paraphrase of the sage's account of the after-life in *Arcana Coelestia* has been cited by F. A. C. Wilson in illustration of this debt:

> 'The most minute particulars which enter the memory remain there and are never obliterated' [making] us live again all our transgressions and see our victims 'as if they were present, together with the place, words and motives', and that suddenly, 'as when a scene bursts upon the sight' and yet continues 'for hours together'. And like the transgressions, all the pleasure and pain of sensible life awaken again and again, all our passionate events rush up about us, and not as seeming imagination, for imagination is now the world.[2]

Certainly the passage could stand as an account of what goes on in *The Words Upon the Window-pane* where, in a séance, the spirit of Swift is tapped and his conversations with Stella and Vanessa reported to the audience by a medium. Yet the Swedenborgian-cum-

Yeatsian notion of 'dreaming-back' one's earthly experiences after one's death is not simply a dramatic device existing in isolation from any larger body of belief. Swedenborgian *correspondence* provided a means whereby a central doctrine (which stated that the forms of Man, of Heaven, and of Hell are structurally analogous) is extended to account for every detail of the visible world: 'The whole natural world corresponds to the spiritual world, not only the natural world in general but also in every particular. Therefore, whatever in the natural world comes into existence from the spiritual world is said to be in correspondence with it.'[3]

In part, this belief derives from Swedenborg's famous vision; in part, it is only a vast extrapolation from literalist readings of scripture. The consequence, however, is an encyclopaedia of interpretations whereby hands, heavenly bodies, herbs, hills, houses, numbers – not to mention odours and stones – can all be de- and en-coded spiritually.[4] For Yeats, the common attachment of such a system and the literalism of certain Protestant sects was enough to discount Swedenborgianism as a profound statement of the theory of the unity of all. One who had early rebelled against the scientific positivism of his father's generation was unlikely to take on board Swedenborg's infinite cargo of laborious correspondences. Nevertheless, the subjective realism which might be winnowed from all that chaff was a doctrine he dearly sought to establish.

In this, he was of course an heir to several Victorian anxieties and desires. System in Lyell's geology had gravely shaken orthodox belief, and Darwin's demonstration that the secular view of the universe was not just an account of events in the remote past but a theory of continuing evolution further challenged man's notion of his own place in the order of things. As early as Tennyson's *In Memoriam* (1850) literature had explicitly debated issues centred on the conflict of scientific and traditional authority. Not least among the questions raised by the natural sciences was one of language. If the Bible did not fully account for the creation of the earth, the animal kingdom, mankind and the rest of it, then a challenge to the theory of language inherent in orthodoxy was mounted above the quibbling about fossils. In the second chapter of Genesis, God had brought all the animals before Adam so that their names might be established. The act of nomination, however, is reported within another rather different, two-part chronicle:

And the Lord said, It is not good that the man should be alone: I will make him an help meet for him.

And out of the ground the Lord God formed every beast of the field, and every fowl of the air; and brought them unto Adam to see what he would call them: and whatsoever Adam called every living creature, that was the name thereof.

And Adam gave names to all cattle, and to the fowl of the air, and to every beast of the field; but for Adam there was no found an help meet for him.

And the Lord God caused a deep sleep to fall upon Adam, and he slept: and he took one of his ribs, and closed up the flesh instead thereof;

And the rib, which the Lord God had taken from man, made he a woman, and brought her unto the man.

And Adam said, This is now bone of my bones, and flesh of my flesh: she shall be called Woman, because she was taken out of Man.

The purpose in quoting these six verses is not to initiate some intricate exegesis of a deep meaning but rather to demonstrate the problems which were all too obvious to Victorian doubters. How is it that God can not or will not name the beasts, but requires that Adam should do so? Why should the business of providing Adam with a female of his species be interrupted by the naming of the beasts? What, finally, is the relationship between naming and gender? Among Le Fanu's stories and novels, those collected in *In a Glass Darkly* (1872) will be shown to address this problem. For what it was worth, Swedenborg had offered an interpretation of the chapter, and particularly of the two verses immediately following those quoted, in terms of the conjunction of good or truth with man or angel, and continues 'this conjunction may be likened to a man's thinking what he wills and willing what he thinks'. Genesis 2: 24 was then cited, with the conclusion: 'This is a description both of the heavenly marriage in which the angels are [,] and of the marriage of good and truth. "Man's not putting asunder what God has joined together" means that good is not to be separated from truth.'[5]

This may not convince, yet it may (in certain circumstances) reassure. For Swedenborgian correspondence is not so much a system relating material objects to spiritual values, as it is a comprehensive attempt to relate words to objects in a manner which is permanent, authorised and complete. Victorian theories of language were progressively hostile to such notions of an absolute relation (tantamount to identity) between language and a non-linguistic reality. Linda Dowling has shown how the great strides taken by romantic philogists and poets (Herder, Wordsworth) were rendered problematic by mid century. Already John Horne Tooke (1736–1812) had advanced a basically materialist philosophy of language, but in 1838 one central tenet of Tooke's etymology (that *truth* derives from *troweth*, i.e. the verb *to trow* or to trust, believe etc.) was vanquished in the name of religious orthodoxy by F. D. Maurice (1805–72). The triumph was pyrrhic, for no sooner were the Utilitarians routed than Friedrich Max Müller (1823-1900) arrived from the continent. It was a fundamental premise with Max Müller that 'language was organized on purely linguistic principles independent of both men and representation'.[6] Back in the 1790s the far from materialist Edmund Burke had been happy to employ Tooke's notion that words were like coins and might be counterfeited to denounce the impudence of anti-reformers in Ireland:

> A word has been lately struck in the mint of the Castle of Dublin; thence it was conveyed to the Tholsel, or city-hall, where, having passed the touch of the corporation, so respectably stamped and vouched, it soon became current in parliament, and was carried back by the Speaker of the House of Commons in great pomp, as an offering of homage from whence it came. The word is *Ascendency*.[7]

Merging the idiom of word-as-token with a rhetorical trope based on the fashion of election parades, Burke confidently made his case for the preservation of British liberties through reform. Mid-Victorians found little comfort in current linguistic research in their efforts to defend 'the logos-within-history of a noble English cultural destiny'. Yet Max Müller attempted to reconcile his 'science of language' to the conventions of religious belief, and in many respects he remained pre-scientific as in his '*a priori* assumption that language was thought and thought language'.[8] Before he died, he had been supplanted by the Neo-Grammarians, and the way lay open to Saussurean linguistics.

If Max Müller turned out to be a false prophet, in other areas less colourful figures added their concerns to the debate about language. Richard Chenevix Trench (1807–86) first published his lectures *On the Study of Words* in 1851. As befitted a future archbishop of Dublin, he was resolute in his own undertaking and even more reassuring to his flock. On the surface, Trench provided the accommodation between belief and the study of language which Müller ultimately failed to deliver. Yet Trench, in his way, also launched a revolution in the study of language by proposing, in 1857, the compilation of a word-list which was finally completed in 1928 as the *New English Dictionary*.[9] Trench was particularly interested in the historical evolution of language. The fourth lecture in his *English Past and Present* (1855) was entitled 'Changes in the Meaning of English Words', while the previous lecture had listed many feminine nouns lost from the language over the centuries. The dictionary project turned out to be more massive than Trench and his associates imagined; it required the reading of vast numbers of books on the basis of which it would be possible to illustrate the use of words without reference to their alleged intrinsic merit (a good word or a spurious one) but solely on the basis of changes of meaning and implication. *On the Study of Words* had devoted some pages to showing the extent to which there is 'history in words'. One of Trench's examples was *ascendancy* in which a 'faith in the influence of the stars' formally survives.[10]

The *Oxford English Dictionary* (as it has come to be known) marked one major shift in English lexicography, the replacement of the compiler's personal assessment of style (cf. Samuel Johnson or Thomas Sheridan) by the weight evidence simply of usage. Not only acknowledged works of literature, but newspapers, technical manuals and other low publications were scanned and dissected. The task lay well beyond the individual control even of James Murray, generally credited as the dictionary's presiding genius. In a remote Irish rectory, not far from the family home of Dictionary Sheridan, the Reverend George Sidney Smith (1804/5–75) laboured to compile a list of words beginning Pa. He left the parish of Aghalurcher in 1867, and was no doubt further unsettled by Disestablishment of the Church of Ireland two years later. His great pile of paper slips was eventually traced to a stable in County Cavan some time after his death in 1875, but most of it had already been used to light fires. 'A great number of books had to be re-read to make good the loss.'[11] Such accidents oddly dramatise the place of language in the concerns of Victorians. Words may be used if they are traced, but it is increasingly clear that tracing them is an impossible task and no one man can master the language in its entirety. Indeed, even if it were traced in some hypothetical completeness, one is only confronted with layer upon layer of historical instability, of shifted meaning, loss and variation. Certainty, fixity are no more realisable than completeness.

Among the zealots of the Philological Society, even more technical aspects of grammar gave rise to discussion. E. L. Brandreth, in a paper 'On Gender' published in the transactions for 1880–1, divided the languages of the world into a gendered group and an ungendered (including English). So much was unremarkable, it might seem, providing one was working exclusively within one language. But Jakob Grimm had lamented in his *Deutsche Grammatik* (1819–37) that German used *Geschlect* for both sex and gender, requiring him to introduce a terminological distinction between *natürliches Geschlect* (sex) and *grammatisches Geschlect* (gender).[12]

Awareness of this problem in grammar complicates the cross-language reading of a text like Balzac's *Séraphita*. Let us take the opening of a relatively simple sentence and display it generously on the page:

| La personne | que Minna nommait | Séraphitüs |
| s'appuya sur | son talon droit ... [13] | |

An English translation can be easily supplied:

| The person | whom Minna had addressed as | Seraphitus |
| poised himself | on his right heel ... [14] | |

In French, the first noun (a common noun) is of the feminine gender irrespective of the referant's sex. In English, the equivalent noun does not manifest a gender in its own form or that of the definite article. Thus a comparison of the first line in each language shows that French easily accommodates a feminine noun for a referant who will in a moment be named with a masculine-form (via Latin) name. No difference is implicated in this distinction. In English the relationship between the common noun and proper noun is of another kind, though none the less easy. The first (common) noun functions without reference to gender or sex and so accommodates the masculine proper noun just as it would a feminine one. It is, however, on the second line that the contrast between the languages begins to emerge. In 'son talon' the possessive adjective derives its gender (generally speaking) from the noun it qualifies and not from the noun for which it deputises. Thus, in isolation, 'son talon' might be translated into English as 'her heel' or as 'his heel'. Feminine nouns in French take 'sa' as a rule but certain feminine nouns take 'son' (i.e. those which begin with a vowel etc.).

We have then a comparative pattern which will not reduce to simple mirror translations, even in the elementary example analysed above. Though 'his/her' corresponds to 'son/sa' in one function, 'his' does not correspond to 'son' referentially. The doctrine of correspondences in Swedenborg ultimately breaks down in the same manner, owing to the unverifiability of any common structure in the two corresponding codes (items of the material/visual and spiritual worlds). In Balzac, this aspect of Swedenborgianism is subordinate to the union of the angel with God and the parallel union of Minna and Wilfrid. In Le Fanu, however, the arbitrary, unverifiable and treacherous operation of correspondences will throw up endlessly reiterated plots of disunion, division and displacement.

As we have seen, Séraphita's hermaphrodite state was an anticipation of his/her union with God – for all is homogeneous in that region. Yeats's interest in such doctrines frequently concentrated on the idea of angelic marriage. Writing of George Russell (AE) in the *Autobiographies*, he commented on his friend's alternation of exquisite and commonplace work, and added: 'Was it precisely because in Swedenborg alone the conscious and the subconscious became one – as in that marriage of the angels, which he has described as a contact of the whole being – so completely one indeed that Coleridge thought Swedenborg both man and woman?'[15] Not only in arcane pursuits but in experiences of the common people did Yeats find this symbolism. One night, while he and old George Pollexfen were at work laboriously upon their visions, the dreams of a servant (Mary Battle) had paralleled their 'allegorical marriage of Heaven and Earth'. She had imagined that her good Catholic bishop (of Sligo) was wed to 'a very high-up lady, and she not too young, either'. As a consequence, 'it will be no use going to confession'.[16] Marriage in both these passages is symbolic of the removal of difference. But as Curtius observed in his characterisation of the theory of the unity of all, such monism generates a complementary dualism. The apocalypse which Séraphita inaugurates in her union with God, signalled at a low mimetic level in Wilfrid's desire for conquest and world domination, must lead to the Last Judgement: all will be equal in the eyes of the Lord, but there will follow a division of the blessed and the damned. Heaven exists by courtesy of Hell.

It is not the purpose of this study to pursue Swedenborg very much further. Yet one of the crucial elements in Le Fanu's reading of his doctrines is the tension between attraction and repulsion. Little of this could be proved, for specific references to the doctrines are restricted to perhaps two or three stories or novels, the most notable being *Uncle Silas*. If Swedenborg was for Balzac a visonary in whose scheme of things one might eventually descry some unity behind the frenzy of contemporary change, for Le Fanu he was a blind leader of the blind – and all but recognised as such. Le Fanu is concerned exclusively with the dark side of the vision, with the revelations which follow death, the reinactments of crime and the confrontation once again with one's victim. It is a suitable ingredient for a mid-Victorian novelist attached (however indignantly) to the sensational school of Charles Reade and Wilkie Collins. To borrow a trope from the jargon of drug addiction, Le Fanu's Swedenborgianism was a bad trip. One reason for this undoubtedly is the loss of faith in systems, even in a system which offered a virtual identity of language and reality. Language can no longer be seen in such a light: if it is systematic, then the system excludes the individual human being, or in so far as it includes him he is annihilated, a sacrifice to his own inclusion. In fiction, it is the concept of character which crucially bears the burden of language's inability to sustain a reliable link with whatever is the real.

Something of this can be detected beneath Le Fanu's sensational plots together with evidence of the discovery's repression. *Uncle Silas*, being the best known of the novels, can stand as typical, and it has the additional merit of explicitly citing Swedenborgian texts. Set in the rural north midlands of Victorian England, the basic story has been taken over from an earlier one of Le Fanu's set in eighteenth-century Ireland. The Ruthyn brothers have been somehow politically ostracised, and this isolation is intensified by the unorthodox religious affiliation (to Swedenborgianism) of at least one of them. At a certain level, the shifts of setting and period together with the extreme de-socialisation of the family both represent and conceal the role of the landowning élite in Ireland at the time. The introduction of a Swedenborgian minister – the vulgar but honest Dr Hans Emmanuel Bryerly – goes some way towards puncturing the hermetic solitude of the Ruthyn households. It does so, however, by augmenting what is least representative of either of the societies (Irish, English) in which the action has been set.

As in Balzac's *Séraphita*, there is some mention of angels amid this anomalous community of widowers and orphans. The narrator concludes with a resounding paragraph:

> This world is a parable – the habitation of symbols – the phantoms of spiritual things immortal shown in material shape. May the blessed second-sight be mine – to recognise under these beautiful forms of earth the ANGELS who wear them; for I am sure we may walk with them if we will, and hear them speak![17]

But Maud Ruthyn has seen no angels in the course of the events she has related. Unlike *Séraphita*, Le Fanu's novel does not provide a means whereby the reader can distinguish the mere mortals from the mere angels. No inconsistency of gender reveals a figure who is to each what complements him or her. Certainly the novel can be read as possessing a symmetry of action based on the kind of correspondences propounded by Swedenborg in *Heaven and Hell*; certainly the plot can be interpreted as essentially an enactment of those processes which Swedenborg believed the soul experienced as it underwent judgement after death. But whereas *Séraphita* advanced 'good' Swedenborgianism, *Uncle Silas* tells of damnation, or – to be more correct – it is a tale narrated by one who is all but damned by her failure to see spiritual evil in her uncle. If Le Fanu has been rescued from the trammels of a gothic sub-tradition, he has simultaneously embraced a web of unverifiable correspondences. Here is no inaugurating springtime, but autumnal bereavement and enclosure. Elizabeth Bowen called it 'ever-autumn' which may be compared closely with the 'ever-after' cliché of folktale and pie in the sky.

There is, however, the possibility of a more radical reading of the novel than the merely atmospheric. Not only has Le Fanu utilised the plot of an early short story – and in doing so transferred the action from eighteenth-century Ireland to Victorian England – *Uncle Silas* itself turns on a drastic change of location. Superficially, young Maud the narrator travels from her late father's house (Knowl) to her uncle's (Bartram). But by means of a host of symmetrical details linking these two houses, the novel advances the implication that they differ not on a physical plane, but in their spiritual orientation. Similarly, Uncle Silas is not a character distinct from the narrator's father: he is the post-mortem state of the father. The unfolding of Silas's plan to rob and murder Maud is not just another sensationalist plot: it is 'the dreaming back' of the seemingly pious father's violent inner disposition towards his daughter. The novel, thus interpreted, becomes dark metaphysical romance; death is its fulcrum, the apocalypse its moment and momentum. Time rewinds on the bobbin of Ruthyn's soul, with the effect of synchronising its progressive aspect (earthly career) and its eternal (judgement). If *Uncle Silas* co-exists as sensational novel and metaphysical romance, the question remains as to how we place such a work of literature in a reconsideration of Irish literary history.

On literary history

We have then two distinct interventions, one of which may be still in need of elaboration. Balzac's *Melmoth reconcilé* takes up the problem of Maturin's gothic hero, floats it on the stock-exchange, and in doing so unsettles the assumed lineage of Le Fanu's fiction. But the second intervention, that which both obstructs and mediates the line of connection between Balzac and Yeats, is enacted by Le Fanu himself. For, as the reference to hair-raising stories in 'Swedenborg, Mediums, and the Desolate Places' indicated, it was in *Uncle Silas*, *In a Glass Darkly* and a few other scattered pieces by Le Fanu that Swedenborg finds temporary refuge in Victorian Irish culture. The central section of the present book attends in detail to the fiction which constitutes that second intervention.

Yet one may still ask – why Le Fanu, why not (for example) James Clarence Mangan, or Maturin himself? Le Fanu's fiction deals with a number of themes which occur prominently in Balzac. These include Swedenborgian doctrines concerning not only ultimate spiritual truth but matters as immediate as marriage and sexuality. In addition there is a shared preoccupation with painters and paintings, and a distaste for the unfolding politics of an increasingly bourgeois and democratic society. There are of course formal resemblances between the two bodies of fiction but these will be discussed in a later chapter when the reader is more familiar with the peculiarities of Le Fanu's plots. The most pressing reason for choosing Le Fanu is that his fiction is charged with historical concerns which are promptly disguised, dispersed, and denied. Many of these concerns relate to the emergence of that problematic social constituency, the Protestant Ascendancy, to which Yeats recruited the dead Synge.

Notes

1 W. B. Yeats *A Vision* (1937 version) London: Macmillan, 1962 p. 157.
2 See F. A. C. Wilson *Yeats and Tradition* London: Gollancz, 1958 pp. 145–6.
3 Quoted in W. J. Mc Cormack *Sheridan Le Fanu and Victorian Ireland* (2nd rev. ed.) Dublin: Lilliput Press, 1991 pp. 177–8. See chapter 5 of that work (pp. 148–94) for a further account of *Uncle Silas* in relation to Swedenborgianism.
4 Hands signify power; stars and constellations sigify cognitions of good and truth; herbs signify scientific truths ... and so on. See the index to Emanuel Swedenborg *Heaven and Hell* London: Swedenborg Society, 1958.
5 Swedenborg *Heaven and Hell* p. 201.
6 Linda Dowling *Language and Decadence in the Victorian Fin de Siècle* Princeton: Princeton University Press, 1986 p. 61.
7 Edmund Burke 'Letter to Richard Burke' (1792) quoted in W. J. Mc Cormack *Ascendancy and Tradition in Anglo-Irish Literary History from 1789 to 1939* Oxford:

Clarendon Press, 1985 p. 78.

8 Dowling op. cit. p. 70.

9 K. M. Elizabeth Murray *Caught in the Web of Words: James A. H. Murray and the Oxford English Dictionary* New Haven, London: Yale University Press, 1977 p. 135.

10 Richard Chenevix Trench *On the Study of Words* [and] *English Past and Present* London: Dent, 1927 p. 63.

11 Murray op. cit. p. 177 for the quotation. See also *Transactions of the Philological Society* (1880–1) p. 129

12 *Transactions* (1880–1) p. 248.

13 Honoré de Balzac *Séraphita* Paris: Librairie Gründ, (n.d.) p. 21.

14 Balzac *Séraphita* [*and other tales*] (trans. Clara Bell) Sawtry: Dedalus, 1989 p. 10.

15 W. B. Yeats *Autobiographies* London: Macmillan, 1955 p. 244.

16 Ibid. p. 260. It is odd that Yeats doesn't recognise Mary Battle's dream as a folk-memory of the scandalous marriage of John Butler (1720–1800, 12th baron Dunboyne and Catholic bishop of Cork from 1763 to 1787) – odd because Yeats strove manfully to prove that he belonged to the same Butler family.

17 J. Sheridan Le Fanu *Uncle Silas; a Tale of Bartram-Haugh*. Oxford: World's Classics, 1981. p. 424. (Original emphasis.)

PART TWO

Sheridan Le Fanu
and his art

4

Mediating the past:
The House by the Church-yard

Balzac was born on the eve of the nineteenth century, and in *Séraphita* he celebrated that occasion as virtually apocalyptic. Nothing so exciting as an *annus mirabilis* ever befell Sheridan Le Fanu. Yet in the period immediately following the death of his mother, he resumed the writing of novels after a fifteen-year abstinence. From 1863 until his own death early in 1873, he maintained a steady output of fiction of uneven quality. A good proportion of this will be examined in the course of this and the next six chapters, including incidental stories and neglected novels. Much will strike the reader as distinctly unstriking. Yet the first three novels of the resumed author constitute a distinctive achievement: *The House by the Church-yard* (1863), *Wylder's Hand* (1864) and *Uncle Silas* (also 1864).

In 'A Prologue' to the earliest of these, the elderly narrator gradually introduces himself as Charles de Cresseron (*sic*). In his youth, he had gone with his Uncle Charles to the churchyard and there inspected some recently unearthed remains in the presence of the sexton, Lemuel Mattocks. Personal, literary and military histories converge in these few names. The first of the author's family to reach Ireland had been a Charles de Cresserons (*sic*) who fought for King William at the Battle of the Boyne (1690). When the Williamite regime had been consolidated in both England and Ireland, it gave rise to a whig oligarchy deserving in its arrogance the scorn heaped upon it by Jonathan Swift in the *Travels* (1726) narrated by Lemuel Gulliver. Set among the casually unearthed bones of a graveyard, where murder, trepanning, personation and disgrace are immediately recalled, the prologue draws the name of Swift's narrator into the narrative delivered by William's soldier.

Before passing on to consider the novel, we should look again at the choice of narrative-pseudonym. In the serial version, the name

Charles de Cresseron is placed so as to indicate the *author's* name, with its recurrence as the *narrator's* name modulated internally with an effect of minimising any tension between the two. The name does not exactly reproduce that of the ancestral Charles de Cresserons, and such deliberate minute deviations are not unknown elsewhere in Le Fanu's spelling of proper names and citation of authorities. What might motivate such careful employment of the name? With de Cresseron, Le Fanu invoked the first generation of his Huguenot ancestors to reach Ireland, a generation actively involved in the military imposition of the Williamite regime. Born in Caen in 1653, Charles de Cresserons died in 1738, having served for sixteen or seventeen years (1689-1706) in a dragoon regiment. By 1861, the name itself had died out in Ireland, being replaced so to speak by that of the cautious and sedentary Le Fanus. Militant Protestantism, together with the experience of exile and migration, could be summoned up from the family tree only by recourse to the remote de Cresserons. And whereas de Cresserons came straight like the sword into Ireland, the early-eighteenth-century Le Fanus had travelled more circumspectly and demurely.

At one, subliminal level of allegory, the opening pages of *The House by the Church-yard* are a *dies irae*, day of wrath, or even Day of Judgement for the Irish eighteenth century. Graves have been opened and the secrets of the illustrious dead are about to be narrated. Yet the novel's labyrinthine plot resists revelation even as it releases it, and the grand dénouement is postponed and delayed by many elaborate little scenes of domestic emotion, bar-room entertainments, gossip and diversion. In strict literary terms, *The House by the Church-yard* owes less to Scott than to the costume novels of Harrison Ainsworth, and also to the (anti-)puritan fiction of Nathaniel Hawthorne. Its tapestry-like chapters contain vignettes of mundane life, the passage of ordinary time, even as they accumulate to form an apocalyptic exposé of a dynasty. If Sturke and Archer and Dangerfield are the names of the latter-day actors in the drama, then the initials and figures on the coffin plate transcribed in the second chapter of the novel bespeak an earlier and more elevated level of action:

R. D.
obiit May 11th,
A.D. 1746.
aetat 38.

The latter-day grave-attendants debate whether a device above these details is 'a fourpenny cherub', 'a star ... a Freemason's order', or (as the parish clerk *knows*) a coronet. The details themselves remain cryptic, for all that we learn of Richard, Lord Dunoran, wrongfully imprisoned to await execution for a murder he did not commit.[1] Perhaps the year of his death may be noted as that in which Jacobite hopes of restoration were finally annihilated at Culloden – indeed he died within a month of the great defeat – but the attentive reader of Le Fanu's fiction will more quickly recognise certain names. 'Some Account of the Latter Days of the Hon. Richard Marston of Dunoran' had been written in the wake of the 1848 rebellion, and republished with an English setting as 'The Evil Guest' in *Ghost Stories and Tales of Mystery* (1851). The story is reworked for the novel *A Lost Name* (1868) while Marston's name is resurrected in Le Fanu's last novel, *Willing to Die* (1873), and elsewhere.

It is tempting to recruit the term *nominalism* to denote this pervasive practice of Le Fanu's. By it, however, one could not mean a coherent philosophical position, somehow related to the scholastic doctrine, adopted by the novelist and employed throughout his fiction. Some remarks on professional philosophers' treatment of proper names will be found at the conclusion of Chapter 7 below. For the moment at least, I simply mean by nominalism Le Fanu's peculiarly intense use of proper names, especially personal ones. In *The House by the Church-yard*, the names of two distinguished sixteenth-century figures are given to characters in the eighteenth-century action. The rector bears the surname Walsingham, as if he were to be seen subsisting under the aegis of Sir Francis Walsingham (1530?–90), secretary of state to Queen Elizabeth. His daughter Lilias is listlessly wooed by Captain Devereux, who in this imaginative genealogy may be read as a transcript or descendant of those earls of Essex (Walter Devereux, 1541?–76; Robert Devereux, 1566-1601) for whom Ireland was not a happy hunting-ground. To these might added the marginal case of Dan Loftus, the rector's eccentric yet learned jack-of-all-trades, for the Loftus family had been distinguished in the early stages of the Irish reformation. No one-to-one correspondence between historical figure and fictional character is attempted by Le Fanu or observed by his reader, yet certain broader patterns are discernible.

This nominalism intersects with a line of references to painting and the visual arts generally in a series of points where portraits are invoked. Le Fanu as a Victorian novelist, writing in a contemporary setting, frequently plots his stories and novels so that the sins of the past are worked out in the present. Characters return from the grave, it seems, sometimes by appearing to be portraits or representations of a figure long thought dead or even known to be dead. *Guy Deverell* (1865) provides a typical case, in which all the Victorian trappings of roadside inns, cigars and saucy housekeepers are on display. However, in *The House by the Church-yard* with its ostentatious historical setting of one hundred years earlier than the period of composition, these historical names from a period nearly two hundred years earlier still – Walsingham, Devereux and even Loftus – are associated with a kind of serene resignation or melancholic contentment. The rector will, of course, be desolate at the death of Lilias, and Devereux has his worries. But the major and minor villains of the novel bear bluntly unresonant names – Dillon, Archer, Sturk. If there is a hint given in the process of naming (as with Dangerfield) it is a literal and not an allusive one. Allied to this ability of the eighteenth-century setting to accommodate harmoniously characters who are named after cunning, secretive, violent and assertive figures of Elizabethan *Realpolitik* is its provision of a comfortably domestic and middle-class milieu. The narrator relies in part on recollections of his namesake and uncle: but if this suggests a direct line of communication down the generations we should note how the narrator's uncle was a mere curate where the major clerical figure in the drama of the 1760s had been the rector. Such a demotion, as it were, is in keeping with a pervasive sense of reduced social status and eroded security.

In this connection, as in its association of a bloody inheritance with quaint architecture, cosy interiors and an ambling narrative, *The House of the Seven Gables* (1851) invites comparison. In Hawthorne's tale, Hepzibah Pyncheon has been reduced by the consequences of Maule's curse on the family to the indignity of opening a shop. Her brother Clifford has just been released from prison where he had paid the price for a crime he did not commit. With old Judge Pyncheon as the villain and Phoebe Pyncheon as the young ray of hope, Hawthorne's novel has a more closely knitted cast of family members than anything Le Fanu attempts for Walsingham and his daughter. Nevertheless, puritan–colonial America generally, and its nineteenth-century legacy, might provide a useful parallel for the discussion of Irish literature.

But, to return to the milieu of *The House by the Church-yard*. There are servants and aristocrats in the novel; the social norm, however, is unmistakably bourgeois. De Cresseron's narrative, drawing in turn on other memoranda, sets a tone of pious yet gleeful quietude. Industrialisation in the present is deplored but not so as to draw unnecessary attention to that phenomenon. The narrator has retrospective business, and he moves quickly to establish a skyline darkened by storms and fears but not by factory chimneys. The rector, the doctor, the innkeeper and even the Catholic priest congregate to vivify a miniature *polis*. It is, to be sure, only a village, but it is a barracks village, almost a suburb, and so indicative of the metropolis nearby.

The House by the Church-yard therefore combines two never wholly reconcilable aspects. It excavates the past, laying bare the evidence of deceit and homocide. It assimilates the past, transforming the ruddy-handed Eliabethan lord of creation into a dreamy *pater familias* or love-struck soldier. The tension between these two approaches to history enlivens the book even as it disturbs its formal unity. For Le Fanu incorporated into the novel a virtually independent chapter subtitled 'An Authentic Narrative of the Ghost of a Hand'. The link between certain records of psychological unease in the novelist's own family and this account of a (literally) disembodied hand has already been noted in *Sheridan Le Fanu and Victorian Ireland*. If the toad-like 'fattish hand' has a shiver-inducing and sensational *frisson* it also points towards intriguing possibilities for a classification of Le Fanu's oddly constructed fiction.

The hand is complete in itself but it is, by another reading which cannot be utterly disgarded, a fragment. For one cannot identify a hand except with reference to wrist, arm, elbow and so forth which delimit or define it. The hand in Chapter XII of the novel is therefore the fragment of an unapparent, absent or non-existent body. There is a once familiar classical allusion by which one refers to fragments as *disjecta membra*, scattered remains as they might be found on a battlefield. Behind that Latin cliché lies a specific line of Horace's: 'disjecta membra poetae,'[2] which translates first as 'the dismembered remains of a poet' but then also (by an transferred epithet) as 'the remains of a dismembered poet'. This in turn may be interpreted at either a literal level (his arms, legs etc.) or a literary level (his texts in fragmentary form). And if we look back at the chapter about the hand, the *membrum disjectum* that terrified Mrs Prosser, we find that the chapter itself is curiously cut off from the larger body (the novel) to which we expect to find it attached. This disjunction operates in several ways – the Prossers are nowhere else involved in the many plots and subplots of *The House by the Church-yard* – the hand manifests itself never again – the chapter impinges not at all on any of the characters. The incident, occurring long before the novel's action commences, took place in the Tiled House at Ballyfermot, of which the mysterious Mr Mervyn has become tenant. Mervyn of course is passing *incognito* for he cannot reveal his actual name (Mordaunt) and still hope to trap the murderer for whose crime Mordaunt/Mervyn's father had been condemned. The 'ghost of a hand' story is an interpolation, just as the hand is. Elsewhere in the fiction, single words, captions and so forth insist on a similar intrusion to a degree which requires examination as a quality of the composition intruded upon.

Compositional unity may indeed be jeopardised in this way precisely so as to interrupt any full sequential account of events (implying causation, responsibility, identity, etc.) running from origin itself to the recording of origin. The innumerable elements and sub-elements into which *The House by the Church-yard* might be analysed are arranged in a centrifugal pattern (with their energies of dispersal withheld from moment to moment by the ambling narrative) precisely so as to screen from scrutiny the actual (if actual) centre from which they issue. This is a fiction of plural not singular concentration, including but not assimilating disparate items and tonalities. Its dialectic is contradiction and not reconciliation. We will need to reconsider how Le Fanu's fiction is to be classified, for neither 'sensational school' nor 'Big House' nor 'historical romance' does justice to this configuration.

Even an elegantly dispersed constellation may be disrupted by the intervention of one further item. And here the role of names is implicated yet again: while the fictional character Mordaunt awaits his rehabilitation to the imaginary title, Lord Dunoran, he passes himself not just as Mr Mervyn but as 'A. Mervyn'. At first, this has the inscrutable generality of suggesting that he is simply a Mervyn among many of that name – that is, his pseudonymity is deepened and pushed towards anonymity. But then it also aligns him with the nominal Elizabethans, Walsingham, Devereux and Loftus. Audley Mervyn (d. 1675) served the Stuart monarchs rather than the Tudors; but successively as M.P. for Tyrone, governor of Derry and speaker of the Irish House of Commons, he was a latter-day consolidator of Walsingham cunning and Devereux bravado. In choosing a pseudonym (like his creator, Le Fanu) Mordaunt has dragged in another intervening history which complicates his mission to redeem his father's title.

One is assisted in taking this matter further. Mordaunt had been the family name of the earls of Peterborough, and the historical Audley Mervyn actually came from Peterborough. Moreover, Mordaunts and Mervyns fought on opposite sides of the English Civil War, and so when the character Mordaunt adopts the name A. Mervyn he mimics a switch of specific and locally active loyalties. If Le Fanu found these names in Clarendon's *History of the Great Rebellion*, he would only have been following in the footsteps of Samuel Richardson who derived a series of fictional character names from the same source. Incidentally, the title of Clarendon's *History* in itself points to rival terms (rebellion ... civil war) for the same event.

The happy union of the young Lord Dunoran and Miss Gertrude Chattesworth brings Le Fanu's novel to a conclusion made all the more conventional by its being repeated in the marriage of Aunt Rebecca Chattesworth to humble and bumbling Lieutenant Puddock. Thus the Chattesworth ladies wed both upwards and downwards in society, the niece into the titled aristocracy and the aunt into the solid yet modest ranks of the soldiery. As sister to a general, Rebecca has made the more decisive shift. Chattesworth of course also names the English seat of the dukes of Devonshire, and this instance of a placename becoming a family name not only contributes to a generalised pattern of reassuringly familiar 'posh' names (in the manner of Richardson) but implicates the attainder of the Courtenays (earlier earls of Devon) whose motto will feature so cryptically in *Uncle Silas*. These latter-day Chattesworths live at Belmont, and this echo of Portia's house in *The Merchant of Venice* further extends the mosaic of Elizabethan allusions in the novel. Before the end of Chapter V – had we but paused to notice – at least six Shakespearean plays were alluded to, *Hamlet, Macbeth, The Merchant of Venice, Othello, Richard III* and *The Winter's Tale*.

Puddock, a low-ranking pillar of the military establishment surely, has theatrical ambitions: he wants to act Tamerlane. The allusion of course is to the Scythian king who gives variants of his name to plays by Christopher Marlowe and Nicholas Rowe. Marlowe's *Tamburlaine the Great* (1587–90) is well known for such heroic as:

Is it not passing brave to be a king,
And ride in triumph through Persepolis?[3]

But Puddock's preference is in fact for Rowe's play of 1702, where
the hero is presented as a calm philosopher–prince and presented
also as modelled on William III! In Puddock and Dunoran, the
Chattesworth ladies have chosen husbands who mediate between
the undeniable violence of the Elizabethan era when Ireland was
finally conquered and the uneasy, smoke-clouded politics of an in-
dustrialised village on the outskirts of Victorian Dublin. For all its
cameo scenes, its faithful recital of dates and newspaper items, *The
House by the Church-yard* is not a novel about the eighteenth century
as such. No novel which renders benign a Walsingham or a
Devereux has exclusively eighteenth-century tasks in hand.

The earlier establishment in Ireland of the reformation, state
governance, the English language and the technology of printing,
and the bearing of that on the uncertainties of Le Fanu's middle-
class, Protestant heritage – *that* is the substance of the novel. Like
Mordaunt pretending to be Mervyn, its ostensible setting in the
1760s is in many ways a disguise, a pseudonym. The self-enclosed
village idealises a 'Protestant Ascendancy' Ireland even before that
concept had been fully articulated. Chapelizod is therefore exclusive
and vulnerable, though the thing it finally thrills to is a kind of
internal sabotage, aptly if casually likened to vampirism. We should
not allow the cinematographic potential of Le Fanu's imagery obscure the manner in which his fiction can be related to an emergent
historiography. Oddly in tandem with the historian W. E. H. Lecky's
Leaders of Public Opinion in Ireland (first published while Le Fanu's
novel was being serialised), *The House by the Church-yard* is an imaginative and tactical reassessment of Irish history, with the eighteenth
century chosen not so much as theme but as a forum of debate.
Lecky, in the introduction to his 1871 edition, observes that 'the
upper classes have lost their sympathy with and their moral ascendency over their tenants, and are thrown for the most part into a
policy of obstruction'.[4] The decade following publication of his
book and Le Fanu's saw Fenianism and Church disestablishment
shake the foundations of what now gradually and hesitantly was
beginning to call itself the Protestant Ascendancy. Yet, Lecky felt,
'probably no country in Europe has advanced so rapidly as Ireland
within the last ten years, and the tone of general cheerfulness, the

improvement of the houses, the dress, and the general condition of the people must have struck every observer'.[5]

Both of these exercises in historical reassessment could be characterised as 'Protestant', Lecky in a sense negotiating terms of renewal for what was becoming a palpable minority in the age of electoral reform, and Le Fanu seeking some imaginative or imaginary vantage point – locus of retreat, if necessary – for the same constituency. If Lecky's improvement struck Sheridan Le Fanu, it did not distract him from the increasingly guilt-charged inquiries into inheritance, identity and motivation. Publishing economics, not ameliorism, conditioned his fictional output after *The House by the Church-yard*.

The novels thereafter were set in England. Yet one minor detail in *The House by the Church-yard* points to an avenue through which Le Fanu managed to extend his apprehension of the Irish countryside and its culture. Dan Loftus is initially described as a 'simple, meek, semi-barbarous young scholar', an associate of the rector who has put him through college and encouraged his researches. He is, more particularly, 'a good Irish scholar' whose ability to comprehend 'Celtic MSS.' assists Walsingham in his inquiries concerning the origins of Chapelizod Castle.[6] Like the Catholic priest, Father Roach, whom the soldiers consult on all matters involving dogs and their ailments, Loftus is possessed of arcane data which ease his admission into Establishment circles – conditional and temporary admission of course. Loftus the antiquarian underlines the concern with historical causation evident both in the gruesome central plot and the names of incidental characters; he also reflects the revival of archaeological and philological research in the mid-Victorian period. Back in the 1840s, Le Fanu had consulted Charles Gavan Duffy on details of historical verisimilitude for *The Fortunes of Colonel Torlogh O'Brien*. This interest clearly had not waned twenty years later, for in November 1861 a suggestion was made to the scholar John Gilbert in connection with the proposed publication of Eugene O'Curry's *Lectures on the Manners and Customs of the Ancient Irish*: 'what of inserting the prospectus in the *Dublin University Magazine*[?] I am sure if Lefanu's own attention were drawn to it, he would do so at once, out of friendly feeling to O'Curry.'[7]

In a number of short stories, Le Fanu drew extensively on Irish folk traditions. An enhanced appreciation of Patrick Kennedy's qualities as a scholar and researcher can only confirm the opinion expressed in 1980 that his influence was decisive in directing Le Fanu's imagination back into this reservoir of ideas. Antiquarianism, bookishness, local historical research leading into the study of folklore – all these will recur in Le Fanu's fiction and in the larger cultural enterprise about to commence a decade after his death. Scholarship will be a new kind of moral ascendancy – witness the central role of Samuel Ferguson, Standish Hayes O'Grady, Douglas Hyde and a dozen less eminent figures. In the meantime, Dan Loftus of the 1861-3 novel is an amusing tribute to the author's debt.

Given the historical setting of the novel, Loftus must also be read as the author's half-satirical acknowledgment of his own anachronistic position. Indeed, Le Fanu offered the humblest of services to John T. Gilbert when the future knight was embarking on one of his scholarly inquisitions of the Irish past. He was neither a diligent archivist like Gilbert, nor a professional historian as Lecky was to become, nor an inspirational savant like O'Grady. He lacked the linguistic skills of Ferguson and Hyde, and lacked also the direct communion with folklore which his friend Patrick Kennedy possessed and processed. Nevertheless, Le Fanu's engagement in historical writing in the 1860s deserves attention not least because of the light it can throw upon the early concerns of Lecky. The fiction, however, progressively detaches itself from antiquarianism, finally to manifest a highly nervous, fragile and yet palpable sense of the historicity of the present. In such late novels as *Checkmate* (1871), Le Fanu was explicitly rewriting in contemporary settings work which he had first attempted during the years of Young Ireland's greatest influence.

Below the academic achievements of scholars, there lay a more popular and inchoate sense that the common people of Ireland – those who bore Gaelic names at least – were the dispossessed descendants of a cultural and material order which could be imaginatively reconstructed by means of research and propaganda. Loftus's apparent poverty in *The House by the Church-yard* signals something of the kind. And unlike the Fergusons and Hydes, Le Fanu shared one feature with the conventional image of the Gaelic *savant* – residual memories of lost status and dignity in a realm from which his ancestors had been expelled. For many of the claimants to Irish royal blood, of course, the belief was romantically inflated. Yet Le Fanu, who could trace expulsion on the map of Europe and produce French certificates of early ennoblement, never once builds a fiction round this paradigmatic Huguenot experience. When characters of French extraction or background appear in the novels they are more often villains than victims, they are more often – to be exact – villainesses. This avoidance of his own familial past casts its own shadow on the recurrent plot of inherited guilt.

Notes

1 J. Sheridan Le Fanu *The House by the Church-yard* (with introduction by Elizabeth Bowen) London: Blond, 1968 p. 15.

2 *Satires* I iv 62. See Mc Cormack *Sheridan Le Fanu and Victorian Ireland* (2nd rev. ed.) Dublin: Lilliput Press, 1991 pp. 142–3 for an incident involving the novelist's wife's dream of her dead father's hand.

3 Christopher Marlowe *Tamburlaine* (ed. J. W. Harper) London: Benn, 1971 p. 135 (Act II, sc. v, ll. 53–4).

4 W. E. H. Lecky *The Leaders of Public Opinion in Ireland – Swift – Flood – Grattan – O'Connell* London: Longmans, Green, 1871 p. ix.

5 Ibid. pp. xi–xii.

6 *The House by the Church-yard* p. 29.

7 John Edward Piggot to J. Gilbert 14 November 1861. See Rosa Mulholland Gilbert *Life of Sir John T. Gilbert* London: Longmans, 1905 pp. 55, 95 etc. for relations between Le Fanu and Gilbert.

5

The parochial and the exotic: two tales of 1861–2

In *A Lost Name* (1868), there is a phrase which neatly summarises much of what we have just seen of Le Fanu's fiction – 'The present is the inheritance of evil.'[1] It is not a profound remark, but then perhaps its most chilling implication is that spiritual resources for the future are already contaminated or at a low ebb. What a later generation will call entropy can be detected everywhere in Le Fanu's fiction. Nevertheless, his resumed activity as a novelist at the beginning of the 1860s did seem to manifest real energy and real commitment. While *The House by the Church-yard* was appearing as a serial in *The Dublin University Magazine*, he published two short stories in the same columns; set in County Limerick and seventeenth-century Milan respectively, 'Ultor de Lacy' and 'Borrhomeo the Astrologer' indicate a breadth of reference which also impresses.

'Ultor de Lacy' is centred on Cappercullen, Murroa and Abington, districts in County Limerick where the author had grown up in the disturbed 1820s:

> In my youth I heard a great many Irish family traditions, more or less of a supernatural character, some of them very peculiar, and all, to a child at least, very interesting. One of these I will now relate, though the translation to cold type from oral narrative, with all the aids of animated human voice and countenance, and the appropriate *mise-en-scène* of the old-fashioned parlour fireside and its listening circle of excited faces, and, outside, the wintry blast and the moan of leafless boughs, with the occasional rattle of the clumsy old window-frame behind shutter and curtain, as the blast swept by, is at best a trying one.[2]

Plausible autobiography and folk-narrative convention are perfectly reconciled in this opening paragraph. The conclusion also conforms to the established pattern of the folk-narrator's providing authority for his recitation:

[45]

Old Miss Croker, of Ross House, who was near seventy in the year 1821, when she related this story to me, had seen and conversed with Alice De Lacy, a professed nun, under the name of Sister Agnes, in a religious house in King-street, in Dublin, founded by the famous Duchess of Tyrconnell, and had the narrative from her own lips. I thought the tale worth preserving, and have no more to say.[3]

Knowing Le Fanu to have been only six years old at the time specified, we are initially confident of the story's fictional status. But it is not without autobiographical traces. The de Lacy castle is placed where the Barringtons were to build Glenstal Castle in the 1830s and 1840s: William Le Fanu had married Banky Barrington in 1857, and in 1861 (the year his brother acquired *The Dublin University Magazine* and published 'Ultor de Lacy' anonymously in its columns) William spent a good deal of time with his in-laws, fishing the little rivers of their childhood and returning to Abington church occasionally on a Sunday. Like any successful Victorian professional man, his vacation came second to his vocation: in 1866 he threw up a fine stone bridge on the Barringtons' burgeoning estate. On Easter Sunday 1861, he had lent his author–brother a further £50 and by August noted in his diary that 'Joe owes me £1,000'. The fortunes of the two brothers could be symbolised in their contrasting attitudes to the Cappercullen/Abington district of their youth.[4]

Retrospect conditioned Sheridan Le Fanu's interest in this familiar site rather than prospects social or architectural. The story is essentially one of revenge conducted across the centuries by a participant in the Elizabethan wars against the daughter of an eighteenth-century Jacobite. When Una de Lacy is spirited away by the fiend, she leaves behind a message chalked on her bedhead – 'Ultor de Lacy, Ultor O'Donnell'. This implied identity of two victims leads on to the surviving daughter's inheritance of a box containing a portrait:

> When she looked on it, she recoiled in horror. There, in the plenitude of its sinister peculiarities, was faithfully portrayed the phantom who lived with a vivid and horrible accuracy in her remembrance. Folded in the same box was a brief narrative, stating that, 'A.D. 1601, in the month of December, Walter De Lacy, of Cappercullen, made many prisoners at the ford of Ownhey, or Abington ... among the number one Roderic O'Donnell ... who, claiming kindred through his mother to De Lacy, sued for his life ... but was by De Lacy, through great zeal for the queen, as some thought, cruelly put to death ...'[5]

The parochial and the exotic

Abington, the parish where Dean Le Fanu had upheld the interests of the reformation, was accordingly the site on which the fictional de Lacy of Cappercullen butchered his kinsman in the Protestant queen's name. The shape of the victim's posthumous revenge is evidently a transfer of roles between victim and villain – the pattern is familiar from better known stories such as 'The Haunted Baronet' and the name Abington is allocated to a pretty woman casually mentioned in 'Mr Justice Harbottle'. But these last-named are a good deal more sophisticated in their detail than 'Ultor de Lacy' and the question will be raised whether the English setting of one and the autobiographical provenance of the other do not together constitute the chief ground of distinction between them.

With its glimpse of Elizabethan massacre 'Ultor de Lacy' remains an isolated item in Le Fanu's writing. The purported incident upon which it is based is of the kind chronicled in Thomas Stafford's *Pacata Hibernica* (1633), the editing of which was to constitute in 1896 Standish James O'Grady's most striking contribution to the Irish literary revival. Stafford had been an obscure traveller and soldier who, inheriting certain papers from the archives of the Elizabethan commander Sir George Carew, had assembled a vivid account of the war in Munster and the final destruction of Gaelic Ireland and its elaborately traditional culture. Le Fanu's combination of historical zeal and narrative fantasy anticipates a good deal in O'Grady generally, but the hero's name defies the exhaustive lists and genealogies of English and Gaelic chronicler alike.

'De Lacy' ostentatiously refers to one of the greatest Norman families of the Irish twelfth century and after, with territories centred on County Meath. 'Ultor' is used in the story as if it were a Christian name, and to that extent it is, just as 'Increase' or 'Cotton' were Christian names in the Mather family of New England. But to trace the source of the fictional de Lacy's Christian name, we look not to the puritan virtues (increase etc.) but to the Roman classics. 'Ultor' is a Latin noun, sometimes used as an additional proper name for Mars, the god of war, but more generally used to mean 'avenger'. Within this detail of Latin vocabulary, the reader makes little sense of the story's early observation that a de Lacy who left Ireland for France at the time of 'the establishment of the revolution in Ireland' (i.e. the 1690s) gave his son 'the strange but significant name of Ultor'. Its aptness for the gradually unfolded story of earlier de Lacys and their harsh treatment of the O'Donnells after the Battle of Kinsale (24 December 1601) is also evident, especially when we notice that the name is distributed to both antagonist parties in the words chalked on Una's bed-head. Dispossession of Cappercullen at the time of the Williamite settlement having proved only a temporary revenge, the O'Donnell spirit has (it seems) taken a human booty.

Read in both Latin and English (or Norman-French) the title of the story now reads more like a summary declaration. Yet inscriptions of this kind were far from rare, though ghost story and sensational narrative were not the usual context in which one found 'Ultor' linked to a name. There is a picture by Peter Paul Rubens, available as an etching cut by Bernard Baron, showing Achilles killing Hector.[6] The captions are printed below the picture in Latin and English, with a fuller account of the event continuing in separate columns:

Achilles Ultor	*Achilles Revenging*
Achilles Patrocli ultor,	Achilles under the protection
Minervae praesidio,	of Pallas, runs Hector through
Hectorem hasta trajicit …	and revengeth Patroclus's death …

Not only does the caption mirror Le Fanu's but a comparison of the two accounts of this event from the Trojan War further exemplifies, at the level of linguistic structure, the doubling of revenge enacted in the Irish story by the bed-head caption with Ultor attached to both de Lacy and O'Donnell. Indeed we can now see the crude chalk letters as an rendering into the folk-style, adopted by and from old Miss Croker, of a convention used in etchings and other reproducible depictions of heroic or epic events. Latin and English texts diverge however, and in several ways. Latin first indicates 'Achilles Ultor' (i.e. Achilles the Avenger), but permits, according to its flexible word-order, to attach the noun 'ultor' to the name of Patroclus (i.e. the avenged). Doing so, in an essentially English reading context, it gives something like the appearance of roles reversed between the two heroes. English, for its part, diverges on a different name. Latin had naturally referred to the goddess of wisdom by her Latin name (Minerva), but the Greek equivalent name (Pallas, or more fully Pallas Athene) is inserted by English in acknowledgement that the event originally took place – so to speak – neither in Latin nor English but in Homer's Greek.

The name of the story is the name of a central character. Ultor De Lacy was neither the butcher of 1601 nor the victim of O'Donnell's supernatural revenge: he lived between these savage events, implicated in the 1745 Jacobite rising it is true, but a middling fellow, a central character in that apparently immunising sense. But the name is inscrutable as to whether a word order permissible in Latin might not operate simultaneously with the commonplace order of Christian- and then family-name. Names yet again take on quizzical features, one attaches itself to two family names (de Lacy and O'Donnell) whereas the goddess of wisdom may in her singularity be referred to by several names and epithets.

Names also slide, are abbreviated or mistransmitted. In addition to the Latin epithet (not name, except perhaps in the case of Mars), middling de Lacy's strange but significant name resembles another piece of display nomenclature, name as it is formally rendered in caption or motto or citation. 'Ultor' resembles the Latin abbreviation 'Ulton.' signifying Ulster (Ultonia). Within Le Fanu's story, such a reading of the name is encouraged finally by the (otherwise inexplicable) transfer of the Christian name from a de Lacy to an O'Donnell. At the time of the massacre from which the later events of the story derive, the O'Donnells of west Ulster were in retreat after their defeat (under Hugh O'Neill, earl of Tyrone). The Ulster provenance of these disguised allusions to the historical past – the O'Donnells, the O'Neills etc. – is perhaps conceded in the distorted reading of Ulton. as Ultor. By this secondary interpretation, more tentative than the first, de Lacy inscribes on his son the territorial identity of the family's victim. But this name is evidenced in a corrupted version, and so only half-evident, as if to mitigate the guilt which would be displayed by florishing the pure version. The slippage from Ulton. to Ultor can also be read in terms of revenge of course but only if we see dispossessed de Lacy's pact with his young son as an admission that their family deserves *to be avenged upon*.

The Ulton/Ultor double reading may seem excessive, but Le Fanu's use of names is often overdetermined. For example, Cappercullen was the place where his brother's Barrington in-laws built their mock-baronial castle – the billiard room entrance was modelled on a door in Ely Cathedral! However, Cappercullen is firmly part of County Limerick, while the story insinuates that the de Lacy property was in the far poorer County Clare, on the far side of the River Shannon.[7] We thus have excessive concentration in a name (fiction and family) given that we also have inadequate concentration in a name (is it Limerick or Clare?). Le Fanu's story had been published anonymously, and so the name Le Fanu nowhere appears. Instead, the narrator acknowledges a debt to old Miss Croker. Now William Le Fanu's brother-in-law, one of the Barringtons of Glenstal (as the castle built at Cappercullen was henceforth to be called) was Croker Barrington. The story takes its name, and names, from what one might imagine as a damaged or faulty document or one half-competently transcribed from one culture to another.

The second story of 1861–2, 'Borrhomeo the Astrologer', appears to exist quite outside such patently local issues. Set in Milan at the time (1630) of the plague so powerfully evoked by Alessandro Manzoni in *The Column of Infamy* (1842), the sequel to his famous novel *The Betrothed* (1827), Le Fanu's anonymous story retells a basically Faustian plot of soul-selling and damnation. The presence in Manzoni's novel of Archbishop Federico Borromeo confirms a relationship between the two bodies of fiction, Irish and Italian, though the intrusion of the letter 'h' into the famous ecclesiatical family name should be noted in Le Fanu's title.

Two details link Le Fanu's 'Borrhomeo' to his own 'Ultor de Lacy' seemingly remote back home in County Limerick – or Clare. First, we have been told casually that de Lacy had served as a soldier in Italy; second, 'Borrhomeo' elaborates the device of a miniature portrait noted at the end of 'Ultor de Lacy', and even repeats the term enamel in describing it. When a strange young man offers to show the astrologer 'everything' that alchemy can hope for, he opens a snuffbox-like object with 'the small enamel portrait of a beautiful but sinister face' inside. Borrhomeo 'thought he saw the face steadily dilating as if it would gradually fill the lid of the box, and even expand to human dimensions'.[8] As a specifically female image, this may remind us of the picture in 'A Strange Event in the Life of Schalken the Painter' (1839) or even prompt anticipations of 'Carmilla' (1871–2). The stories of 1862, however, also refer specifically to miniature and anonymous works, portable images of apparently malevolent character. Their portability emphasises their possession by some particular individual: the eldest male of the de Lacys in the first case, and a far less definable owner in the second who, nevertheless, articulates a theory about the paintings and possession.

In the present story the image (she/it) is swiftly superseded by an incident occurring on the astrologer's journey to receive his Satanic instructions:

The parochial and the exotic

It was well known to Borrhomeo – a house of evil resort, where the philosopher sometimes stole, disguised, by night, to be no longer a necromancer, but a man, and so, from a man to become a beast.

They passed through the shop. The host, with a fat pale face, and a villainous smile, was drawing wine, which a handsome damsel was waiting to take away with her. He kissed her as she paid, and she gave him a cuff on his fat white chops, and laughed.

'What's become of Signor Borrhomeo,' said the girl, 'that he never comes here now.'

'Why, here he is!' cries Borrhomeo, with a saturnine smile, and he slaps his broad palm on her shoulder.

But the girl only shrugged, with a little shiver, and said, 'What a chill down my back …'[9]

Speaking of himself in the third person singular, Borrhomeo has already become invisible to *la femme moyenne sensuelle* who has now replaced the initial enamel portrait. That has a certain thematic significance, of course, but one should not miss the resemblance of the scene itself to paintings of low life, moralistic or celebratory, associated with the art of the seventeenth century. The moralistic tone is certainly present in the characterisation of a brothel, but 'Borrhomeo the Astrologer' is presented as part anonymous narrative and part translated quotation from an original manuscript – to whom can the moralising be attributed?

The picture which Borrhomeo has already been shown is duplicated a moment later when his conductor through the bawdy house hands him 'a thin round film of human skin'. Having breathed on the little object, Borrhomeo is able to stretch it 'to the size of a sheet of paper'. Instructed to cover his face with it 'as with a napkin', he is rewarded with the sight of a picture which shrinks 'until its disc was just the same as that of the lady's miniature in the lid of the box' on top of which it is placed by the conductor. The latter provides an explanation of these procedures, and then undergoes a transformation of his own:

'Every adept has his portrait here,' said the young man. 'So good a likeness is always pleasant; but these have a power beside, and establish a sympathy between their originals and their possessor which secures discipline and silence.'

'How does it work?' asked Borrhomeo.

'Have I not been your good angel?' said the young man, sitting before him. He extends his legs – pushing out his feet, and letting his chin sink on his chest – he fixes his eyes upon him with a horrible and sarcastic glare, and one of his feet contracts and divides into a goatish stump.

Borrhomeo would have burst into a yell, but he could not.

'It is a nightmare, is it not?' said the stranger, who seemed delighted to hold him, minute after minute, in that spell. At last the shoe and hose that seemed to have shrunk apart like burning parchment, closed over the goatish shin and hoof.[10]

Conventional tropes of gothic literature mingle here with extraordinary evidences of a self-conscious literary *Angst*. It is significant that the incident is prefaced with a note in square brackets in which the infinitely remote editor comments as follows: '[How the honest monk who wrote the tale, or even Borrhomeo himself, knew this and many other matters he describes, 'tis for him to say.]' For, cloven hooves apart, the entire focus of the passage is concentrated upon the means of constructing a manuscript as the essential preliminary to interpreting it. The skin acquires the size of paper (the common writing material of the modern editor's epoch) and traps Borrhomeo's face (skin etc.), but the young man's shoe and leggings have shrunk like parchment (the material of a decisively earlier epoch). Le Fanu neatly exploits the 'goat's hoof' of conventional devils to introduce the material basis of vellums and parchments, and the re-emergence of an earlier medium of writing (by way of reference to parchment) robs Borrhomeo of all independent powers of speech and movement. Yet it was in relation to the paper/skin image that the securing of 'discipline and silence' had been claimed. The suspension of the individual's powers results from a 'sympathy' established between the possessor of a picture and its subject/original, a notion (as we saw) also at work in Balzac's *Le Peau de chagrin*. Within the narrative Borrhomeo's ravenous appetite for longevity leaves no room for moral considerations, but the narrative also provides a further account of suspended moral response and does so explicitly in terms of power vested in pictures made by a parchment-characterised agent. If the narrative is gapped in certain details and places, then even that account of absolute control is jeopardised.

Le Fanu's fiction naturally possesses features which are to found elsewhere in the literary – and indeed non-literary – culture of the age. Certain virtually unconscious ideological nostrums are built into any text, and these in one form or another pervade its context also. Thus, it would hardly be surprising to find that some of the concerns identified in the fiction surface in other authors and other texts. Yet, one striking feature of Le Fanu's relation to the immediate period in which these stories were written lies in his apparent anticipation of such concerns. For example, one way of summarising 'Borrhomeo the Astrologer' would focus on the question of punishment after death – its eternal or less than eternal duration. To be sure, the irony of the villain's dilemma is that he is punished at length *before* death, but this nice detail does not disguise a familiar theological dispute.

Theologians as far back as William Whiston (1667–1752) had advanced an interpretation of doctrine which tried to mitigate the awful severity of everlasting punishment for sinners, and similar views had reappeared more recently and locally in the thought of Richard Whateley (1787-1863) who was archbishop of Dublin from 1831 until his death. But for readers of English literature, the *locus classicus* in this context is the poetry of Tennyson, especially those pieces associated one way or another with his friend F. D. Maurice. In his *Theological Essays* (1853), Maurice had argued that the popular belief in the endlessness of damnation was mere superstition; instead, the word translated from Greek as 'eternal' more strictly referred to qualitative rather than durational aspects of our future punishment. But the significance of this controversy – Maurice was dismissed from a Cambridge profesorship – does not lie simply in its substance being echoed in these stories of Le Fanu's. In the 1850s and 1860s, Tennyson wrote a number of narrative poems in which stories of a return from death feature; these not only reflect some of the contemporary tropes of the sensational novel but specifically (in the poem 'Aylmer's Field', 1864) allude to the doctrines of Emanuel Swedenborg and the crisis of the French Revolution. Le Fanu's unacknowledged stories of 1861-2 should be read thus as part of an anxious Victorian reconsideration of major theological and political themes.

Nor was Dublin immune to these English concerns. In 1864, the publication of two sermons preached in Trinity College by George Salmon (1819–1904) provoked a minor pamphlet skirmish among the established clergy. The historian J. W. Barlow (1826–1913) advanced a case suggesting that punishment after death might indeed be finite, ending in some cases in restoration of the sinner to heavenly bliss, and in others to annihilation. He was replied to firmly by the Reverend George Sidney Smith (1804/5–75), whose current preoccupation with words beginning Pa- was shortly to be committed to fires less than hellish but yet consuming. Smith, who was professor of biblical Greek in the university, sought to argue on 'the principles of sound hermeneutics; or, in other words, of honest common sense'. In practice, this involved a return to Salmon's chosen text (Matthew 25: 46) and its regrettable use of both the word *everlasting* and the word *eternal* for what on the surface appeared to be the same thing. Immediately, the problem was referred back to the one Greek word of the original gospel and the linguistic base of the difficulty was at once compounded and exposed. Salmon had already had to concede that the Bible was no longer the primary authority on matters concerning astronomy, but he continued to hold that its authority as scripture was intact. The intimately related questions of eternal punishment and of textual authority (or, perhaps, textual integrity) occur in both Le Fanu and Salmon. In Le Fanu, we might add, they are not burked.[11]

The Salmon controversy, though particular to Dublin, was then part of a wider and familiar literary debate, reaching at least as far as 1850 when Tennyson's *In Memoriam* had tunefully expressed many anxieties concerning the orthodox reassurance offered to the bereaved. In 1861 John William Colenso's *Commentary on the Epistle to the Romans* inaugurated two decades of bitter dispute within the Church of England, by challenging the theology of sacraments, of sin and punishment, and – ultimately – by applying a highly damaging textual analysis to great portions of the Old Testament. The Dublin flurry had its own distinctive features, with an extreme anti-Catholic attitude voiced by the Reverend William Digby, and a philosophical response embodied in the work of a barrister, Edward Falconer Litton. The latter touched on matters of considerable interest to Le Fanu, when he demolished the argument by analogy according to which the soul survives death uncorrupted just as the body survives in a cataleptic trance. Le Fanu's 'The Room in the Dragon Volant' investigates the paralysed consciousness of just such a victim.[12]

Ireland had no Tennyson to offer the Victorian age, nor can one rank Le Fanu among the best novelists of the time. Oddly, given the intellectual torpor of mid-Victorian Ireland, it was in the field of historical research that her contribution to these debates was first noted. When the young Edward Lecky published *The Rise and Influence of the Spirit of Rationalism in Europe* in 1865, the question of eternal punishment still deserved extensive treatment. Lecky's serene professionalism earned him a lengthy rebuke from Charles Daubeny, F.R.S., an important botanist and former professor of chemistry at Oxford who had also been a friend of Archbishop

The parochial and the exotic

Whately of Dublin. The heart of the matter may be summarised in a few sentences from *The Spirit of Rationalism*. First, 'the rapid growth of a morphological conception of the universe' had deeply affected speculative opinion. Secondly, 'when modern science acquired an ascendency over theological developments ... the attention of men was then directed chiefly to those multitudinous contrivances which are designed for the wellbeing of all created things, while the terrorism once produced by the calamities of life was at least greatly dimished'. And, thirdly, the notion that the scriptural chronicle contained 'an occult meaning, a notion 'which in modern times has been systematised and developed with great ingenuity by Swedenborg in his "Doctrine of Correspondences"' gives rise to very important questions 'concerning the comparative authority of the historical and the spiritual meanings'. Lecky's repeated emphasis on the modernity of these issues in 1865 underlines their urgency in the minds of more timid thinkers.[13]

Which brings us back to Sheridan Le Fanu who, for all the exactness of his fictional terrors, is recognisably shaken by their implications. Within the narrative of 'Ultor de Lacy', a similar crisis of authority can now be discerned. For it is not enough to classify the story under some heading like The Present-As-Evil-Inheritance. Too much intervenes between 1601 and the post-Jacobite occasion of Una's seduction for her to be a Norman-Irish victim of a Gaelic Maule's curse, too much that is innocuous or slight or at worst, venial. No single line of retribution descends from the scaffold, on which O'Donnell uttered his presumably Satanic prayer, to the bed from which Una de Lacy disappears. What continuity there is is vitiated by two factors – (1) the largely undisclosed nature of the picture which Ultor is shown by his dying father; and (2) the convergence of both de Lacy and O'Donnell in the words on the bed-head. Not the *lex talionis* of ancient Rome and the revenge tragedies of Jacobean England, but a more intimate and abstract terror is worked out in the story of Una de Lacy. The code requiring vengeance possesses logic, it distinguishes absolutely between victim and villain and seeks a righting of balances between them. The problem with Le Fanu's story is that one cannot finally tell whether one is dealing with an 'Achilles Ultor' or a 'Patrocli Ultor', the essential distinction upon which the authority of the avenging agent relies has been blurred, as if a Latin word-order had spasmodically become an English grammar.

'Borrhomeo' has its affiliation to this model, clearly, but it fits additionally into another group of texts. Let me draw attention to a number of Le Fanu's stories which share a common continental setting with 'Borrhomeo'. These are 'A Strange Event', 'Spalatro', 'The Room in the Dragon Volant' and 'Carmilla'. Claude Lévi-Strauss has elaborated a theory concerning the structure of myth in which the incompleteness of any one statement of a myth indicates its signficance. To 'reconstruct' a myth wholly, one needs to tabulate all statements of it: as with an orchestral score no one line in this tabulation carries the entire message or melody, but by arranging all the statements in an ideal form all the individual gaps and absences are supplied or at least detected.[14] In the accompanying tabulation, large and small 'X's indicate the prominence or otherwise of the named topics:

	Blood	Sex	Satan	Painting
'A Strange Event'	–	X	X	X
'Spalatro'	X	x	x	–
'Borrhomeo'	x	–	X	x
'The Room'	x	x	–	x
'Carmilla'	x	X	–	X

These topics are somewhat simplified in the schema. By blood is meant spilled blood, though Lévi-Strauss would insist that the overvaluation of 'blood-relationship' (in incest etc.) ought to be incorporated somewhere in a related sub-heading. Certainly Le Fanu alludes to shared ancestry among a number of his tensely related characters; casually enough in the case of O'Donnell who cited relationship through his mother as a reason for clemency, more suggestively in the case of the narrator of 'Carmilla' and Carmilla herself, for here incest would be added to the injuries of vampiric lesbianism. However crude the above schema may be it still indicates that the co-ordination of a single fiction, in which all four elements – violence (blood-letting), active sexual attraction, Satan (or a junior devil, like the Demon Lover), and the art of painting – are active, is frustrated in each possible case by the exclusion of one element.

The orchestral score can then be read in either (or both) of two ways; to identify each of these headings with all the others (i.e. Satan = Painting = Murder = Sexuality) and/or to indicate the innocuousness of the missing theme within the particular story from which it is missing (e.g. killing would have been justifiable in Schalken's position: even Satan might be preferable to the nameless sexual irregularities of 'Carmilla'). Indeed, the simultaneous validity of *both* readings may have to be considered. What is more readily grasped is the systematic exclusion of some one item from a text which is thereby robbed of authority *and* rendered tolerable.

This question of textual authority is more than an internal feature of 'Borrhomeo the Astrologer'. Le Fanu's monkish tale bears several resemblances to Manzoni's novel, not the least significant of which is their common presentation of themselves as editions of a manuscript. This authentic, hand-written and first-person-singular source cannot – for whatever reasons – be made directly available to the reader. As a narrative device, the lost manuscript had long been a stock-in-gothic-trade by which personal testimony and exotic atmosphere could be intensified, but its larger implications for the business of writing itself have not gone unnoted. In Manzoni's case, the narrator complains of the original chronicler's baroque style, and demonstrates this by opening with a lengthy and burdensome quotation. In Le Fanu's case, the 'manuscript' has of course passed through translation, though other obscurities and lacunae are also referred to in passing. Manzoni is keen to show that the 'original' may be less intelligible than its rewriting, while Le Fanu virtually denies that an 'original' can be conceived of. The history of Borrhomeo's dreadful fate is de-authorised even in the process of its presentation; authority for the event is as elusive as any release from his punishment, and this with some implication that damnation and authorship are analogous one to the other in some respects. The villain's ultimate fate – to live entranced for a thousand years even though he be 'hanged, impaled, and buried, according to his sentence' – parodies psychic integrity or personal immortality. In this, it reinscribes Melmoth's dilemma not so much through the reintroduction of the old gothic tropes as by a disinclination to take up the implications of Balzac's commercialisation of them. 'Borrhomeo' is in flight from its age, but it finds refuge only in the dreadful permanence of a future no less rigid than the past. It might be possible to reconcile this ironic definition of damnation with the historical reversals of 'Ultor de Lacy', but central to any synoptic account of the stories would be a problematic of identity.

Le Fanu and his art

Notes

1 Sheridan Le Fanu *A Lost Name* London, 1868 vol. 1 p. 243.
2 'Ultor de Lacy; a Legend of Cappercullen' in *Best Ghost Stories of J. S. Le Fanu* (ed. E. F. Bleieler) New York: Dover, 1964 p. 444. The notion that Le Fanu's choice of female Christian name derives from the Una of Edmund Spenser's *Faerie Queene* (see Book 1), composed in part during the poet's Irish residence in the 1580s, has the merit of drawing attention to an Elizabethan text. But Spenser's Una is the embodiment of a metaphysical unity of truth and virtue, whereas Le Fanu's ... isn't. It seems more likely that Le Fanu's source is directly the common Gaelic name Úna which was popular from medieval times onwards.
3 Ibid. p. 466. It is tempting to consider what Le Fanu's sources for this story may have been. The major chronicles of the Elizabethan wars do not record an incident resembling that lying behind the plot of retribution. The *Pacata Hibernica*, attributed to Thomas Stafford and first published in 1633, had been republished in Dublin in 1810. In the second volume there are references to Hugh O'Donnell marching his men across Slieve Felim at night and slipping 'through a straight, neere to the abbey of Ownhy' [i. e. Abington] and eluding an ambush; this incident, in which the Ulsterman trusted a deep frost to make boggy land negotiable, was 'the greatest march with carriage ... that hath been heard of'. But that was *before* the Battle of Kinsale, and the Ulstermen were then heading southwards. Much later, *c.* 9–12 July 1602, some of O'Neill's men and carriage were lost at Abington. Neither incident, nor its date, fits Le Fanu's historical background. O'Sullivan Bere's narrative mentions one or two members of the De Lacy family, but in other connections; and *The Annals of the Four Masters* add nothing. (See *Pacata Hibernica; or a History of the Wars in Ireland during the Reign of Queen Elizabeth* Dublin: Hibernia-Press, 1810, vol. 2 pp. 377, 378, 430.) We can conclude then that Le Fanu may have had access to some local legend, and that he created a pseudo-historical framework for a theme related to the pressure of history itself.
4 William Le Fanu's diaries are preserved in the Library, Trinity College, Dublin.
5 'Ultor de Lacy' p. 465.
6 I saw the engraving in a Cork restaurant in 1989, appropriately one named The Huguenot.
7 'Ultor de Lacy' p. 447.
8 J. Sheridan Le Fanu *Borrhomeo the Astrologer: A Monkish Tale* (ed. W. J. Mc Cormack) Edinburgh: Tragara Press, 1985 p. 23.
9 Ibid. p. 27.
10 Ibid. pp. 28–9. The closing of the skin may echo the account in Genesis of the operation in which Adam's 'spare rib' is removed to become woman (see above p. 23).
11 See George Salmon, *The Eternity of Future Punishment, and, The Place which that Doctrine Ought to Hold in Christian Teaching: Two Sermons Preached in the Chapel of Trinity College Dublin* Dublin: Hodges, Smith, 1865 (2nd ed.). James William Barlow, *Eternal Punishment and Eternal Death: an Essay* London: Longman, 1865. Barlow, *Remarks on Some Recent Publications Concerning Future Punishment* Dublin: Mc Gee, 1865. George Sidney Smith, *The Doctrine of Eternal Punishment*

The parochial and the exotic

Examined Chiefly in relation to the Testimony of Scripture Dublin: Herbert, 1865. The quotation from Smith will be found on p. 3 of his pamphlet. See also Thomas Ryan *Annihilation and Universalism; or A Review of the Works of Messrs. Barlow and Litton, and Others, in a Letter to a Friend* London: Paul, 1866. For a general account of the controversy (which neglects the Irish theatre of conflict) see Geoffrey Rowell *Hell and the Victorians; a Study of the Nineteenth-Century Theological Controversies Concerning Eternal Punishment and the Future Life* Oxford: Clarendon Press, 1974.

12   See William Digby *Thoughts on Ancient and Modern Demonology, as Exposed in the Light of Holy Scripture* Dublin: Curry, 1863. Edward Falconer Litton *Life or Death: the Destiny of the Soul in the Future State* London: Longman, 1866. Digby's is a short pamphlet, and by p. 13 he is asking such demonological questions as 'Why cannot Ireland prosper?' and two pages later analysing the 1641 rebellion. Litton's, on the other hand, is a lengthy and thoughtful work with references to Plato, J. S. Mill, the Danish philosopher Oersted, as well as several nineteenth-century Irish authorities (Richard Whately, William Archer Butler etc.).

13   William Edward Hartpole Lecky *The Rise and Influence of the Spirit of Rationalism in Europe* London: Longman, 1910 (2 vols in 1) vol. 1 pp. 287, 264; see pp. 311–51 for Lecky on Hell; see also Charles Daubeny *Christianity and Rationalism in their Relations to Natural Science; being a Protest against Certain Principles advocated in Mr. Lecky's History of the Rise and Influence of the Spirit of Rationalism in Europe* Oxford: Parker, 1867.

14   The tabulation is modified from that given in my introduction to *Borrhomeo the Astrologer* (p. 10). For the orchestral score see Edmund Leach *Lévi-Strauss* Glasgow: Fontana/Colins, 1974 (rev. ed.) pp. 59–60.

6

Beginning
the English novels

The House by the Church-yard had included less concentrated inquiries of a kind similar to those conducted in the stories of 1861–2. Whether for financial reasons alone or otherwise, Le Fanu was obliged to abandon Irish historical settings in all his subsequent full-length novels. The last instalment of the Chapelizod saga appeared in the February 1863 number of *The Dublin University Magazine*, and on the 26th of that month he signed the contract with Bentley's of London which resulted in *Wylder's Hand*. In place of the Irish disciple of Scott, however deviant, an English novelist was born.

Retained as narrator, Charles de Cresseron becomes little more than a technical device as far as the plot is concerned. He aligns himself, against history, with an earnest yet unassertive present normality. And the opening paragraphs trumpet Le Fanu's compliance with his publisher's insistence on a 'story of an English subject and in modern times':

> It was late in the autumn, and I was skimming along, through a rich English county, in a postchaise, among tall hedgerows gilded, like all the landscape, with the slanting beams of sunset. The road makes a long and easy descent into the little town of Gylingden ... An undulating landscape, with a homely farmstead here and there, and plenty of old English timber scattered grandly over it ... [1]

Though there is a powerful contrast between this novel and its renowned successor, *Uncle Silas*, Le Fanu's first attempt at a novel of English contemporary life deserves attention. The business of opening with an English scene is relatively simple, the question remains as to where the action commences. For all his conventionality, de Cresseron has become no less retrospective in his translation from Chapelizod to Gylingden, for as soon as he heard of a Miss Lake: 'there rose before me an image of an old General Lake, and a dim recollection of some reverse of fortune. He was – I was sure of that – connected with the Brandon family; and was, with the usual fatality, a bit of a *mauvais sujet* ... '[2] However subliminally, this opening English scene has promptly implicated an earlier Irish historical action. The narrator's associative memory can be more fully appreciated if a seemingly unconnected episode from *Uncle Silas* is drawn into the discussion. Near the close of Maud Ruthyn's ordeal, she journeyed ostensibly to Dover en route for France; in fact she had been taken circuitously back (in effect, a prisoner) to the unrecognised inner-quarters of the house she had earlier quit. Now, General Gerard (later Viscount) Lake (1744–1808) had not only served in Ireland during the United Irishmen's 1798 rebellion and distinguished himself for savagery at the Battle of Vinegar Hill, he had also crossed with R. B. Sheridan over a lucrative sinecure which the Prince of Wales had tried to transfer from Lake to the dramatist.

This episode in turn can be associated with another from Sheridan's colourful career. After the death of his first wife, he fell in love with the famous Pamela, daughter of Madame de Genlis, then visiting England. When the ladies set out to return to France, their coach to Dover was secretly diverted at Sheridan's instigation, and Pamela's departure delayed for a period.[3] In *Uncle Silas*, Maud's transfer to a French school – really a subterfuge preparatory to her murder – is deliberately short-circuited in the same way. The irony goes deeper, for Pamela ultimately married Lord Edward Fitzgerald, rumoured to have been Sheridan's wife's lover, and of course renowned as the romantic leader of the United Irishmen at the beginning of 1798. The novel *Wylder's Hand*, in allowing its narrator to associate freely round the name of Rachel Lake, displays its open frontier to Irish history and intrigue.

Sheridan of course was a distinguished kinsman whose name the novelist bore. One other autobiographical trace in *Wylder's Hand* deserves mention. In 1845, Sheridan Le Fanu and his brother had each inherited a ring from their father; William's was 'a cornelian seal with Persian characters' which had earlier belonged to Thomas Sheridan.[4] Mark Wylder of course has been dead throughout most of the novel, a fact disguised by the regular delivery of letters purporting to come from him and evidently written in his hand. At the climax of the novel his cousin and covert rival, Stanley Lake, is thrown from a horse at a point in Redman's Dell where Wylder's corpse has become partly exposed:

In this livid hand, rising from the earth there was a character both of menace and appeal; and on the finger, as I afterwards saw at the inquest, glimmered the talismanic legend 'Resurgam – I will rise again!' ... discoloured and disfigured as were both clothes and body, I was sure that the dead man was no other than Mark Wylder. When the clay with which it was clotted was a little removed, it became indubitable. The great whiskers; the teeth so white and even ... The left hand, on which was the ring of 'the Persian magician,' was bare ... [5]

The 'hand' of the novel's title is both Wylder's forged handwriting (by which Lake conceals his murder of Mark) and the anatomical limb (*disjectum membrum*) which points up from the concealed corpse to throw the murderer from his mount. This doubled usage is oddly duplicated in the rings. At first, de Cresseron tells us of a ring with a pious Christian inscription, particularly apt in that Mark is virtually rising from the grave even as the ring is noticed. But a few paragraphs later, he speaks of the Persian magician's ring, challenging the reader to identity a Christian theme with a Persian or magical one. Mark's body is remarkably preserved, not only recalling the indestructable and tortured body of Borrhomeo in his thousand-year trance but also mocking the earth or clay which conventionally should have received and dissolved his 'clay'. All in all, this novel of an English subject and modern times manages casual Irish historical allusion through a surname and a comprehensive inversion of Christian hopes for the future life. What's more the means of its doing so centrally involve verbal oscillations – hand/hand, clay/clay – as if to point mutely to the treacherous identity of word and object.

In his craggiest style Raymond Williams wrote of the realist novel in terms which, at first glance at least, are helpful in discussing *Wylder's Hand*:

neither the society nor the individual is there as a priority. The society is not a background against which the personal relationships are studied, nor are the individuals merely illustrations of aspects of the way of life. Every aspect of personal life is radically affected by the quality of the general life, yet the general life is seen at its most important in completely personal terms.[6]

The contemporary setting, the treatment of social occasion, the observation of character all conform to Williams's ideal. One is aware of limitations to Le Fanu's familiarity with the English shires, even as one would have to concede that his knowledge of Irish popular culture was second-hand. Despite – or because of – the efforts to integrate his plot into an English setting, there are signs of discontinuity, there are elisions, silences and unexplained gestures. The realism which *Wylder's Hand* ironically achieves is that of neither English manners nor Irish; the novel moves between these two terms and unwittingly explores the metaphorical ground of their union. Marriage is proposed, postponed; absence is enforced, explained. Of the social bustle, the narrator observes 'there is no privacy like it ... provided only that you command your countenance'.[7] That the entire ballyhoo of ballots and ballrooms and backbars and backbiting lawyers should revolve round a dead man in Redman's Dell, believed to be touring Europe, draws the novel back towards the central enigma of *The House by the Church-yard*.

But *Wylder's Hand* also anticipates some of Le Fanu's bolder strokes. The conclusion in which two women – Dorcas Brandon and Rachel Lake – become the ultimate focus of the novel suggests the feminine narrative of *Uncle Silas* which will proceed from the pen of Maud Ruthyn herself. Women, however they may be crowded round by suitors and 'advisers', are implicitly regarded as a positive locus of action. Indeed, de Cresseron in the early chapters of *Wylder's Hand* casually associates female beauty with 'the image of God'.[8] No libidinous worship of Miss Brandon can be ascribed to the narrator; on the contrary, the paragraph (which also cites George Sand) constitutes one of those earliest transferences from male to female (to the near self-effacement of the male) which will characterise Le Fanu's 'English' novels. In treating sexuality, as in treating the surfaces of English upper-class life, Le Fanu actually engages in a realism of the unreal. That is to say, the usual conventions are haunted by repressed or subversive values, or are mocked by evidences of a superior power whose lineaments can hardly be hinted at in so mundane a chronicle as the novel of entertainment.

Without suggesting any code or *clef*, we can see that Wylder's eternal sleep and earthy resurrection function not unlike nationalist Irish passion within the iron casket of the United Kingdom. While notional England and Ireland are endlessly represented in Victorian novels, few novelists even strove to grapple with the existence of the larger and economically actual entity, with the complex relationship of the Union itself – Trollope is perhaps the exception.[9] Yet in *Wylder's Hand* the conventionality of the landscape betrays not so much the author's unfamiliarity with the English countryside as the purely decorative status of parkland within the economic life of the state known – but not in fiction – as the United Kingdom. Obliged to shift from Irish historical settings to English contemporary ones, the novelist resists the trajectory of the very class-allegiance which is disputed, emergent, still inchoate in the 1860s. Ascendancy will come to revere the short-lived and self-defining glories of the eighteenth-century Irish Protestant parliament. But not yet. In Le Fanu's fiction, that tradition has not been invented, and the coercion evident in the alternative focus on 'old England' is everywhere evident.

This is not a matter simply of political institutions. Le Fanu's unconscious feminism acts to undermine old patriarchal assumptions just as the allure of a bogus representationalism blinds other characters to the deadness of the titular hero. The political forms of representationalism are of course implicated. Stanley Lake has parliamentary ambitions. It is not his electoral opponent (Sir Harry Bracton) who denies Lake a seat but his murdered victim who unseats him. The past and not the future lies beyond his control. This verbal play on parliament and horse as providing 'a seat' is reproduced elsewhere. Hand, inscribed ring and family motto are each in turn ironised. For Mark Wylder's hand ultimately signals his long-buried death and not his continuing life, his presence beneath the native sod and not his absence abroad. In the strictest sense, his *resurgam* is 'not to be'. (In imitation of George Berkeley's formulation, this might written out as *resurgere = non esse*.) In contrast to this annihilation of the principal male actors of an English crisis, the final paragraph shows Rachel and Dorcas drifting happily on the lagoon at Venice. *Their* being abroad signals release, and de Cresseron obliquely emphasises the defeat of male power generally in his brief description of the place 'where so many rings of Doges lie lost beneath the waves'.[10]

The abstract trajectory inscribed in this novel might be cryptically particularised as travelling from lake to lagoon, that is, from the echo of General Gerard Lake to the Venetian scene with Dorcas and Rachel. In strict fairness, it should be noted that the text does not use the word 'lagoon', preferring 'the waters ... the forsaken sea'. (Yet lagoon is the usual term employed for the inner reaches of the Adriatic on which the city is built.) With this reservation then the trajectory can be more fully described as moving from the hard connotations of the warlord to the liquid and enfolding patterns of civic waterways. This then is one instance of character in dissolution, a process worked out through the collapse of his schemes and through the textures of a few nouns. As an enactment of the eclipse of male aggression in the novel, the verbal detail could hardly be bettered. Moreover, Mark Wylder's ring – Christian or magical – now takes its place among the 'many rings' which doges of Venice have cast into the sea. This latter ceremony, an annual event since 1177, was performed on Ascension Day which, in the Christian calendar was (so to speak) the occasion of a second and greater resurrection.

Thus the *resurgam* of Mark Wylder's ring is not just mocked in his grisly emergence in Redman's Dell but is more comprehensively incorporated in the novel's final glimpse of the female characters. The twoness of this feminist emphasis has its own significance. Venice was, by the protocols of the cememony of rings, 'bride of the Adriatic'. Yet in the line from Byron's *Childe Harold* which Le Fanu incorporates in his final paragraph 'The spouseless Adriatic mourns her lord'. On this evidence, the city is both bride and lord or, less androgynously, both city and sea are characterised as feminine. Byron is not to blame for this apparent profusion, for the lord in question in the poem is Bucentaur, the state galley used by the doge, the last of its name being destroyed by the French in 1798, the year of General Lake's triumph in Wexford. Thus Le Fanu has elided the man-ox war-vessel and substituted as a consequence a doubled feminine in Venice / Adriatic. The happiness of Rachel and Dorcas is a mere reflection of a profounder nominalist logic. Nevertheless, the basis of this logic cannot be admitted into a Victorian novel of entertainment and so the final scene drifts into sentimental vapourings. The association of lake / lagoon with the Latin terminology of manuscript description leads one to see *lacuna* not only as pool but as gap or repression, a sense in which Freud was to use it much later. *Wylder's Hand* follows an highly original trajectory, but cannot name it. Perhaps only Lacan can.

In this connection, some features of the superficial plot take on their own somewhat larger significance. The financial machinations of Lawyer Larkin had been called a 'whole structure of rapine and duplicity', and the elimination of sexual violence by the concentration on one sex only is thus philologically implicit in the novel's description of what business corruption is. The initially inert narrator also achieves a deeper rationale: recounting his encounter with the two women in Venice, he writes 'unseen I saw'. The purification of narrative into non-intrusive vision is an aspiration which the novelist pursues even in fiction where the narrator is a female character.[11]

Le Fanu's energy at this time deserves notice. The last instalment of *Wylder's Hand* appeared in February 1864 and the first of what was to become *Uncle Silas* in July. The new serial was initially called *Maud Ruthyn* and the female narrator was fully acknowledged in the novelist's choice of title. Bentley's of London thought otherwise, and the three-decker version appeared as *Uncle Silas*. The change of name disguises Le Fanu's commitment to the feminist aspect of his new fiction, and it is worth asking if the use of non-Irish settings had not relieved him somehow from the implications of his own patrimony. With the ancestral narrator finally pushed aside, *Uncle Silas* remains his most impressive achievement. Not surprisingly, this is the novel which has attracted republication, reconsideration and even a television film – starring Peter O'Toole! – since the first appearance of the biography in 1980. Two particular contributions deserve to be brought together here.

In the introduction to the World's Classics edition, the editor demonstrates how the initial presentation of Austin Ruthyn derives from a passage in Chateaubriand's *Mémoires d'Outre Tombe* (1849–50).[12] The details of the proof need not detain us again; it is sufficient to say that the debt is unchallengeable, and that Le Fanu promptly turned the material to his own very distinctive purpose. In both the *Mémoires* and *Uncle Silas*, the narrator describes his/her father perambulating in a dimly lit room, but the further description of Chateaubriand's father is split in Le Fanu's treatment so that part attaches to the figure of Austin Ruthyn and part to Silas, his brother. In terms of textual source, this is a specific demonstration of the process – described at length in the fifth chapter of the biography – whereby character is presented in duplicate as if to encourage the proliferation of Swedenborgian correspondences. The process involves both differentiation and identification in a manner suggesting that the implications of bringing all aspects of character together were textually repressed in the dispersion into twin-figures.

Moreover, both the male figures generated from the Chateaubriand passage are placed in framing devices repeatedly – in the first instance Austin emerges 'for a few minutes, like a portrait with a background of shadow'.[13] The internal significance of this has been discussed in the chapter of *Sheridan Le Fanu and Victorian Ireland* just cited, and one simply adds that Chateaubriand is not responsible for the pervasive use of such allusions to portraiture, painting and framing in this or in any other of Le Fanu's fictions. It is obsessively the author's own – if author there be. For a paradox is thereby introduced. In what way is it 'original' of an artist to introduce the names of other artists into his work? To be sure, we are speaking of a novelist who repeatedly invokes a painter (Rembrandt, Wouvermans, Van Dyck, etc.), but the element of jeopardy remains. The novelist *creates* character, we are told, but if the character in question is 'à la Wouvermans' has not the novelist's creative power been implicitly limited or frustrated? Certainly, the presentation of characters in *Uncle Silas* repeatedly discounts their freedom; they are cast against backgrounds, framed in windows, described as 'monumental', and in other ways related to portrayed figures. Movement is achieved only after great exercises in narrative. Or it is sometimes spasmodic as if some controlling energy had momentarily relaxed. Elizabeth Bowen has something similar in mind when she writes of Le Fanu adopting 'an oblique and more than semi-mistrustful view of character'. 'Oblique' and 'view' are precise terms of his relationship to the human personages of his fiction, they are visual terms.[14]

The second point of further appreciation of *Uncle Silas* in its textual duplicity clarifies something even more obscure. In Chapter 19 taciturn Austin Ruthyn is about to speak frankly to his daughter:

> He turned on me such an approving smile as you might fancy lighting up the rugged features of a pale old Rembrandt.
>
> 'I can tell you, Maud; if my life could have done it, it should not have been undone – *ubi lapsus, quid feci*. But I had almost made up my mind to change my plan, and leave all to time ... I don't speak of fortune, that is not involved – but is there any other honourable sacrifice you would shrink from to dispel the disgrace under which our most ancient and honourable name must otherwise continue to languish?'
>
> 'Oh, none – none indeed, sir – I am delighted!'
>
> Again I saw the Rembrandt smile.[15]

The quick succession of allusions to the great Dutch painter is hypnotic, especially as the second almost persuades one that a painting – 'the Rembrandt' – is the subject/nominative of the verb to smile. But no, these are further embellishments of the narrator's portrayal of her father, a portrayal sustained by the paradoxical constant reinscription of artists' names. What he says, proposes etc. remains in the background while the signatures attract admiration. In such company as Rembrandt's, it would not be surprising if the Latin tag were ignored also. And indeed it resists interpretation, unlike the familiar Ovidian *edax rerum* which follows it obligingly.

The Courtenays of Powderham, sometime earls of Devon, took as their motto the double question *Ubi lapsus? Quid Feci?* translatable as 'Where is my fault? What have I done [to deserve this]?' These words which express astonishment at a sudden and undeserved fall are said to have been adopted by the family when they lost the earldom. The historical association of the Courtenays with Ireland and with County Limerick has been discussed elsewhere, and its relevance to the plot of *Uncle Silas* assessed. Suffice it to say here that the fall of the Courtenays in the sixteenth century, with the notoriety attached to their name and Irish property in the nineteenth century, instances once again that reproduction of Elizabethan allusions which we traced in *The House by the Church-yard* and 'Ultor de Lacy'.[16]

In several senses, the Latin tag raises the question of genealogy. Officially it serves as a family motto, recognisable to the genealogist rather than the classical scholar. In a manner more strictly apt than most family mottoes, it addresses itself to the family's condition and how this condition has come about; that is, it comments on the genealogy of Courtenay genealogy. Beyond family pride, it summarises the condition of fallen humanity which, as a consequence of its sin, cannot know the full extent of its loss, its offence against God. But the novel *misquotes* the Courtenay family motto, crucially omitting the query marks. The effect is to render the utterer (Austin Ruthyn) apparently more complacent in his unconscious echo of the phrase. On the surface, Maud's father appears to speak frankly and in his own person, whereas textually he repeats with error a text concerning error.

A general summary may be useful at this moment. In *Sheridan Le Fanu and Victorian Ireland* it was demonstrated at some length that *Uncle Silas* owes complex debts to Emanuel Swedenborg, author of *Heaven and Hell* (1758).[17] In addition we now note René Chateaubriand, the visissitudes of English nobility, and an hundred or so casual literary allusions. So much is textual. Add to this again the smaller, more concentrated body of reference to portraiture. Structurally, the doctrines of Swedenborg have a pre-eminent place in this network rivalled only by the consistent painterly accounts of character. Each of these aspects of *Uncle Silas* insinuates a notion of secondary existence; the external world for Swedenborg is only one level of a vast system of correspondences while a portrait presupposes (even if it does not always strictly require) an original sitter. Austin and Silas, as presented in the novel, conform to such a binary pattern. When their relationship was under examination, the question arose as to the kind of offence in Austin which could give rise to Silas. The question, *qua* question, is given textual status in the inaccurate allusion to the Courtenay motto just as the discovery of a Chateaubriand 'original' for the initial presentation of Austin unveils a compositional methodology.

This is a fiction of secondary existences predicated on the withdrawal, absence, inaccessibility – or even *impossibility* – of anything which might be called primary existences. The implications of this for the treatment of character may be considered in a moment: for the present let us look at more strictly textual and structural matters. Unlike *Wylder's Hand* with its ostentatious creation of an English landscape, *Uncle Silas* derives from two earlier stories by Le Fanu. These were 'Passage in the Secret History of an Irish Countess' (1838) and 'The Murdered Cousin' (1851), both set in Ireland. Working back from the novel, one can see a growing admission of textual diversity. The novel has hermetic ambitions as we have seen, the story of 1851 emphasises in its title the close relationship between the victim and the narrator (the intended victim), while the earliest version of the plot exists in several larger narrative con-texts. First, it is but a 'passage' from some longer narrative, a *secret history* rather than a self-sustaining *objet d'art*. Secondly, it forms part of the series of anonymous tales presented as extracts from the papers of Fr Francis Purcell of Drumcoollagh, with introductory matter contributed by an anonymous editor, friend of the late Fr Purcell. Passage, extract, paper, etc. – all of these terms underline the unavailability of a complete text, even the impossibility of such a thing.

Fiction had long been presented as edited fact, and the fragment became a central preoccupation of the romantic writers. In William Wordsworth's poetry, the apprehension of certain 'spots of time' leads to a harmonious vision of reality in which the irritations of ordinary life and the limitations of personality are transcended. It goes without saying that Le Fanu knows no such blessing. The incompleteness which his stories and novels repeatedly accomplish allows for no union between an intractable world and the seriality which replaces the individual. Every character in Le Fanu is pre-ceded; literary convention sees to much of this, supplying stage-hand domestics either faithful or treacherous, wicked uncles and endangered heiresses; but even the seemingly distinctive details of *Uncle Silas* are, on examination, subsumed under one or another de-originating rubric. The solipsism of *Heaven and Hell* is reduced to the endless chronicles of Irish history. Character is repeatedly signed in the name of some renowned artist, and the names of characters reproduced from fiction to fiction. Notoriously, 'Marston' appears in more than half a dozen, and it is augmented by the names of another half dozen dramatists. Such references do not indicate or identify a theme, they show the limitless opportunities fiction has to mediate between the filters and screens which themselves mediate 'fact' to it.

In an instance examined earlier for other purposes, *The House by the Church-yard* has Dan Loftus put through college by Dr Walsingham. But the college in question is likely the one (Trinity) of which Adam Loftus became the first provost in 1592. Does Dan Loftus derive his name from this subliminal literary effect? (Or, perhaps, from his other namesake, yet another Adam Loftus, lord chancellor of Ireland in 1619?)[18] Faced with these irresolvable op-tions, the reader may even come to realise that the title of the novel does not univocally refer to any one house, the title exists in a more complex relation to the habitations of the living characters. With the same double option, 'Borrhomeo the Astrologer' may in his name echo either of two archbishops of Milan with similar names (Carlo Borromeo (1538–84), and his nephew/successor Federico Borromeo) who were active in the history which forms the back-ground to the tale. But if Le Fanu misspells the Italian family name, does he do so to disguise a debt to Alessandro Manzoni or to implicate a notion of *homo*geneity, a condition of sameness, an elusive but underlying identity of all things? Balzac's *Séraphita* had announced that there all was homogeneous but *here*, in the interim world of a self-divided Anglo-Ireland at work upon an emergent ideology which will serve to eclipse any dangerous talk of social class, the unity of all things is a consummation, not an end in itself.

The question initially raised about names and misspellings can be taken further. In the first two of his 'English' novels, Sheridan Le Fanu strove 'to begin again' and eloquently demonstrated the fatal contradiction involved. Despite the energetic propagation of an 'olde Englande' sentimentality in the nineteenth century generally, Le Fanu's fiction demonstrates that the English landscape and its 'noble timber' cannot be created afresh; from any image of such a pristine condition there will arise an emblem of decay, an ironic echo of resurgence. The implosive order of *Uncle Silas* demonstrates a corollary, that symmetry sustains itself only in destruction. Yet in his efforts towards a singular universe Le Fanu unveils evidences of serial character and plural textuality which may prove to be innovative.

The depth of this crisis in Le Fanu's work can be gauged from the falling-off evident in *Guy Deverell* (1865). If this is listed by Nelson Browne among the author's 'five great novels' we should perhaps inquire as to what constitutes greatness in fiction.[19] As with *Wylder's Hand*, the opening scene is an English roadside, but whereas de Cresseron's narrative engendered a tension between locale and narrator, the coaching inn of *Guy Deverell* is biscuit-box picturesque and nothing more. A young man's appearance greatly disturbs Sir Jekyl Marlowe's self-esteem because he resembles someone whom the baronet killed unfairly in a duel many years earlier. The explanation – Guy Strangways is the son of that Guy Deverell – is both obvious and ludicrously withheld. Lady Alice's encounter with him in church permits the indulgence of 'resurrection' as a hyperbolic account of her dead son's image. There is no ambiguity or evasion about the matter: 'she therefore saw the moving image of her dead son before her, with an agonizing distinctness that told like a blight of palsy on her face' and again in her own words 'I have seen the most extraordinary resemblance to my beautiful, *murdered* Guy'.[20] Yet this blood-relationship is promptly forgotten, or at least veiled in the non-congruence of names. Lady Alice is a Redcliffe whereas the dead man (and his 'resurrected' image or son) is Guy Deverell. If the scene in church is contrived and showy, perhaps this stems from its function as a distraction from an admission the novel ultimately cannot make. Less sentimental – because less heavily worked than the balcony vision of the dead – is a reference to 'the enamelled miniature on her bosom' as rival to the sight before Lady Alice's eyes.[21]

Browne astutely recognises 'an indeterminate quality about the mystery itself, as if the author could not quite make up his mind whether or not it was worth while to unravel the knot of intrigue'.[22] The plot is once again centred on the notion of vengeance, but the machinery of criminal investigation can be heard too audibly whirring in the background to allow for any complexity of treatment of the kind concentrated in 'Ultor de Lacy'. It is true that the impersonal narrative implicates Guy Strangways in a reflection upon character, and its relationship to language:

> Perhaps it was a bore. But habitual courtesy is somewhat more than 'mouth honour, breath.' Language and thought react upon one another marvellously. To restrain its expression is in part to restrain the feeling; and thus a well-bred man is not only in words and demeanour, but inwardly and sincerely, more gracious and noble than others.[23]

This begins well enough, and promises something like a recognition that mental life is not a totally autonomous and sovereign domain: if we are not wholly in communion with the linguists and the neo-grammarians, it is because the insight is almost instantly cancelled. Instead of pursuing the matter, the passage veers off into a rationale of gentility and ends up in unwitting endorsement of repression. This is not out of place in the romantic subplot of *Guy Deverell* because, if he is attracted to pretty Beatrix Marlowe, then the revelation of his true identity must also unveil a liaison of first cousins. What is resisting disclosure is not just the baronet's past crime but a passion (Guy's) which fails to comply with the strict code of exogamy. Against this one must also note Strangways's passivity, as if a second layer of repression were on the point of discovery, and the overvaluation of blood relationship in his attraction towards Beatrix were to be read as a cover for a more illicit introversion. The radical treatment of women in the two preceding novels is here deflected into a sort of suspended sexuality in the titular hero.

Just as the girl is strolling into the garden and Guy is about to read to her grandmother, he reflects on his feeling towards Beatrix and hers towards him: 'I'm sure she *dis*likes me. So much the better – Heaven knows I'm glad of it.'[24] In the previous sentence the narrative has paralleled their relationship with a curiously chosen classical one: 'He bowed and smiled faintly too, and for a moment stood gazing after her into the now vacant shadow of the old oak wainscotting, as young Numa might after his vanished Egeria, with an unspoken, burning grief, and a longing at his heart.'[25]

In Byron's *Childe Harold* (already called into play at the close of *Wylder's Hand*) the meeting of the proto-historical Roman king and the goddess in a sacred grove symbolises the human search for an *ideal* love. In Juvenal, the tryst had given rise only to amusement, though Romans generally held that Egeria had advised Numa on religious matters. What is significant here is that the classical allusion does not involve passionate human sexuality. Guy's curious gazing into 'the now vacant shadow of the old oak wainscotting' fails to conform with the conventional 'gazing after her' by an excess of unexpected detail concerning the location. The sacred grove has been interiorised to become a timber wall. In *Uncle Silas* and elsewhere, wainscotting had often acted as a background against which characters were formally disposed, its panelling framing them as in a portrait.[26] The theme of Numa and Egeria strikes one not just as literary but as pictorial, fit subject for a Rubens or Van Dyck. But, as if paradoxically to draw attention to the unbridgeable gulf between the verbal and the visual, the passage settles for the convention of 'unspoken … longing'.

Oddly enough, when the story concludes with an account of Beatrix's wedding, her bridesmaids and so forth, no *explicit* statement of Guy's status as husband is made. The reader is left in no doubt, of course, especially as the birth of a son allows the narrative to conclude: 'as in these pages we have heard something of a father, a son, and a grandson, each bearing the same name, I think I can't do better than call this tale after them – GUY DEVERELL.'[27] The consolidation of the past with the present, and its projection happily into the future, is premissed effectively upon an identity of names, despite the earlier conflict of evidence between 'Redcliffe' and 'Deverell' as the name of Lady Alice's son. Beyond that, the characterisation of the novel never escapes from Pre-Raphaelite felicities and crime-novel motivations. The forgotten enamel miniature is forgotten precisely in tandem with the repression of sexual introversion.

If one regards *Guy Deverell* as an unsatisfactory successor to *Uncle Silas*, there is none the less one feature which takes the reader back to *The House by the Church-yard*. Immediately after Beatrix's Egerian retirement to the garden, Guy had gone to Lady Alice's room where she asked him to read to her. The book chosen by him is written in 'very old French' so that he is obliged to translate for her into English. The chapter then proceeds to inscribe a lengthy passage from the recitation, duly headed 'Concerning a Remarkable Revenge after Sepulture'. The story uncannily parallels the murder of Lady Alice's son (Guy's father and namesake) in an unfairly conducted duel, the marriage of the surviving duellist and the birth of his exceptionally beautiful daughter etc. etc. But the setting of the tale read and translated by Guy is fifteenth-century Normandy, the victim is 'a young gentleman of Styrian descent', and the mode of revenge to be employed explicitly supernatural and vampiric.[28] It is indeed precisely when the infernal arts are being rehearsed in the recitation that Lady Alice interrupts to demand to know who Guy Strangways really is. With a contradictory stamp of his foot and speaking 'very gently', he confirms for her that he is indeed Guy Deverell.

This interpolated story counterbalances the 'Authentic Narrative of the Ghost of a Hand' in *The House by the Church-yard* in that it acts as a micro-text to the enfolding longer narrative whereas the haunting of Mrs Prosser was totally unconnected with the greater diverse actions of the novel into which it is transcribed. Different kinds of textual mimicry are at work in each case: as we have said Chapter 12 intrudes into the earlier novel just as the hand does into Mrs Prossser's bed: now the old French chronicle duplicates in supernatural terms the basic plot of the Victorian mystery story in which it is incorporated. The specific acting-out of a vampiric revenge upon wicked old Chavelier de St Aubrache is averted by Lady Alice's interruption, by which she imposes the name Deverell on Guy who confirms it but with contradictory gestures. Strangways had been his alias, and if he were really her son's son Redcliffe should be his legal name, yet Deverell he becomes at a moment which thus averts both vampirism in his recitation and incest in his relationship with Beatrix/Egeria. Coincidentally, the young woman has returned from the garden/grove to witness this scene of nominalisation.

But one cannot leave the interpolated narrative to rest merely upon its structuralist laurels, even if an intriguing anticipation of the Styrian setting of 'Carmilla' is added to the reverse parallel with Chapter 12 of *The House by the Church-yard*. Le Fanu and de Cresseron alike hailed from Normandy, and just as the odd detail about a father-in-law in the story of Mrs Prosser hinted at the novelist's family and *his* father-in-law, so the background to the story of the Chavelier de St Aubrache is associated with Le Fanu's own origins. If, in alluding to General Lake and Thomas Moore, *Wylder's Hand* and *Uncle Silas* smuggled into their ostensibly English setting a homeopathic dose of Irish history, then the limpid civilities of *Guy Deverell* actually incorporate a far more antique and far more violent emblem of authorial pedigree. Indeed, the view of Nelson Browne again that Sir Jekyl Marlowe 'is too luxurious by temperament, too much of the self-indulgent voluptuary, to be a complete monster of wickedness ... he is a naughty baronet, not a bold, bad one' might be taken further.[29] Sir Jekyl and his brother (a bishop named Dives), simpering Guy Deverell and the solider Varbarriere may be read as amiable foils for the briefly glimpsed St Aubrache and his Hungaro-vampiric adversary. It is the novel, however, which we are required to read at three-volume length, while the old French chronicle occupies a single page.

Notes

1 J. Sheridan Le Fanu *Wylder's Hand* London: Gollancz, 1963 p. 1.
2 Ibid. p. 11.
3 See Madeleine Bingham *Sheridan; the Track of a Comet* London: Allen & Unwin, 1972 pp. 330–2.
4 See W. J. Mc Cormack *Sheridan Le Fanu and Victorian Ireland* Dublin: Lilliput Press, 1991 (2nd ed.) p. 88.
5 *Wylder's Hand* pp. 369–72.
6 Raymond Williams *The Long Revolution* Harmondsworth: Penguin Books, 1965 pp. 304–5.
7 *Wylder's Hand* p. 13.
8 Ibid. p. 10.
9 See 'The Myth of England', the introduction to Anthony Trollope *The Eustace Diamonds* (ed. W. J. Mc Cormack) Oxford: World's Classics, 1983.
10 *Wylder's Hand* p. 387.
11 Ibid. pp. 386–7.
12 See the introduction to J. Sheridan Le Fanu *Uncle Silas; a Tale of Bartram-Haugh* (ed. W. J. Mc Cormack) Oxford: World's Classics, 1981 pp. vii–ix.
13 Ibid. p. 2.
14 Elizabeth Bowen 'Introduction' to J. Sheridan Le Fanu *The House by the Church-yard* London: Blond, 1968 p. vii.
15 *Uncle Silas* pp. 102–3.
16 W. J. Mc Cormack *Ascendancy and Tradition in Anglo-Irish Literary History from 1789 to 1939* Oxford: Clarendon Press, 1985 pp. 187–94.
17 *Sheridan Le Fanu and Victorian Ireland* pp. 173–87.
18 *The House by the Church-yard* p. 29 etc.
19 Nelson Browne *Sheridan Le Fanu* London: Barker, 1951 p. 115.
20 J. Sheridan Le Fanu *Guy Deverell* New York: Dover, 1984 pp. 20, 18.
21 Ibid. p. 20.
22 Browne op. cit. p. 54.
23 *Guy Deverell* p. 228.
24 Ibid. p. 229.
25 Ibid. pp. 228–9.
26 For two examples, chosen almost at random, involving windows as frames see *Uncle Silas* pp. 118, 122.
27 *Guy Deverell* p. 414.
28 Ibid. p. 230.
29 Browne op. cit. p. 54.

7

Characters beheaded
with mottoes

The revelation of character has been presented as the supreme achievement of the novelist's art, its depth and complexity surpassing even the remarkable personalities of the ordinary world. (Who, in life, rivals Dorothea Brooke of *Middlemarch* or Strether of *The Ambassadors*?) Though it is now largely conceded that not all novels are written within 'the great tradition' of Dr Leavis's prescription, and though it certainly is not maintained here that Sheridan Le Fanu was a novelist of the first rank – any first rank – difficulties remain in presenting his treatment of character sympathetically. At first glance, such difficulties can hardly be eased by a decision to link consideration of character with the use of mottoes or epigraphs. For the inexhaustable riches of novelistic character are incomparable to the brittle and sententious trophies of the phrase-hunter. Perhaps so, but the elaborate literary creation which is character in the classic account of fiction is known by a simple name – we recognise Dorothea, not Chapter the Fifth. And the sentiment blazoned in an epigraph is usually less striking than the name appearing below – Homer, Shakespeare or Patience Strong. Less flippantly one might argue that character, as the conventional critic presents it, has one experience in common with the epigraph – both have been ripped from a larger context for mendacious purposes.

It is already clear that personal names in Le Fanu's fiction behave strikingly and yet in an undefined fashion. For example, a combination of names from one fiction breaks down and resurfaces in its separate elements in other stories and novels. To take a distinctive case, in 'The Watcher' (1847) passing reference is made to Sylvester Yelland, a sailor once employed on an eighteenth-century ship: in the novel *Checkmate* (1871) Yelland Mace emerges as the former name of a central character, Walter Longcluse. The repetition of the odd name Yelland, together with the name-changing plot, sets up a disturbing kinetic between works which the reader is entitled to think of as discrete. The name Marston is the most frequently encountered, and though there is a certain consistency of theme (treachery/bigamy) in some of the fictions involved, this is far from universal – consider Mrs Marston, the good old housekeeper in *Wylder's Hand*. If Richard Marston was master of Dunoran in the story bearing those names, he was accompanied by two similar sounding fellows – Merton and Mervyn. And meanwhile Toby Marston rules Gylingden Hall in 'Squire Toby's Will', despite the fact that Gylingden had been a village serving Brandon Hall where Mrs Marston was housekeeper.

Nor is the process of log-rolling names from one fiction to another wholly confined to personal names. In 'The Haunted Baronet' young Philip Feltram disappears into the lake, while in *Uncle Silas* a town called Feltram constitutes the nearest centre of population to the Ruthyn household. Scarsdale, a place referred to in *Uncle Silas*, also names a character in the serial previously unattributed to Le Fanu – *Loved and Lost*. In both cases an element of the uncanny is involved. Feltram returns apparently from the dead, an episode common enough in the shorter fiction. In the two novels sharing the name Scarsdale, the term 'cousin' serves as a link, for Maud Ruthyn meets her cousin at Church Scarsdale, and in *Loved and Lost* the female narrator meets a cousin called Scarsdale.

Perhaps the novelist took a fancy to particular names and overused them; perhaps a verdict of laziness or even incompetence should be returned. After all, better novelists have striven to build up an extensive fictional setting in which placenames recur, and to populate this with interconnected families where names are transmitted from generation to generation and from branch to family branch. Such is or was life, and the Le Fanus themselves provided a model of such practice. Similarly, personal names have in the past arisen from place-names (or vice versa), and there are quite ordinary circumstances (not excluding marriage) in which name changes occur.

Yet when the 'big black fella, as high as the kipples, came out o' the wood near Deadman's Grike' and declared to Mother Carke that 'one name's as good as another for one that was never christened' more than social convention is hinted at. In the world of faery the activities of changelings sabotage human attempts to stabilise name and identity, and the novelist may have been careless in dividing off his folklore-based fiction from those novels seemingly fixed in the reliable certitudes of Victorian domestic life. In the story just quoted, a young girl known as Laura Lew goes with her friend Bessie Hennock to the bank of a stream: Bessie sees on the other bank 'a very tall big-boned man, with an ill-favoured smirched face, and dressed in worn and rusty black' where Laura sees 'a conny lad … his bonny velvet, his sword and sash'. But Laura, a foundling, is also known as Laura Silver Bell because of 'a tiny silver bell, once gilt, which was found among her poor mother's little treasures after her death, and which the child wore on a ribbon round her neck'. Unlike Bessie, she has two names, and thus has access to a second world from which she never returns. The supernatural basis of 'Laura Silver Bell' is not exclusive to the stories based on folklore, and its implications for character can be taken up in a moment.[1]

In the novels and stories with more or less contemporary and mundane settings, such explicit naming by association (with the bell etc.) is of course rare. For Victorians, names were imposed by inheritance or marriage, and the coercive implications in relation to a sense of character may be noted. Nor is an individual character openly equipped with alternative names. The distinctive character-istics of Sheridan Le Fanu's fictional use of names are its lack of system *combined with* its pervasive reduplication: both constitute forms of coercion. Indeed, one might say that an underlying tendency across the fiction as a whole is for a name never to be used just once. Of course there are solitary instances, dozens of them, but these are qualitatively outweighed by the visual distinctiveness of recurring frequencies, and in any case the body of fiction cannot be treated as a closed system in itself.

The obsessive names are not simply tics, for very frequently they have summary-like historical associations also. Like *Sheridan* Le Fanu, many of his characters bear names recognisably those of earlier literary or political figures. The names need not always flour-ish their historical associations, though some undoubtedly do. There is, for example, a string of English dramatists – Marlowe, Marston, Sedley, Shirley, Wycherley – and of other more generally 'literary' figures (Berkeley, for example). Those fictional names both proliferate between texts in atomising sub-elements and persist from some previous and external source. Those of *The House by the Church-yard* are reasonably familiar to readers of Irish history, but the list can be extended at the price of boring non-readers of that material. For example, Philip Feltram's antagonist in 'The Haunted Baronet' is Sir Bale Mardykes: John Bale (1495–1563) was a vehemently protestant bishop of Ossory and the author of several plays. In *Willing to Die*, the narrator's father, who commits suicide over an open bible, is Francis Ware: Sir James Ware (1594–1666) was a pioneer of Irish historiography. Of course, the sceptical reader may argue that it is possible to find a distinguished historical bearer of any name, and may suspect that the evidence is adduced simply to support a pre-existent theory. (And what about all those bishops and bookmen whose names don't crop up in Le Fanu's fiction?)

An answer may be found in the pattern of Le Fanu's use of names in which a distinctive feature is the disintegration of a central element into discrete parts. Carmel Sherlock in *A Lost Name* is split up so as to produce the Jesuit Mr Carmel, just as the nonentity Sylvester Yelland has contributed to the making of Yelland Mace. It is not just the reproduction of names in Le Fanu which is remarkable, but the destruction of names also, and their reassembly in new combinations. Given that Walsingham appears alongside Devereux in *The House by the Church-yard* and – far less prominently – alongside Bale in 'The Haunted Baronet', the sixteenth-century provenance can hardly be challenged. At this level, the novels which include historical names resemble historical fiction in which history has been reduced to pure process rather than human action: history is the recurrence of the past, and names are the surviving lees from this dehumanising distillation.

The impact on a notion of character is disturbing as novel converges on novel. Another dramatist born in the sixteenth century (Christopher Marlowe) contributes his name to *Guy Deverell* in such a fashion as to allow one to see Deverell as a variant of Devereux. To be fair, there was also a Deverell family mixed up in Pre-Raphaelite circles, and Le Fanu was not averse to incidental satire at times. Lady Alice, in the same novel, bears the unusual surname Redcliffe – there's no one of the name in the *Dictionary of National Biography*. Yet Redcliffe may also be read as a mutation of Radcliffe (as in Mrs Ann Radcliffe, the novelist who is cited passingly in *Wylder's Hand*). Verbal mutation may 'correspond' with mutations of identity, even of physiognomy, involving illicit transfers between fiction and fiction, fiction and an elusive world of fact. The Charles Archer in *The House by the Church-yard* who is finally identified behind the plethora of aliases would seem to owe something to a 'real' Charles P. Archer, compiler of the *Analytical Digest of all the Reported Cases in the Several Courts of Common Law in Ireland* (Dublin, 1842). Quite how he offended the novelist remains unknown for Archer essentially remains unknown unlike the great literary names in other novels. Surgery plays a part here, as later it does in *Checkmate*, and with such manoeuvres arise anxieties concerning the alterability of biological substance also. *Guy Deverell* being the first of his limply febrile novels, any echoes of Kit Marlowe and the earls of Essex will undergo severe distortion – Deverell may be Devereux just as Strangways claims to be Deverell. From what might be thought of as a solid central core, unique and personal, a name is both reduced or mutilated by misspelling and propagated or dispersed by repro-duction in other fictions.

One interpretation of this would be couched in terms of a com-plex challenge to identity, or at least to the notions of the integral individual which underpin so much post-Renaissance philosophy and politics. If 'name' is taken somehow as the expression of inviola-ble personal identity – e.g. I am Sheridan Le Fanu – then the serial appearance of the name threatens our confidence in such inviolabil-ity. Of course, in 'real life' two or more people may bear the same names (e.g. a father and son), and people who are unrelated may share a forename or family-name. In 'real life' of course, the corpo-ral existences of the two individuals, and the reality of society which both identifies and incorporates different name-groups, rule out any question of serious confusion. Conventionally, the inviolable per-sonality which is me is unaffected by the existence of another person bearing the same name.

In literary discourse, names are distinguishable from other words, but identical words (whether names or not) remain identical. Thus if in *Uncle Silas* a sentence had read 'Ruthyn sat on the table', the reader would have required more than the sentence itself to establish whether Austin or Silas was involved. The problem in Le Fanu's fiction is far more complex in that names not only recur but also alter. In the surname of Sir Wynston Berkely in 'The Evil Guest' we recognise a great deal of George Berkeley (1685–1753), Irish philosopher, though nothing of the bishop's character. Then there is Sir Roke Wycherly in *A Lost Name* who falls just short of repeating the name of William Wycherley (1640?–1716), dramatist.

These variants, occurring in the mid-Victorian period, constitute a regression to earlier centuries when spelling of names had not been standardised. Superficially reproducing an authentic or 'period' indeterminancy of name-rendering, the fiction also reverts to a period when the bourgeois subject was still a historical project in the making. This is an anxious business and not, at least in the immediate terms of the plots, a liberating one. For in those plots, alteration of name generally connotes criminality – as in the cases of Charles Archer and Yelland Mace. The crime, on the surface, is to be concealed by a change of name, but we might ask if there is not a subliminal anxiety that unease at the rigidity of an imposed identity prompts a sense of guilt which is then retrospectively explained by the discovery of a 'crime'. Freud certainly reported similar cases.

Not only between history and fiction can minute alterations of name be traced. Within the body of fiction, one can see not only Devereux becoming Deverell but also the more thoroughly amorphous Charke becoming Carke – or vice versa – or both. Indeed Le Fanu builds up a cluster of very similar names which constitutes something like a continuous series within which a character is momentarily arrested – Mardykes, Marlowe, Marlyn, Marston, Maubray, Medwyn, Merton, Mervyn, Mordaunt. This alphabetical line could be graphed against another in which the consistency of literary names is tabulated, with even a third dimension to the model supplied in a line tracing the use of the same name for multiple characters. In such a model, within such a box, is demonstrated both the unanchored and the imprisoned element of identity. Caught within rigid limits or permutations, it is nevertheless denied a permanent attachment.

In terms of Le Fanu's plot, and especially that of *The House by the Church-yard*, the implication is that history is the challenger to personal identity or to the assumptions upon which such notions have been raised. But history is only one name for a force which cannot be fully specified under any terminology. Character, so to speak, may be but an episode in some greater series of elements – psychically charged locations, gender formations, historical crises or whatever. Such a notion of character in Le Fanu seems at times poised on the brink of discovery, discovery of a more dynamic theory in which personality or identity is constituted or actively constructed in the operations of language, in naming or the condition of being already named, in discourse generally, in dialogue. But there is a second direction in which the new apprehension of character may lead.

Instead of a fuller access to the dynamic of society, leading in turn to a dialectic relation to history in which the past is no longer simply a coercive force but also a responsive forum, some of Le Fanu's characters, sensing the fluidity of character which his writing has made possible, obey an urge to align themselves with an undifferentiated continuum. Perhaps the fate of Laura Lew in 'Laura Silver Bell' illustrates this latter tendency, with the toothless dialect giving the impression that only in a world-view which admits of faery are such urges actual. But the mystical researches of Carmel Sherlock are part and parcel of his own loosening personal identity. Suicide proliferates in the late novels, and perhaps this is the male and contemporary equivalent of Laura Lew's impulsive jumping the bank to be with her lord of faery.

Certainly, the prison-house of names, sketched above, appears to have one exclusive feature – with few exceptions, it contains only males. Outside, greater potential may well lie. The contribution of names to characterisation is particularly tantalising in Le Fanu's treatment of women. Of the names which described the three dimensions of the model only that of Agnes Marlyn (of *A Lost Name*) is exclusively a woman's. Moreover, women characters rarely bear names which are significantly repeated, apart from two Christian names – Maud Ruthyn and Maud Vernon; Eugenie de Barras and Eugenie Countess d'Aulnois. The two Eugenies are of course villainesses of the worst kind, and if their French nationality did not say enough, their bearing the name of Napoleon III's empress specifies the fault.

Among the individually named women, neither guilt nor identity constitutes ground for anxiety in the novels. A sense of emancipation is discernible at the end of *Wylder's Hand* and it is apparently confirmed at the structural level in *Uncle Silas*. Yet for all that Maud Ruthyn narrates the novel, its conclusion merely ties her to a sort of compromise widow- and parent-hood. Maud Vernon in *The Rose and Key* arguably fares less well, for she marries Charles Marston, Lord Warhampton, and bears him many Marstons. In the final novel, the female narrator is increasingly afflicted by loss of consciousness. This apparent derogation from what was becoming the most exploratory feature of the English novels should be recognised as a sign of Le Fanu's advanced and exposed position. No challenge to a concept of character based on the economically independent, biologically free-wheeling bourgeois male could expect to go unpunished or unresisted. Negligible income and plummeting reputation among the reviewers may chart the retaliation in a trivial form; more effectively, it was launched internally. Le Fanu's anxious inquiry into questions of historical responsibility, character construction and sexuality inflicted its own damage on the novelist.

Once again, the diversity of his writing complicates the picture, and the contrast between rival literary forms is always illuminating. If *All in the Dark* and *Willing to Die* seem listless and imminently collapsing, the stories and tales of *In a Glass Darkly* (1872) are among the finest he wrote. These will be examined in closer detail in a later chapter, with special reference to the phenomenon of self-quotation or serialism between the stories. In the best-known of them, 'Carmilla', a female narrator is once again in charge, together with a pattern of names where the pure formalism of an anagram (Carmilla/Millarca) replaces the near-plausible repetitions of Marston–Merton–Mervyn.

The basis in movable type of this new device suggesting a dangerous identity of identities serves to highlight one further feature of Le Fanu's use of character names. Amid the proliferating words, sentences and paragraphs of the three-volume novel or the double-column pages of a monthly magazine, Marston or Borrhomeo or Wycherly stood out as pre-recognised items, at least to some readers. The print is bold in the standard English sense just as the bearers of these names are bold in the idiomatic Irish sense. The names have an iconic presence on the page as if to compensate their bearers for a diminution of substance elsewhere. (In this, still preliminary, sense they act just as the name Rembrandt or Velásquez does when it is invoked to describe a character's appearance.) That Anglo-Irish fiction was structured to address several different readerships is a proposition that has yet to be considered in relation to an author other than Maria Edgeworth.[2] Nevertheless, the literary or historical names in Le Fanu may be said to act as emblems in the eye of the informed reader, not so much in that they convey particular and defined meanings, but because they stimulate certain expectations or associations. These may well be frustrated or ironically rewarded by the plot, yet at a technical level the process of reading is qualitatively altered.

Such names occupy the page with an emphasis which distinguishes them from – say – the behavioural names of theatre (Sir Lucius O'Trigger) or the emotive-descriptive names used by

Charles Dickens (Jaggers, Cheeryble etc.). The difference is evident
of course because Le Fanu uses both of these other naming techniques also. The effect is to have the narrative freighted with items
of a different specific gravity, and these sink or rise (depending on
your preference of metaphor) some distance from the ongoing account of events and objects, commonplace names and words. The
prose of disjunction, of incipiently centrifugal and unaccommodated
detail, is advanced by the stamping of 'Walsingham' on the page. Of
course, the argument about different readerships may be answered
with an accusation of snobbery brought against the novelist – he
flatters readers who know who Francis Walsingham was, and bam-
boozles the others! And there is this element of truth in the accusation. Working in a medium recently converted to the uniformly
produced page-surface of the steam-press, where the individual
weight or touch of an individual worker can be no longer traced, Le
Fanu strives to achieve something of the black-letter effect, of embossed paper, even of the manuscript with its unique signature or
heavy authorising seal. It is, if you like, a conservative reaction
against mechanisation, but it demonstrates how a mode of production (in its most physical sense) may be betrayed into revealing itself
even in a fiction where sweatshops, factories and paper-mills are
unheard of. In other words, it works to break up the serene image of
a uniformly efficient production of literature.

Mottoes of whatever kind also stand off from their background,
more often in a gesture of self-congratulation. They decorate coats
of arms, stained glass windows, title-pages and other declaratory
objects, often representing language itself in an otherwise non-ver-
bal display. The literary use of impressive epigraphs recurs especially where the work in question is conscious of its intrinsic insuffi-
ciency or of an ironic relation to the authority cited. Thus an epigraph conventionally defends the text or assails the reader.

Fanu's most sustained operation of this kind was conducted in
1851 when his anonymous collection of *Ghost Stories and Tales of
Mystery* was published by James M ' Glashan in Dublin. Four pieces
were brought together, each prefaced by an epigraph of the familiar
biblical kind. The second and third of these ('The Murdered Cousin'
and 'A Strange Event') were adapted from the series which had
appeared between January 1838 and October 1840 in *The Dublin
University Magazine*, and which were posthumously collected as *The*

Purcell Papers (1880). The fourth, 'The Evil Guest', was a version of 'Some Account of the Latter Days of the Hon. Richard Marston of Dunoran' (*The Dublin University Magazine*, 1848). The first, 'The Watcher', had appeared the previous November in the same journal.

Each of these pieces can be shown to exist in a state of some textual instability. The first two named have been removed from the comprehensive framework of Fr Purcell's papers, and thus their link with his ostensibly actual career has been broken. Furthermore, according to E. F. Bleiler, the 1851 version incorporates character names from William Godwin's *Caleb Williams* (1794) into 'The Murdered Cousin'.[3] (Two names – the Christian name Emily and the family name Tyrrel – certainly appear in both.) 'The Watcher' later re-emerged as 'The Familiar' in *In a Glass Darkly* (1872). But perhaps the most drastic change occurred when the three-part serial of April–May–June 1848 was shifted from its original Irish setting to one specified as being close to Cheshire. Not only does 'The Evil Guest' introduce the character-name of Marston to Le Fanu's English-set work, it also inaugurates the business of transference from Ireland to England as a locus for fiction.

Having noted these shifts and instabilities, the dutiful reader may be reassured by the solid epigraphs at the top of each story. Admittedly, chapter and verse are not specified but the biblical source is unmistakable. The four tales of Satanic persecution, domestic murder, demonic sexuality and suicide are launched on phrases which appear to guarantee the author's moral and doctrinal orthodoxy. For example, 'A Strange Event' is headed up with the following apt insistence:

> For he is not a man as I am that we should come together; neither is there any that might lay his hand upon us both. Let him, therefore, take his rod away from me, and let not his fear terrify me.

The final phrase echoes the narrative observation that Rose Velderkaust did not share the fear of Vanderhausen which both her uncle and her lover did on the occasion on the demon's first presenting himself to her. Moreover, when she briefly returns to Leiden she insists 'the dead and the living cannot be one', a sentiment which could be reconciled with the first phrase of the epigraph. In other words, the epigraph appears to anticipate pious and innocent Rose's attitude both before and after the demonic compact into which her uncle (knowingly) and Schalken (less culpably) have inscribed her.

But when we look to the Bible for confirmation of this authority, the evidence is ambiguous. In the King James translation to which Le Fanu would naturally turn, Job chapter 9 verses 32–4 reads as follows:

> For he is not a man, as I am, that I should answer him, and we should come together in judgment.
>   Neither is there any daysman betwixt us, that might lay his hand upon us both.
>   Let him take his rod away from me, and let not his fear terrify me.

This is a good deal longer than Le Fanu's version, and the matter omitted has a direct bearing on interpretation. 'Daysman' is glossed as arbitrator or umpire, so that the 'lay his hand' of the middle verse carries no violent implication. Whereas 'come together', appearing above the account of Rose's demonic compact with Wilken Vanderhausen, takes on a sexual meaning, in the Book of Job nothing of the kind is intended. The import of the genuine biblical passage is that God and Job are so utterly different in every manner, that 'a man' cannot presume to answer God himself, nor hope for any coming together on equal terms in a judgement, nor even rely on a go-between. The passage is, in the light of this last reading, strikingly incompatable with the Church doctrine which describes Christ as 'the only mediator between God and man'. Although the verbal details are slight, the discrepancy between the Bible and Le Fanu's epigraph (which, strictly, makes no claim to be biblical) is such that deliberate misquotation can scarcely be gainsaid.

The three other instances confirm this view:

'The Watcher'	Job 7: 14–19

How long wilt thou not depart from me? Thou terrifest me through visions: so that my soul chooseth strangling rather than my life.	Then thou scarest me with dreams, and terrifiest me through visions:
	  So that my soul chooseth strangling, and death rather than my life.
	  I loathe it; I would not live alway: let me alone; for my days are vanity.
	  What is man, that thou shouldest magnify him? and that thou shouldest set thine heart upon him?
	  And that thou shouldest visit

him every morning, and try him
every moment?
  How long wilt thou not depart
from me, nor let me alone till
I swallow down my spittle?

'The Murdered Cousin'
And they lay wait for their own
blood: they lurk privily for
their own lives.
  So are the ways of every one
that is greedy of gain: which
taketh away the life of the
owner thereof.

Proverbs 1: 18–19
And they lay wait for their own
blood; they lurk privily for
their own lives.
  So are the ways of every one that
is greedy of gain; which
taketh away the life of the
owners thereof.

'The Evil Guest'
When Lust hath conceived, it
bringeth forth Sin: and Sin,
when it is finished, bringeth
forth Death.

Epistle of James Ch. 1: 15
Then when lust hath conceived, it
bringeth forth sin: and sin,
when it is finished, bringeth
forth death.

In each case, Le Fanu's epigraph is shorter than its biblical parallel. The changes range from the slight omission of one word (and the use of capital initials) for 'The Evil Guest' to the extreme interference with holy writ which heads up 'The Watcher'. Here, seven biblical verses are reduced to scraps of three of these, the order of which is also rearranged, in some respects reversed. That alteration of the texts was deliberate is ultimately difficult to prove – but equally difficult to doubt. Carelessness by a printer is unlikely to explain the omissions and reverse-ordering of Job 7: 14–19, and in any case *Ghost Stories and Tales of Mystery* was printed in Dublin by Edward Bull, giving the anonymous author maximum opportunity to correct proofs efficiently. Apart from the major alterations just discussed, the change of 'owners' to 'owner' in placing Proverbs 1: 18–19 above 'The Murdered Cousin' surely indicates a calculated adaptation of the text to suit the plot in which just one victim (Emily) is killed although they (her father and brother) wait for their own blood (i.e. the narrator, their relative).

The matter may seem niggling but its implications are profound. Certainly, *accidental* misquotation on the scale suggested would disturb the sincere Christian, especially one brought up in the Bible-revering atmosphere of Irish Protestantism. The propagation of inaccurate biblical knowledge was often charged against opponents of Protestantism, notably the Catholic clergy.[4] Having seen Le Fanu misquote the Courtenay motto and deftly adapt a passage from Chateaubriand, we have some reason to believe that adjusted quotation may feature in his range of techniques. It is also wholly in keeping with his use of recognisable literary names, often mis- or re-spelled, where the substance of the literature seemingly invoked constitutes no sort of authority by way of model or source. Yet even the less exceptional procedure of adjusted quotation contributes to the larger understanding of Le Fanu's assumptions as a novelist. Neither irony nor authority can be adduced from the mottoes systematically placed above each of the stories in the 1851 collection. It is evident that biblical authority does not meet exactly the circumstances of the human disasters anonymously related, yet nothing so reflexive as the fiction's commentary on revealed truth is discernible either.

Uncle Silas has its less precise biblical allusions also. In the sixty-third chapter, and narrating how she went passively to the room where her relatives would lie in wait for her life, Maud refers clearly to a famous passage in St Paul's Epistle to the Hebrews. Once again the comparison is illuminating:

Hebrews 12: 1	Uncle Silas, Ch. LXIII
Wherefore seeing we also are compassed about with so great a cloud of witnesses, let us lay aside every weight, and the sin which doth so easily beset us, and let us run with patience the race that is set before us.	I went in and stood, a phantom, at the window, looking into the dark quadrangle. A thin glimmering crescent hung in the frosty sky, and all heaven was strewn with stars. Over the steep roof at the other side spread on the dark azure of the night this glorious blazonry of the unfathomable Creator. To me a dreadful scroll – inexorable eyes. The cloud of cruel witnesses looking down in freezing brightness on my prayers and agonies.[5]

Here of course, we may argue (as Walter Allen does in *The English Novel*) that Maud Ruthyn's difficulties arise from her misunderstanding of the family's Swedenborgianism and – it would seem – of Paul's epistle also.[6] The preceding chapter of the epistle had concluded with a recital of how the prophets and martyrs had worked wonders through faith – 'Women received their dead raised to life again: and others were tortured, not accepting deliverance; that they might obtain a better resurrection.' Maud, however, is fearful, sees herself already as a phantom, and regards the onlooking stars as cruel – not supportive – witnesses.

This final crisis of the narrator's, near the end of her sojourn at her uncle's house, provides in its biblical allusion a symmetrical partner to words of advice given her as she earlier prepared to leave her father's house. Then, Emmanuel Bryerly had warned her thus:

> Remember, then, that when you fancy yourself alone and wrapt in darkness, you stand, in fact, in the centre of a theatre, as wide as the starry floor of heaven, with an audience, whom no man can number, beholding you under a flood of light. Therefore, though your body be in solitude and your mortal sense in darkness, remember to walk as being in the light, surrounded with a cloud of witnesses.[7]

The concluding words leave us in no doubt that the Swedenborgian minister is citing St Paul, just as Maud will in the later passage. One might argue – still following Walter Allen's reading of the novel – that Maud has foolishly taken Bryerly's advice: she has behaved as though she were safe when in fact she was mortally at risk. Yet Bryerly's oration had gone far towards jeopardising any realist interpretation of the scene:

> Thus walk; and when the hour comes, and you pass forth unprisoned from the tabernacle of the flesh, although it still has its relations and its rights ... you will rejoice; and being clothed upon with your house from on high, you will not be found naked. On the other hand, he that loveth corruption shall have enough thereof. Think upon these things. Good-night.[8]

Much of this vocabulary descends from II Corinthians 5: 1–5 – 'clothed upon with our house which is from heaven'. But the conventional paraphrase adjustments by which the passage is made applicable to the listener – 'clothed upon with your house' – underline the difficulty of biblical quotation which is both accurate and authoritative. The textual presence of St Paul, at Maud's departure from Knowl and at the moment when she fears death in Bartram-Haugh, enacts a wholly internalised correspondence of one house with the other, though one of these is also imprisoning and lethal. It is not surprising that she casts herself as a passive object of sight, involved in no reciprocal process with what she sees; she casts herself, that is, in the role of picture as conceived in a purely me-chanical system of aesthetic reception. The refusal to accept biblical comfort is partly masked by incomplete quotation, but Le Fanu's drastic misquotations in *Ghost Stories and Tales of Mystery* leaves one in little doubt as to the deliberate precision of Maud's unorthodox swerve from scripture.

Apart from the touchy business of misquoting a recognisable verse, Maud may also be in flight from the larger scriptural context of the eleventh and twelfth chapters of Hebrews. The theme of resurrection, touched on already, is ironically present in the opening of *The House by the Church-yard*, in the family motto underpinning *Wylder's Hand* and – as we shall see in a moment – in an early scene of *Guy Deverell* also. Silas's extraordinary posthumous appearance/ existence mimics the theme of course, and here we may see Maud in resistance to her guardian's aggressive resurrection. But she not only mumbles her Pauline text, she also (as compensation perhaps) draws on a passage from the Book of Revelation. Again it is a striking passage:

> And I beheld when he had opened the sixth seal … the moon became as blood; and the stars of heaven fell unto the earth, even as a fig tree casteth her untimely figs, when she is shaken of a mighty wind. And the heaven departed as a scroll when it is rolled together... (Revelations 6: vv. 12–14)

All that survive of this apocalyptic text in Maud's allusion are the stars and the scroll, the latter now dreadful. The ultimate resurrec-tion of the Last Judgement is thus edited out of the narrator's range of allusion.

The biblical quotation or motto is only one instance of Le Fanu's incorporation of brief or fragmentary textual matter into the narra-tive of novel or story. Names like Marston and Berkeley constitute a highly specialised instance of a pervasive technique. As we have seen, *Uncle Silas* is replete with literary tags and the names of paint-ers, heavily embossed into the texture of the sentences, paragraphs and chapters.[9] Certain chapter titles, and even novel titles, operate in a similar fashion. The fifty-second chapter of *Uncle Silas* is entitled 'The Picture of a Wolf': a rationale of this is found in Maud Ruthyn's examination – first – of a coloured print depicting a terrified Swiss girl throwing pieces of meat to a pack of pursuing wolves, and –

second – 'a fine print in my portfolio from Vandyke's noble picture of Belisarius':

> Idly I traced with my pencil, as I leaned back, on an envelope that lay upon the table, this little inscription. It was mere fiddling; and, absurd as it looked, there was nothing but an honest meaning in it: – '£20,000 Date Obolum Belisario!' My dear father had translated the little Latin inscription for me, and I had written it down as a sort of exercise of memory; and also, perhaps, as expressive of that sort of compassion which my uncle's fall and miserable fate excited invaribaly in me. So I threw this queer little memorandum upon the open leaf of the book, and again the flight, the pursuit, and the bait to stay it, engaged my eye. And I heard a voice near the hearth-stone, as I thought, say, in a stern whisper, 'Fly the fangs of Belisarius!'[10]

The mechanics of Maud's page-turning are of no consequence compared to her phrase describing the psychic process – 'perhaps some latent association suggested what seemed a thing so unlikely.' Merging two pictures in her mind, she hears an exhortation which identifies the beggarly Silas with the pursuing wolf. This is not something she can bring herself to write, though the linking of Silas's need (£20,000) with the Latin plea takes her half-way there. The exhortation indeed remained unanchored, heard but not uttered, and like other such admonitions in the narrative conveys some inkling of her father's repressed or dispersed violence. For 'Date Obolum Belisario' had long been exposed as *not* Van Dyck's work despite the early attribution to him: under a sententious motto Austin Ruthyn had been passing off a doubtful item to his vulnerable daughter. William Le Fanu of Chelmsford tells me that an engraving of Belisarius with this caption hung over the fireplace in the house of his uncle Victor Le Fanu at Bray, County Wicklow; as a child he inquired about the meaning of the phrase but did not trouble to establish the artist's name. It is almost certain that the picture descended either from Sheridan Le Fanu's possession, or from his brother's, the successful railway engineer. Its existence in the family raises the issue of contrasting fraternal relationship among the Ruthyns and the Le Fanus.[11]

The wolf of course has a place – honoured or otherwise – in two complementary but contrasting bodies of lore. In popular mythology of the vampire, he plays a part in the undead's repertoire of animal-disguises. In psycho-analysis, he features in the classic case of Sergei Pankejeff.[12] *The House by the Church-yard* is an unlikely hunting ground for either Bram Stoker or Sigmund Freud, yet the arrest of Paul Dangerfield is narrated in a chapter entitled 'The Wher-Wolf', and in the aftermath the residents of Chapelizod are presented as relishing their survival of a monstrous intrusion:

> The wher-wolf had walked the homely streets of their village. The ghoul, unrecognised, had prowled among the graves of their church-yard. One of their fairest princesses, the lady of Belmont, had been on the point of being sacrificed to a vampire. Horror, curiosity, and amaze-ment, were everywhere.[13]

Hyperbole, of course. Yet the effect is to raise some further inquiry as to the general implication of what is usually read as a pleasant mixture of gruesome mystery and gregarious frivolity. The heavy emblemism which is retrospectively heaped on Dangerfield's shoulders is not *totally* incongruous. As an escapee through another man's grave, Dangerfield (originally Charles Archer, namesake of someone who, it seemed, died conveniently in Italy) is so to speak undead, or a changeling. And so a minor uncertainty as to the title of the novel may find some stability in the emblematic mode also. All men and women live on the edge of death, in a house by a churchyard.

If this sounds sententious, then other titles of novels by Le Fanu may suggest a compensating irony. What, for example, of *The Cock and Anchor*, his first novel? Ostensibly the name of a Dublin pub, is it not also a construct of emblems – the cock of resurrection (or betrayal) and the anchor of faith (or immobility)? These reconsider-ations are unlikely to have arisen had it not been for Maud Ruthyn's 'latent association' between two highly emblematic pictures (one a 'counterfeit' with a striking and transferrable caption in words attached, an association which all but articulated more disturbing psychological exchanges.

Modern philosophy has a term which may be borrowed for a moment in this connection. In the early work of Bertrand Russell, one finds a discussion of the 'logically proper name'. This is a name which is so strictly identified with its bearer that, should no bearer exist, the name would be meaningless and – I presume – unidentifiable as a name of any kind. Russell took the view that demonstratives such as 'that' and 'this' were exemplary as logically proper names – a severe position to be sure. Applied to fiction, the theory would require a degree of suspended animation in readers scarcely allow-ing for any act of reading whatever. Nevertheless, in Le Fanu's curious practice with regard to names one can detect a kind of nominalism.

One might point to contrasting operations of the practice, even within the body of work later to be known as Anglo-Irish literature. In Maria Edgeworth's fiction, certain names recur and certain other names carry recognisable historical associations; one function of these names is to address the several different readerships which, in a stratified fashion, constituted her public. Thus the name Nugent is read in categorically different ways by persons attuned to Irish Jacobite history and by non-initiates. Harry Ormond in the Irish-set novel called *Ormond* is explicitly set up as Prince Harry (after Shakespeare) and implicitly related to the great dukes of Ormonde; in the English-set *Belinda*, however, Mrs Ormond carries no such undertone. Edgeworth's practice is more devious perhaps than her admirers have recognised to date: it attends confidently to a fractured culture and an increasingly atomised public. But it is easy to see that this intensive use of names, in other hands, might signal quite the opposite attitude to the public and the world. Thus Le Fanu's is a profoundly nervous nominalism. It is a practice instinct with fears that the universals banished by Russell do not exist, never existed. If this is so, the entire dimension of essences and platonic forms – the unseen and eternal, in other words – does not exist either. Consequently, in Le Fanu's fiction, naming of characters and quoting of holy writ become intimately linked *risks*.

Notes

1 J. Sheridan Le Fanu *Ghost Stories and Mysteries* (ed. E. F. Bleiler) New York: Dover, 1975 pp. 97, 95, 101.

2 See the introduction to Maria Edgeworth *The Absentee* (ed. W. J. Mc Cormack) Oxford: World's Classics, 1988.

3 See pp. viii–ix of Bleiler's introduction to *Ghost Stories and Mysteries*. Note that this collection is not a republication of Le Fanu's anonymous *Ghost Stories and Tales of Mystery* (1851).

4 See, for example, the article 'Romish Misquotation Exposed' *Dublin University Magazine* vol. 15 (June 1840) pp. 685–9.

5 J. Sheridan Le Fanu *Uncle Silas; a Tale of Bartram-Haugh* (ed. W. J. Mc Cormack) Oxford: World's Classics, 1981 p. 411.

6 Walter Allen *The English Novel* Harmondsworth: Penguin, 1958 p. 212.

7 *Uncle Silas* p. 124.

8 Idem.

9 See notes to *Uncle Silas*, where use of Shakespeare, Milton, Bunyan, Swift, Richardson, R. B. Sheridan, Mrs Radcliffe, Walter Scott, Thomas Moore,

Charles Dickens and a dozen others is documented.

10 *Uncle Silas* p. 338.

11 Personal communication, winter 1989. Sheridan Le Fanu's extended indebtedness to his engineer brother, William, together with a certain contrast in personality (the novelist reclusive, the engineer highly genial) lends substance to the notion of a fictional treatment of sibling rivalry in the Ruthyns.

12 See 'From the History of an Infantile Neurosis' (i.e. The Wolf Man) in Sigmund Freud *Case Histories II: Pelican Freud Library Volume 9* Harmondsworth: Penguin, 1979. pp. 227–366.

13 J. Sheridan Le Fanu *The House by the Church-yard* London: Blond, 1968. p. 447.

8

Towards a theory of public opinion

To misspell a renowned literary name, to misquote a familiar verse from the Bible, *is* to risk censure from such a readership as *The Dublin University Magazine*'s and, perhaps, from a devout or anxious spouse also.[1] Why should a novelist run the risk, if not to circumvent some greater one? *Not* to have invoked unalterable holy writ, not to have called up George Berkeley, exactly – these strategies would have left him in the position where authority remains unchallenged, in the last resort untested. The greater risk would have been to test authority, only to find it wanting. Authority here includes religious authority, of course, but it also implicates the author as such, his sense of himself. Yet to attribute deviousness of this kind to Sheridan Le Fanu must jeopardise him in the eyes of his public.

These considerations themselves run a risk or two. First of all, there is the possibility that the present study may be mistaken for a rearguard action in defence of the old criticism, the kind of criticism which approved a novel in direct proportion to its success in creating well-rounded, plausible characters. By this kind of misreading, *Dissolute Characters* could be taken as a rebuke of Le Fanu and a covert endorsement of the more conventional writers who contributed to *The Dublin University Magazine* during the years of his proprietorship. Then, there is the second danger – that of the book's casually giving the appearance of confusing the novelist with the man, husband, bundle of accidents, or – even more catastrophically – confusing narrator and novelist, fictional technique and biographical trivia.

Such problems are germane to the principal topic under discussion, for they can be located on the ideological line which divides (or brings together) the public and the private. The distinction is by now so well established that its status as an item of public opinion often goes unrecognised, with the result that its history is suppressed. Thus rendered permanently contemporary, the public/private divide is conceived of as a constant, and evidence of its emergence in the past, its alterations over the centuries, and its current deployment in ideological debate, is suppressed also. Literary historians are obliged to consider not only the present meaning of a work in the seminar or suburban home – *Moll Flanders*, for example – but also its historical significance in the early eighteenth century. Indeed, they are obliged to have regard to both existences of the work as at once separate and co-existent. With seminarian or suburbanite responsibilities uppermost, they will be aware of the crucial distinction between Moll and Defoe and they will read the text in a state of advanced alertness to the multitudinous instances of narrative irony which this distinction illuminates. But with historical responsibilities reasserting themselves, they also concede that in 1722 *Moll Flanders* was an anonymous fiction purporting to be a signed (by Moll) autobiography. What's more, the line between the public domain in which the novel was read and the private in which it was written did not exist with the clarity now thought obvious.

The history of literature and the history of criticism are thus interconnected in a way far more complex than that which traces critical notions as the effects of literary causes. Both depend upon larger discourses – in social practice, in theological hermeneutic, in the natural sciences. Moreover, the public/private distinction has no single history within which every modernising society fits according to a universal chronology. Jürgen Habermas has brilliantly exposed how in the early days of journalism 'the news' emerged precisely as the residues of a private system of commercial communication between private interests (merchants, traders, bankers etc.). Furthermore he has indicated that in certain instances what is now thought of as private/public was a distinction between *particular* and *common* interests.

Turning to the development of parliamentary reporting, however, Habermas summarises the conventions and restrictions governing eighteenth-century British practice, without paying sufficient attention to the rather different state of affairs existing in Ireland in the 1780s and 1790s. From this difference were generated diverging senses of what is private and what is public. For want of a better word the more *progressive* attitude was that adopted in the Dublin parliament, which in practice facilitated reporters in the House of Commons and which seems to have (on occasion at least) to have exploited the public gallery as a place where commercial interests might be entertained by political magnates like the Hely Hutchinsons.[2] In this, the Irish parliament displayed an engagement with the 'public', conceived both in terms of non-members of the House and in terms of general economic activity, greater than any sanctioned by its sister at Westminster. It is only fair to add that the prolonged crisis of 1789–1803 in Anglo-Irish relations severely blunted the divergence and ultimately led to the growth of a very different dispute between Ireland and Britain.

Habermas's theory of 'the bourgeois social sphere' has much to offer anyone concerned with the cultural history of Ireland from the late eighteenth century onwards, not least those involved in the debate as to how 'the Protestant interest' was superseded – but not immediately – by 'the Protestant Ascendancy'. The latter element becomes an unreflective item in the vocabulary of public opinion, though the pre-history of its imposition / acceptance remains patchily known. The phrase is admitted, grudgingly, into a few early essays by W. B. Yeats who associated it with the middling ranks of society, *and especially the dependent, the hangers-on*, and more specifically with attitudes reflected in the fiction of Charles Lever. Forty years later, in the early 1930s, Protestant Ascendancy has become for Yeats an object of celebration.[3] Between these two positions, of the young and the ageing Yeats, there lies an altered view of the Irish nineteenth century and especially of its fiction. The reduction of Maria Edgeworth to being the author virtually of just one novel (*Castle Rackrent*), a sleight of hand in reassessing Lever, and the elimination of Sheridan Le Fanu from the final version of *The Words Upon the Window-pane* – these are important registrations in Yeats's personal account of Irish literary history.

These revisions interconnect with Yeats's practice as an author in the market-place. It is well known that he aligned himself with William Morris's brand of socialism because it provided an alternative to the vulgarity of commercial production in art and literature. He admired the work of the Kelmscott Press in making available books which were not the product of a standardising factory, and from the outset (1903) he took an active interest in his sisters' Dun Emer Press, contributing *In the Seven Woods* as its inaugurating title.[4] This withdrawal from commercial publishing, however, formed just one movement of a more elaborate strategy. In addition to his support of private presses, Yeats was an early experimenter with the services of a literary agent, A. P. Watt, who also acted for another provincial Olympian (Thomas Hardy), pioneered the business of agency in Great Britain, and greatly increased the poet's income from his work. Literary agents constituted a further mediating factor operating between the writer and his public, one which had a vested interest in maximising royalties and in controlling dissemination of the work. Yeats took one step towards removing his poetry from the hands of commercialism but he took another (and in a different direction) when he placed it in the hands of professional agency. These may be regarded as intensifications of the poet's concern with, in turn, his own privacy and his own publicity.[5]

Sheridan Le Fanu's relations with publishers were more primitive, though tensions between privacy and publicity can be observed in the mid-Victorian period. The serialisation of novels in such magazines as *The Dublin University Magazine* was conducted usually, but not invariably, anonymously or pseudonymously. One factor operating to maintain this state of affairs was the powerful belief that articles of opinion or policy should be anonymous, that is, presented as the expression not of an individual but of the magazine generally and (by implication) objectively. As a rule, fiction was not differentiated from this tradition of journalistic anonymity, though of course a distinctive stylist like Charles Dickens had long ago escaped from the cipher-like identity of Boz. Being not only a contributor to the *The Dublin University Magazine* but also its proprietor and editor, Le Fanu was placed on a major cross-roads of private and public perspectives. His serials were in book-keeping terms free contributions to the magazine which then rewarded him as remote and unlisted proprietor rather than contents-page contributor. However, the maximum financial benefit from writing fiction was achieved only by converting a serial novel into a three-decker, a publication in three volumes inevitably issued from one of the big London publishers. At this point, anonymity was exchanged for explicit naming of the author on his title-pages. In the double publication of a novel, a renegotiation of privacy was required. By using Charles de Cresseron(s) are a signature for the serial version *The House by the Church-yard* Le Fanu pointed to the historical basis for this shifting demarcation line between public and private, while the incorporation of the name into *Wylder's Hand* as the narrator's name marks a further stage in the interiorisation of the public identity; the seeming author becomes seeming character. At the same time, however, the name Le Fanu is thrust on to the London title-pages of the novels in a manner which jeopardises the subtlety of de Cresseron as a name mediating between past and present.

The fiction generally could be read as an episode in the altering relations between private and public domains, an episode transcribed in terms of a different binary pairing – past and present. Nowhere is this more true than in *Uncle Silas* where the futurist doctrines of Emanuel Swedenborg appear to lift the argument into a metaphysical sphere. At several levels, Swedenborgianism is a disguised sociology. *Heaven and Hell* is pervaded by the word 'society' in one form or another, and the doctrine of correspondence sets up innumerable equations between the social world and the spiritual. The notion of judgement which Swedenborg advances is essentially that of rendering public that which has previously been private, and of regarding this transformation as itself a matter of reward or punishment. Within the characterisation of *Uncle Silas*, Austin Ruthyn is a reclusive (or private) figure of great rectitude shadowed by the public reputation for villainy attaching to his brother or alter-ego. After Austin's death, Silas's supposed criminality in the past is transformed into active, that is, present criminality just as in the Swedenborgian afterlife the real moral condition of the dead is gradually unfolded in the reinactment of their deeds. It is at this level, rather than in some mimesis of the sectarian divisions of minority and majority, that *Uncle Silas* can be read as a novel about Ireland.

Le Fanu then is Balzac in reverse and in degraded form. At first one can even find congruence, for there is a hitherto neglected concentration in his fiction of the 1840s on town houses in Dublin with their adjacent poor quarters. 'The Watcher' (later renamed 'The Familiar') is the best known example perhaps, but its companion piece ('The Fatal Bride') makes manifest Le Fanu's debt to R. B. Sheridan and the drama of mistaken occasion. The story is technically flawed, yet it succeeds in narrating an illegitimate birth at a time when the simple fact of pregnancy was virtually inadmissable in fiction. In keeping with this elementary realism, 'The Fatal Bride' also presents the eighteenth-century town as a busy, cluttered place of unsanctioned liaison and chance encounter, rather than the governing centre of a palatial culture extending through the demesnes of big houses out into nature itself.

Le Fanu and his art

Like its companion story from 'the reminiscences of a bachelor', 'The Fatal Bride' involves a journey through the city, from a lane somewhere on the west side of St Stephen's Green (the location of earlier Le Fanu residences) westwards into the Liberties, a poor district associated historically with Jonathan Swift as economic pamphleteer and philanthropist. But the journey enacts a more contemporary shift also as it leaves fashionable, *resort* Dublin and heads for the largest concentration of industry in the Victorian city. Both stories involve a crucial degree of tracking: a character labyrinthinely follows, or is followed by, another through streets broad and narrow. 'The Familiar' casts the follower as an implacable spectre or sprite, a figure not necessarily material but fully effective in its impact on the followed who ultimately dies as a consequence. 'The Fatal Bride' turns on the accidental involvement of the narrator in an assignation off St Stephen's Green, and his passive following of those he has met through to the scene of illegitimate birth. Together the two constitute a contrasting pair of stories, the one 'spiritual' in its motive agencies, the other 'biological'. One displays the city under construction, the other the city in dilapidation. For all their period details of Georgian architecture, these are anatomies of the modern city, comparable to Parisian scenes in Balzac or Baudelaire as well as to the London and Bath locations of Sheridan. Action occurs essentially out-of-doors, on the half-built street or in the parkland of duellists.

But on the heels of the bachelor's reminiscences came reversal. The initial story of Richard Marston, published in anticipation-and-response to the 1848 rebellion, was the first to identify an individual, even isolated, house with a focal character, and it is this identification which makes the Big House a significant literary trope in the fiction which follows thirteen or fourteen years later. (Character, if it lacks authority, may settle for architecture.) The story is quickly 'translated' to an English setting in 1851, and twelve years further on *Wylder's Hand* launches Le Fanu on a second career in which house-and-master will play a central role. Yet for all this synthesis of character and setting, the fiction becomes increasing *bitty*. A law of compensation is at work. As characterisation welds the proprietor to his hereditary estates, other aspects of the fiction reveal the strain imposed by this ideological investment by sheering off and adopting a mock-independence of their own. Character pays a price for its accommodation in the Big House.

Towards a theory of public opinion

This plot of valorised property – simultaneously endangered from without and incorporated to the figure of the master within – is inaugurated at the commencement of a period of legal dispossession and resale, consequent upon the Famine, and often replacing 'traditional' landlords (the Martins of Galway) with a more numerous middle class and professional body of landowners, including individuals like William Wilde and institutions (insurance companies) representing pension investments etc. Early- and mid-Victorian Ireland was a place of Weberian disenchantment to a degree which few cultural historians have recognised. And this too is subject to a law of compensation. Le Fanu's plots often point the finger at some intrusive figure coming between the master and his house, as if to exempt him from responsibility for the sundering which is to come. But the device is rarely crucial. Style has already begun the work of dispossession, just as the shift to serene English shireland begins to unmask the unmentionable reality of the United Kingdom.

It is not easy to classify such fiction, and the problem extends beyond the tiresome debate, now exhausted, about authors who are (or are not) truly Irish. From our examination of *The House by the Church-yard*, the notion of disjunctive literary form emerged. If the exemplary English novel accommodates all that it admits, in conformity to the Pax Britannica of bourgeois society, there is a delinquent merit in the reverse tendency, a fiction which achieves form the way a breaking wave freezes in the air, its spume crystallised in demonstration of the formidable energies which have broken it.[6] The displayed violence of this latter kind of writing recalls (in the most general way) Elizabethan and Jacobean drama rather than Victorian fiction. The recurrence of names is of a piece with this violent formalism, and determined efforts to frame character as if it were portraiture only serve to identify the source of this disruptive yet organising energy.

The city, then, loomed pretty large in Le Fanu's first novel. In most of the English-set novels, however, it is held at bay. *Checkmate* (1871) being a re-write of *The Cock and Anchor* manages to replace Dublin with London *and* Paris. Grammatically, the 1871 novel also opts with odd frequency for a peculiar constancy of the present tense while also concentrating the question of identity powerfully if crudely in the hands of a plastic surgeon. Publicly, the villain of *Checkmate* bears no resemblance to the inner man he was. But a discrepancy between the concealing powers of public (i.e. written) language and the audible revelation of his own unique voice allows a servant to recognise the former Yelland Mace in the present Walter Longcluse, a discrepancy mediating to the reader solely through the written text which he/she encounters privately, but augmented by the testimony of a decayed portrait hanging on the wall of the room in which the recognition occurs.

Past/present … private/public … identity/copy … each of these dichotomies is active in Le Fanu's fiction, and each slides without stability into the next. Balzac's Vautrin posed as the abbé Carlos Herrera whom he had murdered. But Le Fanu's Dangerfield exists at two removes from his victim–alter ego; he certainly had previously been Charles Archer, but it *seems* that this Archer had only come into existence when a previous Archer had been murdered in Italy and his *persona* appropriated. Vautrin finally becomes a policeman and is killed, in a magnificent effect of irony, by a forger. Le Fanu's heroes rarely have such tributes heaped upon them.

The particular conditions of the private/public dichotomy in mid-Victorian Ireland can only be fully appreciated within the larger context of the United Kingdom of which Ireland was so anomalous a part. The final breakdown of the Gaelic language and the accompanying penetration of its territory by English-language newspaper and political posters, by mass-produced goods and the demands of the London markets, will be delicately reflected in the work of J. M. Synge. *The Aran Islands* has more to say about factory trawlers than W. B. Yeats ever conceded, and the recognition of death in *Riders to the Sea* is postponed – but briefly – through the anonymity conferred by indistinguishable clothing purchased in the fairs of Galway. That is to come. Before the dénouement (denuding), a complementary exercise launched under the name of Home Rule attempts to reserve for an Irish parliament certain domestic areas of political concern. Once these aspirations were concentrated in the hands of Charles Stewart Parnell, it was only a matter of time until the Irish search for privacy (*Home* Rule, *domestic* parliament etc.) was wrecked on Victorian hypocrisy over sex and its exclusion from public life. Le Fanu's fiction outlines the swirling unformed precreative mass from which this tragic plot will be cast. Yeats's late perfection of the Parnell myth distorts the closeness between *Checkmate* and the Home Government Association, and the literary revival's general rejection of the novel form further downgrades the mid-Victorian preludes to the great crises and achievements of the 1890s.

Finally, one recognises in the mature Yeats and the young Joyce an obsessive attention to local style – the 'scrupulous meanness' of a phrase, the stitching and unstitching – distressed by what seems the casualness of the Victorian novelist. Only with *Finnegans Wake* does Le Fanu find a place in Joyce's literary kaleidoscope, while his exclusion from *The Words Upon the Window-pane* has been adequately noted already.[7] Both of these (dis)placings of the Victorian past occur in the overheated present of the 1930s, and in texts by Yeats and Joyce where issues of authority are central.

The stylistic alteration between *Uncle Silas* and *Dubliners* can be expressed in economic terms also. As its title makes clear, Joyce's first work of fiction effects a repatriation, but it does so by means of a generic movement as much as a return to Irish settings. The short story is his vehicle and not the novel. The early stories of *Dubliners* had been serialised in the *Irish Homestead* under the pseudonym Stephen Daedalus, and once again one notes the prominence of the domestic/private side of a dichotomy in the journal's name. A novel entitled *Dubliners* would have been inconceivable, one feels, at least in commercial terms. It is no accident that when Joyce turned to begin his epic account of the city, he thought he was writing a further story in the *Dubliners* series. But as the book of stories elaborated itself, the private world of the first-person narrator gradually expanded to embrace a sphere of public action (or, more strictly, inaction) which culminates in 'The Dead', an anatomy of the past as well as a prognosis of character in dissolution-and-reformation. Joyce's difficulties in getting his work published are legendary, but they do not reduce simply to evidence of provincial prudery on the part of George Roberts. Everything that Joyce wrote found its way into the public domain with difficulty and sometimes only with the assistance of private patronage. He too had his version of the mercantilist/neofeudal nexus, with Lucifer and Harriet Shaw Weaver competing for the post of patron saint.

The complexities revealed by even so brief an excursion into the economics of Irish creativity help to confirm Habermas's description of the bourgeois public sphere as 'above all the sphere of private people come together as a public'. As for the historical emergence of the formation:

> they soon claimed the public sphere regulated from above against the
> public authorities themselves, to engage them in a debate over the

general rules governing relations in the basically privatized but publicly relevant sphere of commodity exchange and social labor.[8]

To be sure this is closer to the recognisable world of Balzac than anything we read of in Le Fanu's fiction. But, as should be clear by now, Le Fanu's fiction is written under a series of pressures which force it into the sphere of commodity exchange – the English settings demanded by London publishers, the tension between anonymity and signature, historical allusion and the challenge to authority etc. – while also imposing a blanket ban on any direct reference to industrial production, agricultural labour or indeed to economic activity of the slightest kind. (A proving exception to this rule is the 'rapine' account of legal chicanery in *Wylder's Hand*.) At such a crux, complicated by the preliminary exchanges of a new nationalism and a soon to be redundant Establishment, the Irish arena of public opinion was particularly opaque. In *Ascendancy and Tradition* (1985) I advanced the view that the very notion of public opinion was, at mid-century, so recent as to be radical, and cited George Eliot, H. T. Buckle, and Edward Lecky in support.[9] In truth, however, the sequence of citations from *Felix Holt* and the *History of Civilization in England* represented a second stage in the emergence of public opinion, whose origins lie (as Habermas demonstrates) back in the late decades of the previous century.[10]

Yet it would be pointless simply to amend the argument with a wealth of detail substantiating the earlier dating of public opinion. Though that ideological concept is crucial for the development of bourgeois society, the private/public dichotomy in one form or another can be traced back as early as the Greek city states, just as the philosophical argument about proper names is already under way in Plato's *Cratylus*.[11] Oddly enough, Plato admits (but does not approve) the practice of inserting and removing letters in words and names. A central argument, however, negotiates between the relationship of names and the nature of things, and the relationship between names and painted images. The operations of some primal name-maker of unquestionable authority are considered against the claims of custom and convention. Here lies a too tempting opportunity to establish a line of continuity, and a highly flattering one. A Platonic 'authority' for Le Fanu's spelling of Berkely/Berkeley would be no more use than a battery of evidence tying public opinion to the year 1781. The dichotomy of public and private may be long-lived but it is at every stage historically conditioned. A

Towards a theory of public opinion

theory of public opinion would thus concern itself more with significant fractures in the continuity rather than with yet another seamless chronicle. For this reason one notes in Le Fanu's fiction the convergence of a nominalist obsession, a fondness for character presented as portraiture, and a nervous concern with the interactions of public and private.

Although Le Fanu occasionally alludes to Spanish painters such as Velásquez and even to a pre-Renaissance Italian (Guido), his references to art are more consistently and insistently to be identified with the Low Countries and Protestantism. For the most part, the names are seventeenth-century and thus far removed from the violent upheavals of the reformation. Yet the opening phrases of the story about Godfried Schalcken links the artist explicitly to William of Orange's success in Ireland, and thus to the sectarian wars which the reformation unleashed. Moreover, a dominant feature of Dutch art in the early days of the reformation was its response to new experiences of privacy (in relation to religious life) and publicity (in relation to secular patronage and the market). Even when Le Fanu casually uses the name of Rembrandt to highlight a character or darken a scene, the tradition which the visual artist worked in cannot be dismissed.

Notes

1 An account of Le Fanu's marriage with Susanna Bennett will be found in Mc Cormack *Sheridan Le Fanu and Victorian Ireland* Dublin: Lilliput Press, 1991 (2nd ed.) pp. 111–38; see also the full transcript of some fragmentary religious meditations written shortly after Susanna's death in 1858, published as Appendix Three of the 1991 edition of the biography.

2 I touch on some issues concerning the distinctive practices of the House of Commons in 'Vision and Revision in the Study of Eighteenth-Century Irish Parliamentary Rhetoric' *Eighteenth-Century Ireland / Iris an Da Chultúr* vol. 2 (1987) pp. 7–35.

3 Of Lever Yeats wrote in 1890, 'His books, so full of gayety and animal laughter, are true merely to the life of the party of ascendancy, and to that of their dependants.' (See W. B. Yeats, ed. *Representative Irish Tales* London, New York: Putnam, Knickerbocker Press, 1891 vol. 2 p. 209.) The celebration of ascendancy is found in the prose commentaries of *The King of the Great Tower* (Dublin: Culala Press, 1934).

4 See Liam Miller *The Dun Emer Press, Later the Cuala Press* Dublin: Dolmen Press, 1973 p. 31.

5 I use the term 'publicity' here in the sense endorsed by Habermas's English translator – publicness – and not simply in the sense of advertising etc. The seemingly contrary gestures of Yeats's publishing practice – the agent and the

private press – could be read as a miniature version of a contradiction in late-nineteenth-century economic relations noted by Habermas when he speaks of the co-existence of 'neomercantalism' (state intervention) and 'refeudalization' in society (op. cit. p. 142). The question becomes ideologically acute in the 1930s when Yeats energetically exploits the Cuala Press (run by his sisters) to propagate his political views through commentaries accompanying (and at times spacially overwhelming) poems; see the discussion of material in *The King of the Great Clock Tower, Commentaries and Poems* in Chapter 14 below.

6 My metaphor will strike some readers as odd: the choice of it was determined by a wish, not to accept an organic–natural ideology of literature but rather, to suggest that such ideologies implicate their own limitations.

7 For a re-assessment of attitudes to the novel, see John Wilson Foster *Fictions of the Irish Literary Revival; A Changeling Art* Dublin: Gill and Macmillan, 1987. The standard article on Le Fanu and *Finnegans Wake* is Kevin Sullivan 'The House by the Churchyard*: James Joyce and Sheridan Le Fanu' in R. J. Porter and J. D. Brophy (ed.) *Modern Irish Literature; Essays in Honour of William York Tindall* New York: Iona College Press, 1972. For Yeats's initial use, and then elimination, of Le Fanu's name from *The Words Upon the Window-pane* see W. J. Mc Cormack *Ascendancy and Tradition in Anglo-Irish Literary History from 1789 to 1939* Oxford: Clarendon Press, 1985 pp. 364–7.

8 Habermas op. cit. p. 27.

9 W. J. Mc Cormack *Ascendancy and Tradition in Anglo-Irish Literary History from 1789 to 1939* Oxford: Clarendon Press, 1985 pp. 298–309.

10 Habermas op. cit. pp. 89–102. The evidence is more extensively English than some readers might expect in Habermas, but it is also a crucial aspect of his argument that parallel developments are occurring in other advanced or advancing societies, notably France and Germany.

11 Plato *Cratylus* in *Plato in Twelve Volumes* (with trans. by H. N. Fowler) Cambridge, Mass.: Harvard University Press, 1970. vol. 4 pp. 7–191.

9

'Freezing brightness'

Art seeks to control art in those scenes where Rembrandt's name or Wouvermans' is invoked. But at the beginning of *Guy Deverell*, old Lady Alice is shocked to see on a gallery in church the figure of a man who resembles her dead son: in a passage already referred to she 'gazed and gazed transfixed with astonishment and horror. The enamelled miniature on her bosom was like; but there, in that clear, melancholy face, with its large eyes and wavy hair, was a resurrection.'[1]

Between 'like' and 'resurrection' an entire aesthetic debate is encapsulated, even if the description of Guy Strangways is all too redolent of the Pre-Raphaelite Christ. The conflict between the miniature and the manifestation promises other violent revelations from the past. One can note this further distinction in Le Fanu's use of paintings and painterly idiom: when an artist's name can be specified, the effect generally is to control the character or the incident in question; when no artist is named, when the painting or allusion is anonymous, the effect is disruptive, sinister, even supernatural in its implications; finally, when neither the artist nor the subject can be named, a supernatural malevolence is explicit.

Even in the apparently superficial and immediate world of Brandon Hall, the narrator of *Wylder's Hand* had experienced in sleep the projective violence of art:

> I dreamed that I was arranging my toilet before this glass – just as I had done that evening – when on a sudden the face of the portrait I have mentioned was presented on its surface, confronting me like a real countenance, and advancing towards me with a look of fury; and that the instant I felt myself seized by the throat and unable to stir or to breathe. After a struggle with this infernal garotter, I succeeded in awaking myself; and as I did so, I felt a rather cold hand really resting on my throat ... [2]

In both of these novels, the incidents apparently reactivating pictures are finally explained in mundane terms; in contrast, the short stories remain generally cryptic in their introduction of pictures. Explanation of a picture's significance or apparent power in the novels goes hand-in-hand with their rationalisation of the supernatural, whereas the short work is gnomic as to demons, ghosts and vampires as well as to painters' names and those of their subjects. Le Fanu's use of painting provides the opportunity to consider the problem of classification, of literary genre.

Uncle Silas remains pre-eminent, however. The twenty-second chapter serves to illustrate the various levels at which pictorial similes operate, for it begins with a casual instance and concludes with one of the novel's set-piece canvases. The chapter narrates Maud Ruthyn's reception of a messenger from her uncle, following her father's death, and it concludes with the Swedenborgian Bryerly emerging from the study in which the body lies. It opens: 'When we returned, a "young" gentleman had arrived. We saw him in the parlour as we passed the window. It was simply a glance, but such a one as suffices to make a photograph, which we can study afterwards, at our leisure.'[3] The young gentleman in question is neither young nor genteel, though he is (we will later suppose) Silas's son. Maud's manner of fixing him, which uses the window as if it were a camera lens, is linked to this revelation of character. But the chapter closes with a far more extended scene in which photography has been displaced by the older art of painting. Three women are engaged in a curious vigil:

> It ended by our peeping out, all three in a body, upon the gallery. Through each window in the perspective came its blue sheet of moonshine; but the door on which our attention was fixed was in the shade, and we thought we could discern the glare of a candle through the keyhole. While in whispers we were debating this point together, the door opened, the dusky light of a candle emerged, the shadow of a figure crossed within it, and in another moment the mysterious Doctor Bryerly – angular, ungainly, in the black cloth coat that fitted little better than a coffin – issued from the chamber, candle in hand; murmuring, I suppose, a prayer – it sounded like a farewell – as he looked back, pallid and grim, into the room; and then stepped cautiously upon the gallery floor, shutting and locking the door upon the dead; and then having listened for a second, the saturnine figure, casting a gigantic and distorted shadow upon the ceiling and side-wall from the lowered candle, strode lightly down the long dark passage, away from us.[4]

'Freezing brightness'

The three increasingly long sentences are remarkable in many ways, not least the four occurrences of the word 'candle' in a scene where the narrator's main concern is officially with her dead father and (secondly) with his mysterious adviser. Words associated with painting and the depiction of lighted scenes proliferate – 'perspective', 'shade', 'dusky light', 'shadow', 'shadow' again, 'dark', and even perhaps 'lightly'. The exchange of 'prayer' for 'farewell' instances the commonplace equation of death with a journey. It also exemplifies a system of correspondences between the physio-topographical and the spiritual which pervades the novel and emerges also in 'Carmilla' and elsewhere. In keeping with this, art and its vocabulary are not secondary to some depicted real thing: art is primary though without the authority of the real. The earlier part of the passage conveys this distinctly modern apprehension, the women peeping swiftly almost as a camera momentarily admits light, the blue flash of somehow unnatural light, and the extremely tense focus on a candle seen through a keyhole.

Reversing this last detail, we could describe the painting technique of more than one Dutch painter, who from one room scrutinised through a peep-hole his subject arranged in another room candle-lit or otherwise deprived of natural lighting. Godfried Schalcken was renowned for such paintings. In addition, however, literary history offers instances where the incorporation of 'the beholder' into the fictional occasion is heightened. Diderot's *tableaux* provide many examples, and Le Fanu's relation to an eighteenth-century school of French sentiment deserves attention not least because Diderot also pioneers certains forms of art-criticism which are also evident in Le Fanu's use of the visual.[5]

At this mid-point of the novel, where Maud is about to journey to her uncle's dilapidated house, *Uncle Silas* posits its young narrator as both beholder and subject of the same process. We might call this situation one of exposed privacy, in contrast to the concealed privileged perspective finally vouchsafed to de Cresseron in *Wylder's Hand*. The climax of Maud the narrator's experience in this mode comes at the point where, misquoting St Paul, she regards the stars themselves as a hostile crowd of witnesses. These behold her in their 'freezing brightness', that is, as an object deprived finally of the ability to behold. The heightened particularity of the stars constitutes the necessary and opposite reaction to the near-total elimination of individuality in her self.

Inevitably some brief history of the painting tradition Le Fanu draws on intrudes here, but as justification we may cite the existence of similar themes in the preliminary paragraphs of 'A Strange Event in the Life of Schalken the Painter'. Indeed that very early story, already displaying a proper name in variant if not deviant spelling, remains a central text, not least because it is the first to employ a continental setting. Though there are casual allusions elsewhere to Guido, Murillo and Velásquez, the more persistent reference is to Dutch painting. The Italians and Spaniards, one might say, constitute a rival Catholic group of references; as such they exert less pressure on the author's own cultural inheritance, and appear as decorative features within distinctly 'picturesque' scenes. The story about Godfried Schalcken gives substance to this, and when the narrator begins by linking the painter to his own great-grandfather we recognise an intimacy between Dutch national life and the Williamite dispensation in Ireland and Great Britain. Beyond the political and military events of the late seventeenth century lies the larger question of the Protestant reformation and its attitude to secular culture.

Early Netherlandish art was wedded to the Christian Church just as the art of Italy and Germany was. With the reformation and its attendant wars, a division occurred, Flanders remaining Catholic and the northern provinces adopting Calvinism or some other version of the reformed faith. But even in the work of an individual painter, the conflicts of the age could come together. Peter Aertsen (1508/9–75) and his nephew Joachim Beuckelaer (c. 1535–74) illustrate one powerful tension which can be identified in later metamorphoses through the work of artists to whom Le Fanu explicitly refers. Aertsen began as a painter of altar-panels in which the subject was entirely religious. But in 1550 his *Peasant Feast* became the first panel painting in western art devoted to that subject. The distinction between religious and secular, however, did not come in so simple a fashion. Titles such as *Butcher's Stall with the Flight into Egypt, Market Scene with the Calling of St Matthew* and a dozen others testify to the combination of secular setting and religious theme within the one painting.

Beuckelaer produced at least seven *Market Scenes with Ecce Homo*. In his work, less innovative in some ways than Aertsen's, the foreground is often given over to the meticulous representation of vegetables, fish, meat and other comestibles. Christ in the house of

Martha and Mary, the Supper at Emmaus provided other religious themes before which kitchen materials and incidents were displayed. Critical discussion of such painting has often focused on the competing claims of the religious and the secular subjects, with a tendency to see the proliferation of cabbages as an abandonment of tradition. Yet the extraordinary precision, profusion and 'claritas' of the depicted comestibles, together with the careful representation of clothing, ceramics and other human artefacts, cannot be accounted for simply in the appeal of secularism.[6]

At the price of interrupting this little history of Dutch art in one of its aspects, some interpretation of Beuckelaer's painting should be attempted. Not only does the pictorial element in Le Fanu's work deserve this degree of prepared attention but the interpretative enterprise itself includes the possibility of examining Le Fanu's psychological state at the point of his resumed activity as writer in the early 1860s. In looking more closely at – say – Beuckelaer's *Market Scene* which hangs in the Budapest Szépmüvészeti Múzeum, we can prepare the ground for a consideration of Le Fanu's recourse to Martin Luther's *Table Talk* in the aftermath of his wife's death in 1858.[7] For Le Fanu's allusion to Dutch painting constitutes a retrospective interrogation of the Protestant tradition in moments of its formation and consolidation, just as the contemporary English settings of the novels accommodate the collapse of this tradition amid the discrete presences of Victorian positivism, industrialism, imperialism and occult experiment.

Interpretation includes the interpreter and, in considering Max Weber's classic account of the relationship between the reformation and the growth of capitalism, one does not exclude Weber's own psychological condition, his melancholia and the complex familial energies which animated it. Coincidentally, Weber's background resembled Le Fanu's in a number of details: his mother came of Huguenot stock and retained that piety in the face of her husband's aggressive cheerfulness; two of his sisters died in childhood, with an effect comparable to that of Catherine Le Fanu's in 1841. Over and above any similarity of mood or attitude in the two families, one notes Weber's close incorporation of the interpreter's experience into the methodology which informs his classic account of Calvinist and Lutheran ideology.

A recent influential summary of *The Protestant Ethic and the Spirit of Capitalism* (1904–5) has declared that the book

aims at demonstrating the intimate relationship between the rationali-
zation of modern life (with its resultant *Entzauberung* or desacralization,
its transformation into an organized and disciplined market system) and
the development of the Lutheran or Calvinist notion of a *Beruf* or religiously sanctioned vocation to live ascetically within the world itself.[8]

But instead of echoing the 'vulgar Marxist' notion of protestantism
as a secularised version of medieval christianity, with a consequent
parallel secularising of conduct in the world, Fredric Jameson in thus
paraphrasing Weber endorses the latter's emphasis on the *religion-
isation* of the worldly means (i.e. markets, commerce etc.) and the
thrusting of ultimate ends into the realm of the unknowable. In due
course, Jameson will provide further illumination of Victorian Irish
circumstances, but for our present needs we can rest content with
Weber's own words – 'the process of sanctifying life could thus
almost take on the character of a business enterprise.'[9] Aertsen and
Beuckelaer, as we have seen, are placed on the trailing edge of this
historical transformation, remaining Catholic in their religious practice and yet adopting much of the Calvinist value-symbolism in their
artistic practice.

The foregrounded comestibles of the *Market Scene* have an uncanny clarity. Inert, clean, diverse and yet arranged, they exist between the producer/vendor and the viewer/buyer in a manner
which exceeds their own significance. Far from being evidence of
secularism, far from being replacements (by way of difference) for
the divine imagery of the altar-piece, they are suffused as the symbols of this (now withdrawn and systematised) divinity. Whether as
examples of God's creation or as emblems of a human search for
divinely sanctioned codes of conduct, the loaves and leaves radiate
non-represented divinity. The departure of one representationalism
has intensified another, so that an artichoke or a sprig of cherries is a
unique object and not merely an example. Nevertheless, these are
goods for sale and so constitute something which is even less than
examples, they are items in a chain of supply and demand which the
market setting implicitly reproduces and perpetuates. This divinely
infused vegetable is at the same time part of a serial exchange. Thus,
the light and space these objects are depicted in expresses the
trauma of the divine withdrawal. Bread is not warm, flesh is uniformly as it is. The young man drapes his arm round the milk-maid,
but his face looks upward with an exhausted knowingness. Her
body is full and amply clad, but her expression is at once resigned

and resentful. Perhaps the altar-panel, which by its absence from the background of the picture continues to inform it or inform on it, might have been an early morning Annunciation, with a touch of frost still on the tilled soil. The clarity of Beuckelaer's comestibles is neither epiphanic nor naturalistic but draws on both of the realms implied in these terms to keep them in check. It is a picture of suspended animation, a moment of deep freeze between the commencement of the reformation and its triumph. The picture is displayed for sale even before the vegetables are.[10]

More than half a century separates these painters from Gerard Dou (1613–75), the earliest Dutch artist to whom Le Fanu refers. Aertsen and Beuckelaer remained Catholics all their lives, but in the intervening years divisions had become permanent and apparently absolute. In the balanced views of the Catholic reformer Erasmus of Rotterdam, images in churches might be tolerated but their use was to be strictly supervised lest idolatry creep into the church. The first phase of the Dutch revolt against Spanish occupation began in August 1566, and a fury of image-breaking marked its onset. Organised destruction of statues and pictures of sacred subjects swept from west Flanders throughout most of the provinces. The instigators were Calvinists, the actual iconoclasts included 'unemployed manual workers, habitual drunkards, whores and boys in their early teens', together with emigrés returned from England.[11] The objects of their fury were only humble roadside shrines and commonplace church statuery: the sublime Van Eyck *Adoration of the Mystic Lamb* in St Bavo's Cathedral, Ghent, had to be hastily removed and concealed, a fate which befell it once more during the Nazi years. The Great Iconoclasm of 1566 implemented Calvinist teaching as it had spread out from Geneva into France (where adherents became known as Huguenots) and the Low Countries. Seeming a wholly negative event in the history of art, it enacted a further separation of the religious and aesthetic impulses already evident in such paintings as those of Pieter Aertsen. With the iconoclasm of 1566 and the religious wars everywhere, religious art became a centre of contention. By the 1640s, the Protestant Netherlands had evolved a wholly secular art in which the life of town-dwellers as well as peasants increasingly featured.

One or two seemingly discrete aspects of art history might be further noted before proceeding to discuss the artists whom Le Fanu specifies in 'A Strange Event' and elsewhere. A number of painters came to specialise in portraying church interiors; many of these pictures depicted imaginary churches, and the entire practice derived in one respect from an interest in 'fantasy architecture'. Within the depicted church interior, focus no longer respected the altar. Increasingly, the social function of the church as a place of ambulation was emphasised; human figures dressed colourfully, engaged in conversation or even sightseeing, animated the foreground and middle-distance of the picture. Despite this emphasis on secular behaviour in the church, the pictures often incorporate a moral dimension indicating the 'vanitas' of human endeavour with emblems of death much in evidence – tombstones, commemorative tablets and so forth. This melancholic tone, together with a discreet emblematic ingredient, serves to remind us that baroque culture generally provides the larger context of Dutch painting of this period. If Beuckelaer strikes one as a naive painter, and Schalcken almost as a cynical one, they have in common a reservoir of visual and verbal devices through which painting concentrates the viewer's attention on the problem of artistic meaning. J. A. Emmens has shown that Beuckelaer drew on Francesco Colonna's *Hypnerotomachia Poliphili*, a 'romantic' tale of 1499 for what are (ultimately) Egyptian symbols. One instance of the correlations between the visual and the (implicit) verbal codes given by Keith Moxey is that of the dolphin and anchor which he renders in the adage 'Make Haste Slowly'.[12]

Not all such devices point to traditional or conventional meaning, nor does the visual dimension wholly exclude juxtapositions of the incongruous, even ribald, with the melancholic. In a picture by Antoine de Lorme (d. 1673) preserved in the National Gallery of Ireland, several figures are converging on a floor-inset tombstone, with one man reading a paper as he stands beside the memorial. Two dogs behind him are sniffing each other. De Lorme painted dozens of such pictures, initially with an imaginary setting, but after 1652 he concentrated exclusively on one particular church. The French traveller Balthazar de Monconys recorded that 'he paints nothing but different views of the church in Rotterdam, but these he does well'.[13] The Grot Kerk, dedicated to St Laurens (i.e. Laurence), is the setting in which the final incidents of Le Fanu's story take place. Through the work of de Lorme, Daniel de Blieck and others, it was a familiar item in Dutch painting just as the church itself featured on the 'tourist' itineraries of the day.

'Freezing brightness'

Why link Le Fanu and de Lorme, Le Fanu and Beuckelaer, if Dou or Van Dyck is the earliest Dutch painter to whom the novelist refers? The defence relies on the long axis of a historical dialogue between revelation and representation which, roughly measured for the moment, begins in the sixteenth and dies away in the course of the nineteenth. In Beuckelaer the initial stages of this are evident in the *renewed* seriousness of the represented world, a dimension made possible by the separation of religious and secular spheres and by the concomitant enhancement of vocation in the world. De Lorme, we might say, works at a point of development where this process is stable, sober and yet infused with an acknowledgment of the absent God. Schalcken, as we shall see, stands much further down the road, with cynicism and complacency vying for his attention as he produces to order his amusing representations of a now thoroughly established Protestantism, triumphant in Holland and – if the Irish wars work out all right – in Britain too. Schalcken, in this heuristic placing of Dutch painters, is disturbingly ambiguous; he serves but hardly graces the regime, and his comestibles have been too thoroughly manhandled and packed for market to retain any bloom from God's hands. His master, Dou, being of just one generation earlier (the generation of Rembrandt van Rijn), is perhaps to be taken as the pivotal moment: detached from conventional pieties yet most serious in his worldly avocation. Le Fanu's story can be read as a massive calumny upon Dou's character, and to read it so is to appreciate the degree to which the figure of Schalcken is diminished and hemmed in by what is presented as the elder man's heartless greed. And to take the measure of this generational assault on emergent character – the surrogate father disposing of the young man's future happiness – one has also to bear in mind the veritable gallery of self-portraits by which Rembrandt consolidated his self and his reputation throughout his long life. Within this timetable, Schalcken is represented as premature in his affections and tardy in his actions – another middling man or central character.

The break-up of these Protestant domains may not have been so complete or sudden as it appeared in Irish tory circles in the 1830s. Yet the French Revolution had wholly altered notions of political representation, and 1829 had legislated the return of Catholics to the British parliament. Coleridge and Wordsworth deplored such trends, but among the younger romantic poets medievalist and Hellenic enthusiasms provided a route back towards a civilisation less divisive and brutalised than George IV's Satanic mills. Later in the century, two further movements of aesthetic retrospection advanced the pre-reformation era as an ideal in painting and in life. Of the two, Le Fanu is closer in time to the Pre-Raphaelite Brotherhood, even if William Morris's blend of socialism and medievalism is more local through the early allegiance of W. B. Yeats. The Pre-Raphaelites painted biblical scenes that gave offence, and aimed generally to treat simple themes with a clarity of line and colour reminiscent of European art before Raphael.

Two scenes in Le Fanu's fiction call for consideration in this context. The first occurs very early in *Uncle Silas* when Maud recollects the day when she had just made the acquaintance of Bryerly, her father's Swedenborgian confidant:

> He led me into the garden – the Dutch garden, we used to call it – with a balustrade, and statues at the farther front … We came down the broad flight of Caen stone steps into this, and we walked in silence to the balustrade. The base was too high … for me to see over; but holding my hand, he said, 'Look through that, my child. Well, you can't; but I can see beyond it – shall I tell you what? I see ever so much. I see a cottage with a steep roof … there are tall trees throwing soft shadows round it, and flowering shrubs, I can't say what, only the colours are beautiful, growing by the walls and windows, and two little children are playing among the stems of the trees, and we are on our way there, and in a few minutes shall be under those trees ourselves, and talking to those little children. Yet now to me it is a picture in my brain, and to you but a story told by me, which you believe …'[14]

The child and her conductor advance down the steps, 'along the grass lane between tall trim walls of evergreens … the way was in deep shadow', but suddenly:

> we turned to the left, and there we stood in rich sunlight, among the many objects he had described.
> 'Is this your house, my little men?' he asked of the children – pretty little rosy boys – who assented; and he leaned with his open hand against the stem of one of the trees, and with a grave smile he nodded down to me, saying:
> 'You see now, and hear, and *feel* for yourself that both the vision and the story were quite true …'[15]

The two proceed further and evidently come to a private burial ground where Maud 'had the morning before seen poor mamma laid'. Bryerly then embarks on a further allegorical use of the visual and non-visual to assure the unfortunate child that her mamma was not there. Maud naturally is shocked by this callous piety, and cries aloud: 'I was uttering unconsciously very nearly the question with which Mary, in the grey of that wondrous morning on which she stood by the empty sepulchre, accosted the figure standing near.'[16]

The echo of a biblical event, specifically the resurrection, and the application of a physical obstacle to a scene (the cottage etc.) to the spiritual domain, combine to form something of a paradigm. But there are immediate problems. No valid typological pattern links Christ's resurrection to this merely coincidental occasion. Bryerly has sought to use a visual device (a child's restricted view etc.) as confirmation first of mundane and accessible presences and then of spiritual survival, but the garden landscape where all this takes place, as Maud recalls Bryerly describing it, is woefully vague and undelineated. Tall trees throw soft shadows, there is a grass lane, the trees have 'stems', and the cottage is a bijou concoction of unnameable flowers at the doorway, and 'pretty little rosy boys'. Even when Bryerly's anticipated sighting of all this is visible to Maud, the impression is of a film of talcum. Maud is scarcely confirmed in any belief, about the physical or the spiritual world, and the little rosy boys remain silent, they and their cottage (evidently on the edge of Austin Ruthyn's garden) are never referred to again. Finally we note that the approach to this 'vision' is made by leaving behind the solid, shapely and named landmarks of Caen stone steps and Dutch garden.

The second scene occurs in 'The Haunted Baronet', one of the longer tales in *Chronicles of Golden Friars* (1871) in which Sir Bale Mardykes has gone to Cloostedd Wood, following the veritable resurrection of drowned Philip Feltram:

> Huge oak-trees now began to mingle and show themselves more and more frequently among the other timber ... Vast trunks ... stood like enormous columns, striking out their groining boughs, with the dark vaulting of a crypt.
>
> As he walked under the shadow of these noble trees, suddenly his eye was struck by a strange little flower, nodding quite alone by the knotted root of one of those huge oaks.
>
> He stooped and picked it up. and as he plucked it, with a harsh scream just over his head, a large bird with heavy beating wings broke away from the midst of the branches ...

> The flower was a curious one – a stem fine as a hair supported a little
> bell, that looked like a drop of blood, and never ceased trembling. He
> walked on ... at last the dark slope was all over trembling with these
> little bells ... Mingling with the faint sound of the brook, he now heard
> a harsh human voice calling words at intervals ... and walking on, he
> saw seated upon the grass, a strange figure, corpulent, with a great
> hanging nose, the whole face glowing like copper. He was dressed in a
> bottle-green cut-velvet coat, of the style of Queen Anne's reign ... [17]

Here, an excessive connection between viewer and scene is displayed. At first there is the seemingly atmospheric transformation of
an oak-wood 'roof' into the groined ceiling of a crypt. But from the
perpetual motion of the flower to the discovery of the revenant in
bottle-green, the links between the natural and human domains
have been overactive, a bird's cry transformed into a voice, a ma-
caw's plumage mirrored in Queen Anne costume. These two scenes
constitute the polar opposites within which Le Fanu's concern with
the visual arts is activated. On the one hand there is a would-be
celestial garden unconvincingly foretold by way of a 'picture in my
brain'; on the other, the pulsing, sinister reciprocity of Cloostedd
Wood and Sir Bale's ancestral revenant. In each case, the theme of
resurrection is referred to – piously yet ineffectually by Maud, implicitly and vengefully in the case of Philip Feltram. In *Guy Deverell*, a
miniature painting is juxtaposed against a veritable resurrection; in
'Carmilla' a resurrection occurs from within a portrait. The scene
from *Uncle Silas* reproduces something thematic from the Pre-
Raphaelite repertoire, but wholly lacks its sense of line and form; the
scene from 'The Haunted Baronet' has the precision of natural
depiction for which Sir John Everett Millais's *Ophelia* is renowned,
but insists on its own disruptive supernatural energy also.

Of course, such comparisons of the verbal and visual arts are
wholly illegitimate in themselves, and we should note that we have
no pictures whatsoever before us, only verbal accounts of fictional
scenes partly transmitted through the vocabulary of painting. With
this in mind, we can see that painting in fiction must always constitute an exercise either in failure or in indicating absence. The childhood episode recalled by Maud hints at the proximity of a cottage to
what is also presented as the serenely isolated Great House: such an
admission is made only through the feeble conventions of mid-
Victorian art, and nothing further is heard of any extensive society.
The settings of Le Fanu's English novels persist in this drastic selec-

tivity, eliminating all indications of economic activity save the accumulating debt which, lacking any contextual support or anchor, rolls on from novel to novel until it achieves Francis Ware's suicide in the final novel. Pictures constitute a form of property in themselves of course, but they also act as *mementi mori* and are not only hereditable but retrospective. In Le Fanu they are invariably mournful.

What is it that these verbally constructed images of melancholia exclude? Given the prominence of resurrection as a theme invoked on half a dozen occasions, one is confident that faith is the answer. Yet it is not faith in the straightforward sense of belief in Christian revelation, salvation and the rest of it. Quite apart from any question of God's redemption of man as the ultimate in benefits, the risen Christ looks like a guarantee that, annihilated or traumatically assailed, identity may be restored. Le Fanu's treatment of names, treatment of pictures, treatment of this signal event in a religiously conceived reality – all reach towards this guarantee only to find it conditional, elusive, inadmissible. The work girds itself for a decisive act of selection, 'that those things which cannot be shaken may remain'.[18] Though it has been bolstered by energetic bonds with property and the Great House, assurance of identity (the philosophical position which we associate with the psychological category of personality or – looking towards fiction – character) is manifestly not one of those unshaken things.

Early reformation painters had succeeded in removing objects of superstition or idolatry, images of veneration, even visible representations of the divine (as in the Ghent altar-piece) from their iconography. Yet in doing so, the unrepresented divine had been paradoxically, sublimely, enhanced. Nothing is left in the nineteenth-century legacy of this tradition but vapidity alternating with terror. Not Nature but flower-arranging surrounds Millais's suicidal lover. The exactness of Pre-Raphaelite art is more arithmetical than geometrical, it deals in calculation rather than proportion. Compare – as if one could – Van Eyck's *Adoration of the Mystic Lamb* with Millais's *Christ in the House of His Parents* (1850). Objects are now fiduciary, indicative of some not wholly trusted trust, and related to a symbolic realm only by means of imitation. It is as if art had gone off the gold standard and was all the more financially aware as a consequence: in place of some absolute, there is a prospect of unending relativities. Piety and secularism collude in the absence of actual social existence.

Le Fanu and his art

Notes

1 J. Sheridan Le Fanu *Guy Deverell* New York: Dover, 1984 p. 20.
2 J. Sheridan Le Fanu *Wylder's Hand* London: Gollancz, 1963 pp. 18–19.
3 J. Sheridan Le Fanu *Uncle Silas; a Tale of Bartram-Haugh* (ed. W. J. Mc Cormack) Oxford: World's Classics, 1981 p. 118.
4 Ibid. p. 122.
5 See Jay Caplan *Framed Narratives: Diderot's Genealogy of the Beholder* Manchester: Manchester University Press, 1985. Caplan argues that Diderot's ambition was to re-constitute a (once) Unified Family of Man by the sentimental incorporation of the beholder of his fictional tableux. This project is of course doomed to failure but it illuminates Diderot's 'aesthetics of sacrifice'. See in particular Jochen Schulte-Sasse's afterword to the book, pp. 97–115, 'Art and the Sacrificial Structure of Modernity; a Sociohistorical Supplement to Caplan's *Framed Narratives*'.
6 See K. P. F. Moxey *Pieter Aertsen, Joachim Beuckelaer and the Rise of Secular Painting in the Context of the Reformation* New York: Garland, 1979. On Aertsen and Beuckelaer in relation to subsequent styles of Dutch art see Christopher Brown *Scenes of Everyday Life: Dutch Genre Painting of the Seventeenth Century* London: Faber, 1984; Bob Haak *The Golden Age: Dutch Painters of the Seventeenth Century* London: Thames and Hudson, 1984.
7 See the religious meditations referred to above in Note 1 to Chapter 8.
8 Fredric Jameson 'The Vanishing Mediator; Or, Max Weber as Storyteller' in *The Ideologies of Theory; Essays 1971–1986: volume 2, Syntax of History* London: Routledge, 1988 p. 19.
9 Max Weber *The Protestant Ethic and the Spirit of Capitalism* (trans. Talcott Parsons) London: Allen & Unwin, 1976 p. 124.
10 For an interpretation of emblems in the picture in the Budapest gallery see Ildokó Ember *Delights for the Senses: Dutch and Flemish Still-Life Paintings from Budapest* Budapest: Szépmüvészeti Múzeum, 1989 pp. 20–1. A very similar picture by Beuckelaer hangs in the Pushkin Fine Arts Museum, Moscow.
11 Geoffrey Parker *The Dutch Revolt* London: Penguin, 1985 (rev. ed.) p. 78.
12 Moxey op. cit. p. 85.
13 Quoted (p. 44) in *Dutch Paintings of the Golden Age from the Collection of the National Gallery of Ireland* [Washington, D.C.:] Smithsonian Institution, 1987. See also Homan Potterton *Dutch Seventeenth and Eighteenth-Century Paintings in the National Gallery of Ireland; A Complete Catalogue* Dublin: National Gallery of Ireland, 1986.
14 *Uncle Silas* p. 12.
15 Idem.
16 Ibid. p. 13.
17 *Best Ghost Stories of J. S. Le Fanu* (ed. E. L. Bleiler) New York: Dover, 1964 pp. 136–7.
18 See Hebrews 12: 27. For the significance of the biblical passage in the context of apocalyptic imagery employed by Yeats, see the Epilogue below, p. 246.

10

Godfried Schalcken
in history and fiction

The efflorescence of Dutch art is well known, Rembrandt van Rijn
its chief glory. Yet in addition to the high achievements of the school,
there grew up within it a style of painting and choice of subject-
matter with which Gerard Dou, Gabriel Metsu, Gottfried Schalcken
and Jan Steen are particuarly associated. The setting was entirely
secular, without reference to ceremonial or historical occasions, and
without depiction of actual and known human figures. This was
genre painting, and if the term seems to indicate a secondary level of
operation one should recall that both Rembrandt and Jan Vermeer
have also been regarded as painters of *genre* material.

It is none the less important to note that the term *genre* (from the
eighteenth-century French, and meaning simply 'kind' or 'type')
was not applied in the seventeenth century. Its application to these
scenes of everyday life from which the transcendental and grandiose
are excluded is much closer to the period of Le Fanu's activity as a
fictional commentator on the work of Schalcken and Dou. For
obvious reasons, *genre* painting is pre-eminently (not exclusively)
associated with the Protestant countries of northern Europe where
religious imagery had been banished from the churches and where a
bourgeois art market had developed even before the end of the
sixteenth century. *Genre* nevertheless had origins in the emblematic
tradition as it had flourished through the medium of print. And even
in Schalcken's day, *genre* painting might incorporate a moralistic
device, a verbal message, or – on the other hand – a cheery depiction
of human frailty, sin and enjoyment. In particular, Schalcken was
renowned for his candle-lit scenes. He painted these by placing a
figure alone in a darkened room with just such illumination,
stationing himself in an adjoining sun-lit room, and scrutinising the
subject through a bore-hole in the partitioning wall or door.

The celebrated canvases of *genre* painting frequently depicted domestic interiors, the manners of professional men – doctors, lawyers, artists, etc. – and their bourgeois clients. In Dou and Schalcken, windows are prominently used to frame and control powerful and disruptive figures. These may be astrologers or other quacks, doctors and their patients, or simply luscious girls and their grinning lads. The coming together of popular culture and moral instruction can result in profound ambiguity. A painting often regarded as Schalcken's masterpiece *Lady, Come into the Garden*, derives from a parlour game with clear amorous and erotic implications. Such games were condemned in emblem books, the Calvinist Johan de Brune showing the activity known as 'La Main chaude' under the motto 'A Whore's Lap is the Devil's Boat'. But the dichotomy between behaviour and instruction was not always so strictly depicted, and the *genre* painters were skilled in showing the social actuality of division within a suavely unified composition. In Dou's *The Doctor* (1653), a young male figure is holding up a cylindrical glass vessel to study its contents while a female figure stands behind him looking apprehensively towards him, the whole scene framed in an oval-topped structure resembling a window or balcony. Schalcken's *A Visit to the Doctor* (1669) has an elderly male with a similar vessel, and beside him a young girl dabs at her eye with a scarf. In these and other pictures, two themes converge – that of speculative inquiry (whether alchemical or otherwise) and human frailty (illness, unwelcome pregancy or whatever). Books, sometimes with anatomical diagrams or less physical arcana, tend to buttress the male in his absorbed scrutiny of the female evidences.[1]

The careless dispersal (by his son Philip) of Sheridan Le Fanu's effects after his death prevents us from establishing anything like a full catalogue of the novelist's library or print collection. His brother William was on affable terms with William Dargan (a fellow railway engineer) whose entrepreurial munificence was celebrated with the establishment of the National Gallery of Ireland in 1864. What Sheridan Le Fanu saw in private or public collections cannot be ascertained. Yet we do know that Sheridan Le Fanu possessed a large 'elephant folio' of one hundred engravings after Philips Wouwermans, published in Paris between 1737 and 1762; these have descended intact to his grand-nephew.[2] Wouwermans (1619–68) painted battle scenes, incidents on the roadway (including military and criminal activity), fireside groups of soldiers etc. in a broad manner which yet retained characteristic *genre* features. The incidents of violence out of doors which occur in *Uncle Silas* – assaults, brawls, gypsies at the door of Maud's coach etc. – are comparable to Wouwermans' material, and their careful incorporation into that novel's symmetrical patterns once again suggests art both as a source of disruption and as a means of control.

The survival of the elephant folio in the possession today of William Le Fanu of Chelmsford, together with the latter's account of the Belisarius engraving, suggests a serious interest in such art on the writer's part. These paintings were not solely decorative, and their 'reading' by a Victorian owner is in keeping with their character and provenance. Even in Wouwermans, as in church portraiture and the *mélange* of biblical and local scenes, the emblematic device or motto occasionally found a place. Moreover, caged birds, books propped open, a trumpeter, a broken object … through these as through larger compositional arrangements, paintings such as those by Gerard Dou can legitimately be said to have, or *to have had*, double meanings. And the question of the loss of meaning, or the decay of interpretive skill, is a lively one in approaching a fiction which seeks to provide an exegesis for an imaginary painting.

The preceding paragraphs are not to be taken as an evolutionary account of Dutch painting, not even of a single strand in that development. They are provided specifically to facilitate the closer reading of Le Fanu's fiction, and so have made emphases which might not stand in isolation as valid for the topic generally. Let us first of all look anew at the imaginary picture as it is presented by the anonymous narrator in the opening paragraph of 'A Strange Event':

> The curious management of its lights constitutes, as usual in his pieces, the chief apparent merit of the picture. I say apparent, for in its subject, and not in its handling, however exquisite, consists its real value. The picture represents the interior of what might be a chamber in some antique religious building; and its foreground is occupied by a female figure, in a species of white robe, part of which is arranged so as to form a veil. The dress, however, is not that of any religious order. In her hand the figure bears a lamp, by which alone her figure and face are illuminated; and her features wear such an arch smile, as well becomes a pretty woman when practising some prankish roguery; in the back ground, and excepting where the dim red light of an expiring fire serves

to define the form, in total shadow, stands the figure of a man dressed in the old Flemish fashion, in an attitude of alarm, his hand being placed upon the hilt of his sword, which he appears to be in the act of drawing ...[3]

Without delay, compare this description of the painting with the final account of Schalken's strange adventure: in some kind of waking dream

as soon as he could clearly see what was round him, he perceived a female form, clothed in a kind of light robe of white, part of which was so disposed as to form a veil, and in her right hand she carried a lamp. She was moving rather away from him, in the direction of the flight of steps which conduced towards the vaults. He followed ... the figure paused also, and, turning gently round, displayed, by the light of the lamp it carried, the face and features of his first love, Rose Velderkaust ... She descended the stairs – he followed – and turning to the left, through a narrow passage, she led him, to his infinite surprise, into what appeared to be an old-fashioned Dutch apartment, such as the pictures of Gerard Douw have served to immortalize. Abundance of costly antique furniture was disposed about the room, and in one corner stood a four-post bed, with heavy black cloth curtains around it: the figure frequently turned to him with the same arch smile; and when she came to the side of the bed, she drew the curtains, and by the light of the lamp, which she held towards its contents, she disclosed to the horror-stricken painter, sitting bolt upright in the bed, the livid and demoniac form of Vanderhausen.[4]

The painting attributed to Schalcken in Le Fanu's story conforms to the conventional descriptions of the painter's style, his treatment of lighting, placement of human figures etc. However, the narrated interpretation of the picture which Le Fanu provides runs against the implications outlined above. A woman as it were *beckons* to a startled man who is about to draw a sword evidently in self-defence – so much we learn in the opening paragraph. The violent gesture can hardly be a response to the seductive one, yet no other reason for the drawn sword is provided in this early description of the picture. At the conclusion of the story, we are invited to believe that the woman was leading her erstwhile admirer towards a bed in which 'the livid and demoniac form' of an eternal seducer was sitting. The fearful cause of the self-portraying artist's alarm is now specified, but it is one to which sword-play is a pitifully inadequate response. In the course of winding up, the narrator stresses

Schalken's firm belief in the reality of this vision. Yet a number of anomalies already have emerged. Supernatural figures had no place in *genre* painting, and even in Schalcken's religious work a demon would be inadmissible. There is therefore a fundamental implausibility in the picture ascribed to him, an implausibility of subject-matter, and this despite the narrator's emphasis on the priority of subject over style. In addition, however, the narrator does not recognise that the location – the St Laurence church, in Rotterdam, where Schalken falls asleep awaiting his father's funeral – was a popular setting with many other painters. Though he will specify the place several times in the narrative, he refers to it in the context of the painting simply as 'a chamber in some antique religious building'. At such moments we recall the narrator's distinctly naive attitude towards painting, he regards subject-matter and not its treatment as of primary importance.

On re-examination, the story will confirm in a striking number of ways the importance of the St Laurence church. But for this purpose, a summary of the narrative is now required. Rose Velderkaust, niece and ward of the painter Gerard Douw of Leiden, was loved by Godfrey Schalken, Douw's pupil. The mysterious arrival of an elderly cloak-enclosed stranger pre-empts Schalken's declaration. The stranger, who gives his name as Minheer Vanderhausen of Rotterdam, says that he saw the girl in St Laurence church there, and was much struck by her. On her return, Rose is persuaded by her guardian (who is much impressed by the stranger's gold) to become betrothed to him. But he does not equally impress the girl who declares that she is reminded of 'the old painted wooden figure that used to frighten [her] so much in the Church of St Laurence at Rotterdam'. The pact is agreed between suitor and guardian, it is witnessed by the hapless Schalken, and Rose departs with her minheer for Rotterdam. Nothing is heard from her for a long time, then she suddenly returns in great distress, demands the service of a 'minister of God' and constant attendance by at least one of the painters. Through a blunder she is apparently snatched away again. Years pass by and Schalken, who has been 'residing far away', is summoned to his father's funeral in Rotterdam. The painter arrives at the church (St Laurence's) before the cortège, he is accommodated by a sexton who has a fire going, and he falls asleep. From this he believes himself to have been roused by a gentle shake of the shoulder, and to have witnessed the scene described above and reflected in the painting described in the opening paragraph of the story.

The literary merits of the story are remarkable. But the narrator provides a provenance for the painting which raises the relationship between biography and art, a theme both intrinsic to the account of Schalken's experience and to the narrator's exposition: 'My great grandfather knew the painter well; and from Schalken himself he learned the fearful story of the painting, and from him too he ultimately received the picture itself as a bequest. The story and the picture have become heir-looms in my family ... '[5] When Rose temporarily escaped from the demon lover and reached her former home where Douw and Schalken still reside, a minister ('perhaps more dreaded as a combatant than beloved as a Christian – of pure morality, subtle brain, and frozen heart') is called. But before he can arrive, the woman cries out incoherently 'he is here ... see! there he goes':

> She pointed towards the door of the inner room, and Schalken thought he saw a shadowy and ill-defined form gliding into that apartment. He drew his sword, and, raising the candle so as to throw its light with increased distinctness upon the objects in the room, he entered the chamber ... No figure was there ...[6]

This description of the character Schalken's behaviour in the story exactly matches the painter Schalcken's favourite technique of candle-lit portraiture. The incident, however, is quite distinct from that which allegedly gives rise to the self-portrait with sword. Life, so to speak, imitates art but does so in advance. For Le Fanu's story, the implication surely is that the work of art does not so much derive from the strange event, but that the final paragraphs of the fiction result from the description of the work given at the outset. Le Fanu's stylistic detail augments this kind of reading, by virtue of phrasing, sentence structure and punctuation:

> The window was open, and Schalken sprung to a chair and gazed out upon the street and canal below. He saw no form, but he saw, or thought he saw, the waters of the broad canal beneath settling ring after ring in heavy circles, as if a moment before disturbed by the submission of some ponderous body.[7]

The likely 'submission' of Rose in the canal demonstrates Le Fanu's extraordinary talent in choosing the ambiguous word, for there is a literal sense of 'submission' (cf. emission etc.) which half-conceals the suggestion of 'acceptance' or 'non-resistance'. Similarly, the etymological as well as idiomatic associations of 'ponderous' suggest even a thoughtful submission (i.e. one which has been pondered). Rose, by such ambiguity, is not simply her lover's victim. This bifurcated connotation occurs more radically in the final disclosure of the demon himself. Contained with undifferentiating commas, the phrase 'sitting bolt upright in the bed' first of all attaches itself uncannily to Schalcken before the reader passes on to detach it and re-attach it to 'the livid and demoniac form of Vanderhausen'. Finally, as far as ambiguity is concerned, the suggestion is unmistakable that the minister of God is as much surrogate for the demon as exorcist.

Rose and her lover are linked by name also. Their surnames not only resemble each other (Velderkaust/Vanderhausen) in a casual way, they are marked off from the historically verified names of Dou and Schalcken (though Le Fanu once more exploits variant spellings). The narrator's claim to a family possession of the painting in question, and of an ancestral acquaintance with Schalcken himself inevitably necessitates some account of the two Dutch painters as their careers might have been known to Le Fanu in 1839.

Gerard Dou was born in Leiden in 1613 and died there in 1675. It would appearance that the family's denominational allegiance was Baptist. In addition to a brother (Jan), Dou grew up with two children of his mother's by an earlier marriage: his half-sister married Simon van Tol by whom she had four children. Two of these are relevant to the painter's career, Dominicus van Tol who became Dou's pupil, and Antonia who afterwards lived in his house. His brother had only one daughter, Maria. A good deal can be deduced of Dou's working environment, for he did not leave Leiden for long periods of time. His 'nisstuk' paintings were so called because of the niche-like framing (often involving an arched window or other rounded top-surface) which he used so as to place the viewer looking into a scene, sometimes in direct confrontation with a depicted figure looking out. Dou became a highly successful painter, able to name his price and indeed to command an annual retainer from more than one connoisseur. In the words of a Dutch biographer Dou 'had not to work for his bread':

> For he knew no cares of any kind. He was unmarried and lived quietly in his house by the Galgewater with his niece Antonia van Tol, who kept house for him, and he never troubled himself as to what the world might say of their relations to each other.[8]

This arrangement with his niece is reflected in Dou's wills – he made several over the years. First, he made provision for a reversion to her of 3,000 gulden in the event of her surviving his other niece, Maria, together with all his personal effects, while in the same settlement he nominated just 1,000 gulden for her brother, Dominicus. By the will enacted at his death, he left his housekeeper niece 15,000 gulden for her life. These details are significant for several reasons. First, the historical Gerard Dou was neither short of money nor avaricious – that is, the representation in fiction of his cashing in on his niece's beauty appears to have no foundation. On the other hand, he did have a niece in residence (as the story says) but the relationship was very close – perhaps even adulterously so – and not calculating in any sense. Though it is a commonplace in Leiden, Dou and his niece lived by a canal. There are no references to Rotterdam, which was not a place of great artistic significance anyhow. It was, on the other hand, a very important Huguenot 'refuge' in the second half of the seventeeth century where, even before the Revocation of the Edict of Nantes, Pierre Bayle held a chair of philosophy. Bayle has been recognised as the founder of the Enlightenment school of history, in whose *Dictionary* (1697–1702) even the great Erasmus was not exempt from a revelation of illegitimacy.[9] In this proto-deconstructivist manner, as in the coining of the English term 'refugee', Huguenots moving from the Low Countries to Britain and Ireland sponsored a restlessness of spirit at odds with their renowned piety. After 1685, of course, the French Protestant migration to the Netherlands increased generally, with some refugees ultimately reaching Ireland. Among these were ancestors of Sheridan Le Fanu.

Godfried Schalcken (as it is usually spelled) was born in 1643 at Made near Dordrecht: his father, Cornelis Schalcken (1610–76), was (like Le Fanu's father) a minister of the reformed church. After a spell as pupil to Samuel van Hoogstraten in that town (*c.* 1656–62), he worked in the Leiden studio of Gerard Dou, who thus figures plausibly in Le Fanu's story. However, Schalcken returned to Dordrecht in 1665 and remained there until 1691 by which date Irish and Dutch politics were actively linked in William of Orange. After the prince became William III of England, Schalcken moved to England where he remained from 1692 to 1698 during which period he painted several portraits of the king. He returned to Dordrecht and stayed until his death there in 1706. Both his sister (Maria) and nephew (Jakob) became painters under his tutelege, and he himself painted a portrait of the former. Schalcken married Françoise van Diemen, and attached a pendant portrait of her to a self-portrait. He was a prolific and fashionable artist, whose work included many portraits of named and unnamed subjects. In addition to the representations already mentioned, he also painted his master Gerard Dou, and a Maria Jans, described as the mother of J. Dou.[10]

From all of this one derives no confirmation of any detail in the fiction, apart from the professional link between Dou and Schalcken. The fact of Schalcken's marriage, and the duration of it, argues against what is perhaps an unstated detail in the fiction – that Schalcken remained a bachelor faithful to his early love. That early love, of course, appears from the record to have been Dou's beloved and not his pupil's. The death of Cornelis Schalcken in 1676 serves to 'date' the fictional incident of the vision but, as in our researches into the life of Gerard Dou, nothing substantial emerges to link the painters to Rotterdam or to the church there. There is, however, one tantalising literary link. Balthazar de Monconys, recording his tour of the Low Countries in 1663, first mentions Gerard Dou (whose work he admired) in connection with a Rotterdam dealer who took him to the house of Antoine de Lorme. Indeed it is in this paragraph that the alchemist–physician–traveller makes his one oft-cited remark – about de Lorme's fine paintings of the St Laurence church and nothing but the church. While we cannot establish whether Sheridan Le Fanu read the *Voyages de ... Monconys*, the association of Dou, his niece and his pupil and her demon lover with the Rotterdam church may stem from some such source.

Of course, the sustained references to the St Laurence church have an internal rationale also. In the course of his first conversation with Dou, Vanderhausen explains how he set eyes on Rose: 'you visited the town of Rotterdam some four months ago, and then I saw in the church of St. Laurence your niece, Rose Velderkaust. I desire to marry her...'[11] After Vanderhausen's formal appearance before Douw, Schalken, *and* Rose, the girl exclaims 'when I saw him standing at the door, I could not get it out of my head that I saw the old painted figure that used to frighten me so much in the Church of St. Laurence at Rotterdam'.[12] The habitual tense ('that used to frighten') suggests something more than a brief or recent visit, and the lapse of just four months does not accord with Rose's limited fright at the sight of – so to speak – the wooden figure in the flesh.

Indeed, Rose's reactions are noted by Douw, who is 'not a little pleased, as well as puzzled, to observe that she appeared totally exempt from that mysterious dread of the stranger which ... considerably affected him, as also his pupil Godfrey Schalken'.[13] Rose is an innocent and does not recognise evil, or so one argument might run. But given her evident acceptance of marriage to the uncomely Vanderhausen, and the previous lovers' agreement between her and Schalken, innocence may not explain her conduct totally. The touching inscription of Rose and Godfrey's love for each other is totally abandoned within the fiction once Vanderhausen manifests himself, and no one (not even Godfrey Schalken) remarks on Rose's change of allegiance. This silence on his part may be read as timidity – or passivity – sufficient to stimulate feelings of guilt. In Rose a different but complementary motive can be discerned. At some level she recognises Vanderhausen and accepts him; that level is articulated by reference to statuary in a church purged of images by the iconclastic Calvinists long before 1662. Like so many of Le Fanu's fictions, whether written in the 1830s or thirty years later, the plot hinges round a devious impact of the past upon the present.

The past is conjured by means of an altered architecture. We know that the church in Rotterdam conformed to the post-iconoclasm austerity of decoration. Its new style certainly dates from a period earlier than the lives of Dou and his niece. Rose's recognition of Vanderhausen is established through a wooden figure, and thus is transported back to a former era when – if the church were not still Catholic in the old sense – an Erasmian tolerance still preserved the images of wood and stone. If Vanderhausen somehow signifies the Catholic past, are we to interpret Le Fanu as equating Catholicism with demonic practices? Hardly so; if any character is excoriated in the story it is the minister of God (i.e. a reformed, probably Calvinist minister) who is a 'combatant' rather than a 'Christian', who is possessed of a stony intellect and frozen heart. That the minister's being closeted with Rose leads directly to her second departure (and his) suggests that he is a counterfeit demon. In this connection we note that an account of Vanderhausen occurring early in the story presented him in the odd phrase 'a man of worship', which neatly conjoins his apparent burgher status ('the worshipful mayor of ...' etc.) and an implied allegiance to the Devil – or the Church.[14]

It is true that the final incident of the story takes place in a church which is not named. But the location is specified to the extent that it is 'the church at Rotterdam' which is virtually to specify the Grot Kerk. Moreover, the burial of Schalken's father in Rotterdam is never explained – in so far as he is a verifiable figure, he hails from Dordrecht. Thus, inexplicably, the young Schalken is led back to the site of Vanderhausen's first seeing Rose; it is as if he is compelled by the logic of his vision to be Peeping Tom at the tryst of virgin and old wooden figure.

As with certain stylistic rearrangements of incident inside the story, the historical account may suggest that Le Fanu has transferred items from debit to credit (and vice versa) in a suggestive manner. The illicit liaison between uncle and niece (at least suspected by the townsfolk of Leiden) is dissolved and reassembled into two rival relationships. One of these (Schalken and Rose) is never activated, though its legitimacy and moral validity are all the more firmly established by the behaviour of the two young people. The second, of course, is the demonic pact between Rose Velderkaust and Wilken Vanderhausen: this is greedily sanctioned by the uncle, witnessed by the pupil/lover, and ultimately embraced by the two partners as seen in Schalken's vision. That one detail of the picture arising from vision (Schalken with his sword) should relate to an incident in which he failed to protect Rose points to guilty feeling on his part as to his passive behaviour. But a stylistic detail of the incident's narration (Schalken with a candle) dismisses painterly technique as an efficacious response to crisis. We read casually that Schalken is about to draw his sword, but how do we read precisely the word 'draw'? Does it perch ambiguously between the realm of art and action, vertiginously paralysed and unable to opt for one or the other?

For the story/record is repeatedly on the edge of psychic crisis – in the element of near incest, and so forth. A fiction which has characterised Dou's behaviour as 'sordidness, levity and heartlessness' concludes by transforming a church scene into 'what appeared to be an old-fashioned Dutch apartment, such as the pictures of Gerard Douw have served to immortalize' with an 'abundance of costly antique furniture'.[15] Dou is referred to here (1) as if he had no previous part in the action, that is to say, he is a mere allusion to the style or fashion of a fictional room; and (2) as if he were remote in time from the action described, a factor emphasised in the terms 'old-fashioned' and 'antique'.

This double distancing functions to introduce the passage of time to mitigate or obliterate offence (Dou's alleged selling of his niece). It finds its counter-effect immediately in another obliteration. The vision of a lost beloved woman is occasioned by the death of the visionary's father, whose funeral however is passed over while images of a demoniac sexuality are narrated. When the vision has fled, the painter is found unconscious not by a bed but by a coffin raised 'upon small pillars, a security against the attacks of vermin'. The proper burial and 'last respects' due to the father are obliterated by sleep and vision but their traces may be found in the coffin by which the painter awakes. The evidence of mortality in life may be readily contrasted with the phrase about an art which *immortalises*, these pictures being specified as those of Dou, guardian to the lost girl and professional master to the visionary. A domestic apartment has been conjured into the cellar of a church, but in the end its sinful bed is replaced by a forgotten *memento mori*.

The story, in other words, enacts a network of reversals and inversions. Female, in the picture described, taunts or even tempts male. But she leads him *down-* rather than up-stairs. Male is led forward not only towards a 'roguish' female heading towards bed but also towards a male rival already in bed. Considered initially, 'A Strange Event' appears to deconstruct a painting by extrapolating the biographical sources for its representation: in others words, events generate a picture. The story, however, includes certain passages which begin to jeopardise this interpretation by means of exaggeration. Thus Schalcken, who will be famed for his candle-lit scenes, is written of in terms appropriate to his own painterly technique. Both style and subject of the picture are already implicated at this mid-point of the story, a point already made when we said that the scene of Rose's return *matched* Schalcken's technique of lighting. It might now be more accurate to say that the described technique reverses Schalcken's action on this occasion: then, he carried the candle into the room where his 'subject' was (and loses her); in the paintings he remains outside the room and views it with a candle also kept outside the room. This observation would underline a passive or voyeuristic element in Schalcken's technique, at least it relates to Le Fanu's fictional account of him. Or, if you prefer, the painting described at the outset of the story does not simply arise from the visionary experience of meeting Rose and her Demon in the St Laurence church, but it incorporates a passage from the story in which Schalcken has proved an incompetent protector with both sword and candle. Forced to choose between notions of Schalcken as incompetent painter or incompetent lover, we might conveniently compromise by recognising in Le Fanu's character study a well-known romantic type – 'le poète maudit'. The author's French origins and contemporary French literature engage somewhere behind the heavy drapery and high varnish of the story.

From the accounts available to Le Fanu, it would appear that Schalcken was – however briefly – something of a 'painter laureate' to the new dynasty under whose auspices ancestors of Le Fanu's first reached Ireland. He was known as a painter (one of many) of the king's portrait, and Charles de Cresserons was said to have received such a portrait from the king himself. Yet Schalcken's reputation is one of uncouth manners and sturdy independence, and not of courtly ease. In this, as much as in his royal portraits, his career endorses and celebrates the historical process by which a 'Protestant Ascendancy' might emerge in Ireland. The deeply felt antagonism of Gaelic culture for the upstarts who settled on Irish land is well attested. What is intriguing – and elusive – in 'A Strange Event' is the depiction of a historical epoch (that of Dutch leadership in Protestant Europe) within the fiction of that social constituency (Irish conservativism, verging into Orangeism) in which adherence to the Williamite settlement was the absolute badge of all loyalty and faith. The story thus goes well beyond *The Fortunes of Colonel Torlogh O'Brien* (1847, Le Fanu's second published novel) in relating the origin myth of Williamite Ireland; despite the lavish use of paint, it is a historical fiction albeit a dexterously evasive one, for like the novel it offers little to admire in the régime which commands loyalty. In time, thirty years or more after the writing of the story of Schalcken, this adherence will generate a name by which an apparently distinct ethnic group will be identified – the Protestant Ascendancy.

With that name will come a celebration of the eighteenth century, an assertion of aristocratic or near-aristocratic status, and an attachment to rural estate as the index of security and status. The transfer from urban settings in the two 'reminiscences of a bachelor' (the second published in 1848) to the isolated house-and-master of 'Richard Marston' (also 1848) ties this imminent celebration precisely to the revolutionary events of 1848. Alarmed by his earlier association with some of the Irish rebels, Le Fanu commences a process of revaluation which becomes systematic in *The House by the Church-yard*, a revaluation as yet lacking a term to mark and mask an endangered middle-class fraction. The emergence of Protestant Ascendancy in this comprehensive sense may be seen to begin no earlier than 1868 – in a speech of W. E. Gladstone's. But in *The House by the Church-yard*, written six to seven years earlier, we have found Le Fanu exhuming some of the historical remains upon which Protestant Ascendancy will build its monuments. Now, with 'A Strange Event in the Life of Schalken the Painter', an even earlier stage of the critical process has been uncovered.

The use of a *genre* painter is revealing, for it focuses attention on the issue of secular class. This speaks against the loftier placements implicit in the notion of ascendancy, but it also implicates question of literary form and artistic form generally. Le Fanu's fullest account of a genre painter is of course his story of 1839. But the history of the classification requires further attention. In 1766 Denis Diderot had distinguished between *peinture de genre* and *peinture d'histoire*: natural life, landscapes, what we would now call still life, together with domestic occasions, interiors, the preoccupations of craftsmen etc. all were admitted under the heading of *genre*. Quatremère de Quincy sharpened this implicit definition in 1791 when he insisted that paintings properly described as *genre* are 'those representing *des scènes bourgeoises*'.[16] After this declaration of the revolutionary era, emphasis on social class as a factor identifying the subject-matter of *genre* painting diminished, and 'the modern definition is unequivocally stated in Franz Kugler's influential *Handbuch der Geshichte der Malerei* of 1837: "Genre paintings (in the sense which it is normal to attach to these words) are representations of everyday life."'[17] The German critic's definition of *genre* precedes Le Fanu's story of Schalcken by just two years.

That Le Fanu was of a scholarly bent has been long recognised, though his later years have normally been thought of as the period of his inquiries into Swedeborgianism and other lore. There is good reason, surely, to suppose that 'A Strange Event' results from some youthful study both of Dutch painting and continental literature. In 1831 Balzac published 'Le Chef-d'oeuvre inconnu', one of the *études philosophiques* which go to make up his *Comédie humaine*. It tells of a young painter (Nicolas Poussin) who reluctantly agrees to lend his most beautiful mistress to the elderly, wealthy and wholly invented

painter Frenhofer as a model in return for a privileged viewing of
Frenhofer's work in progress, the portrait of 'Catherine Lescault'.
But when Poussin and another friend are finally shown the picture,
all they can make out from the daubs and blotches on the canvas is
a roughly painted human foot.[18] This tale of the painter/lover's de-
picturing the woman might not have caught Le Fanu's attention
where it not for the direct involvement of a fellow Irish Huguenot in
Balzac's *Melmoth réconcilé* (1835). But it is not simply 'Le Chef-
d'oeuvre inconnu' which leads towards 'A Strange Event'. Some
time *c*. 1820, there appeared an English translation of an anonymous
Dutch tale, 'Jan Schalken's Three Wishes'. In this, a cloaked stranger
gives Schalken three wishes in return for hospitality, and by means
of these Jan and his wife cheat Death on several occasions till
'exactly on their birthday, Jan Schalken and his wife, died quietly in
their bed, and the salt water flowed freely in the little village, in
which they had lived long enough to be considered the father and
mother of all its inhabitants'.[19] The self-defeating efforts of Balzac's
painter and the good fortune of those simple Schalkens who supped
with the Devil are combined in Le Fanu's story with its dispersed
offences, reversals and inversions.

At a more academic level of research, Le Fanu had access to John
Smith's colossal *Catalogue Raisonné* of Dutch art which appeared in
nine volumes between 1829 and 1842. Nevertheless the closeness in
time of Kugler and Le Fanu is important for reasons quite distinct
from those of source or influence. For Diderot – whose *Essais sur la
peinture* did not appear until after de Quincy's definition – *genre*
could accommodate the heroic, the sublime, the subversive, the
cryptic. And in the revolutionary decade of the 1790s, the
bourgeoisie is identified as the herald of these qualities. By the 1830s,
however, the great French Revolution was part of history, and the
July Monarchy was in power in Paris. Le Fanu's fiction of the 1830s
keeps a sharp eye on French politics, even through the medium of
the gothic and the demonic.

If the overall historical context of *The Purcell Papers* is the Irish
eighteenth century, the source of contamination in story after story
is continental Europe, especially France. But a contradiction informs
any correlation of French and Irish politics at this time. While
France lumbered onwards through industrial unrest, riot (1834) and
foreign adventurism towards the next revolution (that of 1848),
Ireland was experiencing a virtually unique experiment in reformist

parliamentary govenment. The dissolution of the Orange Order, the centralisation of police forces, moves towards municipal reform – these developments were embodied in the alliance of Daniel O'Connell and the English whigs, the Lichfield House compact so detested by the Irish tory constituency in which Sheridan Le Fanu was growing up. That alliance accelerated the tendency among Irish tories to identify the middle class in a way which excluded themselves. Le Fanu's shift from the teeming streets of *The Cock and Anchor* and 'The Fatal Bride' to the mansion of Richard Marston (first at Dunoran, then near Chester) enacts this elevating retreat in topographical terms which also concludes in the tories' point of necessary political identification – England. Like Kugler's redefinition of *genre*, the Irish tories were engaged in an exercise of *desembourgeoisement*. Kugler's de-*class*ification of *genre* is thus a matter of the moment, and his emphasis on the 'normal' and the 'everyday' is hardly less important than his continued adherence to the element of representation.

For if seventeenth-century *genre* painting emblemises the middle-class milieu from which Le Fanu came, Victorian *genre* rigorously suppresses emblem and allegory in the cause of sentiment. Now, there is no meaning to be sought in a rigorous study of the picture and its layering of symbols, colours, and even words. Instead there is an instant and appropriately superficial confirmation (as in a mirror) of trite meanings already emplanted in the viewer's box of opinions. Pussy cats and goldfish, wounded soldiers and boys playing with toys – these are the ready-made donées of mass-produced Victorian *genre* work, whether worked into the furbelows of a painting by James Tissot or grainily reproduced in Crimean War supplements to the London *Times*. Evidence of this sentimentalising process is easily enough found in Le Fanu's later fiction, as in the scenes referred to in the previous chapter.

Yet even *Guy Deverell* persists in retaining the theme of resurrection – however vestigially – and in doing so incorporates what is virtually a self-contained short story into the novel's longer narrative. This pattern in the later fiction may now suggest a modified classification. Instead of measuring the divergence of Le Fanu's novels from the example of Walter Scott or the more routine practice of the sensational school, we can see them as the literary equivalent of *genre* work. At their best they excel the cute terriers and coy maidens, retaining some features of the seventeenth-century style in the use of mottoes, devices, interpolated tales, artists' names and so forth. They grapple with the decay of a confidence which stared soberly from the canvases of Rembrandt and grinned from those of Schalcken and Dou, a confidence which once held earthly experience of the self and expectations of salvation in quiet communion. Their heroes can be almost seen skidding into misidentifications, avoiding and accompanying their so-recognisable near-namesakes. Their heroines gaze at portraits in desire and terror, while being also sicklied o'er with the saccharine of nineteenth-century taste. In due course the historical moment, British as well as Irish, of this convergence can be considered in more detail, for it is no coincidence that such a dialectic of repression and recuperation should be written during the decade which concluded in Gladstone's fertile assault on the notion of ascendancy as a poisonous growth.

Notes

1 Christopher Brown *Scenes of Everday Life: Dutch Genre Painting of the Seventeenth Century* London: Faber, 1984. p. 211. For other illustrations see the catalogue *Von Hals bis Vermeer* Berlin: Frölich & Kaufmann, 1984.

2 Personal communication from William Le Fanu.

3 *Best Ghost Stories of J. S. Le Fanu* (ed. E. L. Bleiler) New York: Dover, 1964 p. 29.

4 Ibid. pp. 45–6. Note the exact repetition of 'as to form a veil' within passages which otherwise parallel but do not repeat each other. The words 'form' and 'figure', referring to non-depicted persons, recur prominently as do verbs modifying what it is Schalcken sees ... 'as he thought' etc. The effect is progressively to merge the image and the beholder, and at two levels; (1) Schalcken and what he sees; (2) the reader and the convergent text.

5 Ibid. p. 30.

6 Ibid. p. 43.

7 Ibid. p. 45.

8 W. Martin *Gerard Dou* (trans. Clara Bell) London: George Bell, 1902 pp. 73–4.

9 For Pierre Bayle etc. see Gerald Cerny *Theology, Politics, and Letters at the Crossroads of European Civilization: Jacques Basnage and the Baylean Huguenot Refugees in the Dutch Republic* Dordrecht: Nijhoff, 1987.

10 W. Martin op. cit. pp. 28–9. See for comprehensive lists of the art concerned, C. Hofstede de Groot *A Catalogue Raisonée of the Most Eminent Dutch Painters of the Seventeenth Century* London: Macmillan, 1913 especially vols 1 and 5.

11 *Best Ghost Stories* p. 34.

12 Ibid. p. 39.

13 Ibid. pp. 39–40.

14 Ibid. p. 33.

15 Ibid. p. 46.

16 Quoted Brown op. cit. p. 10. For Diderot's 'Essais sur la peinture' see *Oeuvres*

complètes Paris: Garnier, 1876 vol. 10 pp. 455–520, esp. pp. 482, 507–8.

17 See Brown op. cit. pp. 9–10.

18 See H. de Balzac *Gillette; or The Unknown Masterpiece* (trans. with an essay by Anthony Rudolf) London: Menard Press, 1988.

19 'Jan Schalken's Three Wishes' is included (pp. 317–20) in Peter Haining (ed.) *Great Tales of Terror from Europe and America* Harmondsworth: Penguin, 1973.

PART THREE

The great
enchantment

11

In a Glass Darkly

Karl Marx observed somewhere that Capitalism is the ghost story of reality. Assuming he intended no compliment, where does this leave the ghost story? Best known of the five long tales which make up *In a Glass Darkly* (1872) is 'Carmilla', a covert account of lesbianism, lusciously filmed with Ingrid Pitt and Kate O'Mara under the drably obvious title *The Vampire Lovers*. Does Le Fanu belong midway between the fantasies of Hammar Films and the sickle of revolutionary materialism? Are we to shift from art history to the less stolid virtues of film studies?

On the contrary. Once more Le Fanu's most minute verbal manoeuvres with regard to sacred texts demand the closest attention. As the inattentiveness of at least two of its narrators testifies, names and titles in *In a Glass Darkly* tell, especially when they nervously deflect or omit a detail. In *Ghost Stories and Tales of Mystery* (1851), biblical quotation had been largely confined to the space above the opening paragraph of each story. But the collection of 1872 brought St Paul right on to the title-page. In the first Epistle to the Corinthians we read: 'For now we see through a glass darkly; but then face to face: now I know in part; but then shall I know even as also I am known' (13: 12).

The coherence, or at least the general implication, of the biblical inexactitude provides a useful starting point. At one level, it registers the extent to which the would-be Christian believer can no longer penetrate *through* the darkened glass of earthly evidences and see his Creator and His truth. Biblical scholars differ in interpreting the passage, and the sense of a broader lack of unanimity on the question of revelation underpins much of Le Fanu's work as it does that of his generation generally. St Paul may have been merely chiding the Corinthians on their immaturity, and indicating how much easier their perception of the truth would be when they 'grew up'. On the other hand, an apocalyptic reading would look forward to the Second Coming 'when that which is perfect is come', and such expectations have been attributed to Paul. They have also of course been sustained more recently by some radical Protestant sects from reformation times to the present day. By this second interpretation, whether attributed to Paul or to a contemporary believer, one might well be content to see darkly, to know in part. But if such were to be the case, it would be necessary to see through the glass to some degree. *In*, replacing *through*, appears to deny even this degree of limited penetration. Accordingly, Le Fanu's title, in so far as we can already decipher it, refers to a historical change which has been somehow completed. The aspirant Christian now finds his attention trapped, or obscured, or obstructed, *within* what might have been thought the medium of successful vision. The misquotation, at this level, is quite at one with the religious misgivings of Matthew Arnold's 'Dover Beach', and with the Victorian crisis of faith generally.

This reading is conditioned by the overwhelming dominance of English over the original language employed by Paul, with the success of the King James Bible as the principal villain. Victorian alternative uses of 'through' – denoting the transmission of light or of sight by an aperture or a transparent medium, *or* by means of, by the action of – obscure the issue of returning to a precise meaning of the biblical term. At another level, it is the term 'glass' which throws up problems. Le Fanu has quoted it faithfully enough. Has it kept faith in turn? Even a casual consideration of the topic brings the realisation that window-glass did not exist in New Testament times, that the 'glass' referred to was a mirror or looking-glass, reflecting not transparent. The Authorised Version of the Bible takes a liberty even by using 'glass' (the New Testament Greek is 'esoptron'), for the mirrors of St Paul's days were polished surfaces, metal for the most part. Thus, two levels of interpretive difficulty emerge. One relates to the King James translators' choice of the one 'glass' for the mirror of I Corinthians 13: 12 *and* for the less easily identified material of Revelation 15: 2 – 'And I saw as it were a sea of glass mingled with fire.' The second level of difficulty is Victorian, when the sense of 'through' has been dulled by mechanist associations and when concordances such as Alexander Cruden's (1737) were used to demonstrate the literalist consistency of Holy Scripture. For it is obvious by now that St Paul (or rather his translator) uses 'through' in the sense of 'by means of' and not as involving penetration of a transparent material. Le Fanu's alteration of 'through' to 'in' can at least cite alterations of meaning in the language of the Bible itself as a kind of dubious or self-defeating authority.

We have already looked at another oddly skewed reading of St Paul – if it is not downright misquotation – in the chapter of *Uncle Silas* where Maud Ruthyn contemplates the cloud of witnesses in freezing brightness. From the Acts of the Apostles right through to St Peter's Epistle, a Silas (sometimes called Silvanus) is reported as a faithful supporter and assistant of Paul's, so that the very Christian name of Maud's vicious uncle is an ironic undermining of loyalty, orthodoxy and authority. An earlier episode in the novel virtually enacts the Pauline problem of seeing through glass darkly, and does so in a suitably literal manner: 'I was obliged to keep my cheek against the window-pane to command a view of .the point of debarkation, and my breath upon the glass, which dimmed it again almost as fast as I wiped it away, helped to obscure my vision.'[1] Here, the narrator comes to know the interference of her own body in the business of narration. That 'helped' says a lot about the apprehensive fatalism of Le Fanu's narrators, their tendency in the late novels to faint or otherwise to lose consciousness, but the scene generally anticipates the collective title of the 1872 tales or novellas. The female body takes on a role in 'Carmilla' far more subversive than anything conceded by Maud Ruthyn. A tapestry hanging over the sinister guest's bed will act as a magic mirror, reflecting not only Carmilla the vampire but also the narrator her intended victim.

The narrative possibilities of mirrors and pictures had been exploited long before the Victorian period, yet there was room for experiment. The self-containment, or confirmation, of self guaranteed by the mirror was jeopardised amusingly in a work by Lewis Carroll published in the same year as these grim tales. Going 'through the looking glass' Alice meets humanised chessmen in what amounts to a systematised antithetical world. Le Fanu's figures, in contrast to Carroll's, do not venture so far and perhaps suffer the more for their trepidation. At this level, the Bible-misquoting title suggests a lack of confidence in self-recognition. The self is seen but only 'in a glass darkly', and this in mockery of the actual if limited ability of the early Christian to see God. The implications for a notion of fictional character are obvious.

Misquotation of the Bible is oddly compensated elsewhere in Le Fanu with liberal acts of self-quotation, as if to suggest that text itself constitutes a more reliable form of self than any which might be guaranteed by the authority of scriptural mottoes and their assurances of immortality. This compensation can even be expressed in monetary images, for debts to his own earlier work exemplify a linguistic commerce which is unsleeping. As we see time and again, many of Le Fanu's English stories have Irish antecedents. Even so exotic a collection as *In a Glass Darkly*, with its German-writing exegete-behind-the-narrator and its continental locations, includes a sharp delineation of Georgian Dublin in 'The Familiar', first published in November 1847 in *The Dublin University Magazine* as 'The Watcher'. Other far more minuscule borrowings can be traced to the same journal if not to the self-same author. 'Green Tea', the first story of the collection, relates the haunting by a spectral monkey of the pious Reverend Jennings. In early 1841, the *The Dublin University Magazine* published 'German Ghosts and Ghost Seers', a complex two-part work in which the author (Henry Ferris) incidentally related two stories which can be seen to converge in Le Fanu's of 1872:

> The writer knew an English clergyman who saw, as he lay in bed, his curtains drawn, and two grim hands thrust in, their eyes glaring goblinly upon him. But he was aware that it was 'merely bile in the stomach,' which was very satisfactory to know. There is an English physician at a town on the Continent, who cannot drink green tea, without seeing in the course of the evening, a certain tall woman ...[2]

Ferris, like the vampire Carmilla, operated under an anagrammatic name, for these articles (and others on arcane topics) were signed Irys Herfner. 'German Ghosts and Ghost Seers' is likely one of Le Fanu's earliest sources for the doctrines of Swedenborg (beloved of the Ruthyn brothers and the Reverend Jennings); all in all, the ghostly Ferris must be treated as an influence upon the author of *Uncle Silas* and *In a Glass Darkly*. Yet what is ultimately striking in the relationship is not so much the transfer of names and plot-summaries from Ferris to Le Fanu as the scrambling of discrete details into undifferentiated new amalgamations. Ferris's clergyman and the physician merge in Le Fanu's Reverend Jennings, (cf. Captain Jennings of 'The Fatal Bride') in counteraction to the separate and apparently irreconcilable existences of the many Marstons of Le Fanu's other fictions. These mergers constitute more than an artist's deft appropriation of what is useful to the task in hand; as an examination of 'Carmilla' will demonstrate, plagiarism is the veritable theme of Le Fanu's late work.

Like 'Borrhomeo the Astrologer', *In a Glass Darkly* is ostensibly an example of the editor's art, and the translator's. In place of a manuscript, we have the files of a German physician, Dr Martin Hesselius who, together with Bryerly in *Uncle Silas*, combines medical skill with deep learning in arcane psycho-spiritual matters. A recent historian of 'the fantastic' has seen Hesselius as the precursor of all those psychic doctors and special investigators who teem through the literature of late-Victorian and Edwardian England, applying their uncanny powers to supernatural and criminal mischiefs alike.[3] However, Hesselius makes so little showing in *In a Glass Darkly* that he should be likened more to Mycroft Holmes than to the great sleuth of 221B Baker Street. As with Holmes and his Watson, Hesselius relies on an intermediary, several intermediaries in fact. The anonymous editor is apparently English, originally trained as a physician and surgeon, but forced to abandon his profession following an accident in which he cut himself so badly as to lose two fingers, an involuntary exile consequently, and finally the secretary of Hesselius whose papers he is arranging and indexing.

Thus the stories of *In a Glass Darkly* arise, in several ways, from Hesselius's archive, and the variety of narrative-perspectives adopted in turn complicates the already much-mediated relation between reader and character. For example, 'Green Tea' consists (for the most part) in a series of letters written by Hesselius to a Professor Van Loo of Leyden, 'some in English, some in French, but the greater part in German'. The professor had not been a physician but a chemist who had written a play in his earlier years, and consequently the correspondence was 'necessarily written in a manner more likely to interest an unlearned reader'. Nevertheless, the anonymous narrator indicates that further editorial intrusions have emerged between Hesselius and his new (posthumous) readers: 'I am a faithful, though I am conscious, by no means a graceful translator, and although here and there I omit some passages, and short others, and disguised names, I have interpolated nothing.'[4] The switch of verb tenses within this one sentence places a further obstacle on the reader's access to a reliable chronology. The death of Jennings, we are led to believe, occurred some sixty-four years earlier than the narrator's present moment, and the letters were returned to Hesselius on the death of Van Loo in 1819. In subsequent stories the relation of past event to present is even more contorted until in 'Carmilla' it threatens to become simultaneously absolute and inert: past is to be present.

In the prologue to the second story, 'The Familiar', the narrator informs us that he has chosen it 'out of about two hundred and thirty cases more or less nearly akin ...'[5] Given that the tale originated as 'The Watcher', these cases might even be regarded as Le Fanu's own early and anonymous works. The narrator within the story is identified as the Reverend Thomas Herbert, an Irish clergyman, and by this means the suicidal victim of the first story (the Reverend Jennings) is succeeded and survived by a reliable and unremarkable member of his own profession. Hesselius's notes – we are told – indicate that Captain Barton's nervous condition was probably hereditary, and this speaks against suggestions in Herbert's narrative that Barton's own guilty past is responsible for his mysterious death.

Narrators, on this evidence, are never wholly reliable. 'Mr Justice Harbottle' is prefaced by editorial remarks explaining that the better of two reports dealing this case had been lost, and lost by a doctor at that. This indication of professional carelessness is partly masked by the editor's pompous citation of numerous references (by volume, section and note) to Hesselius's publications or papers. Yet it turns out that the erring doctor did return the better report and that (in the absence of any other explanation) the survival of only the inferior is the responsibility of Hesselius – or his secretary. Meanwhile, biblical misquotation surfaces again in the last sentence of the story, where the word 'also' is dropped from a citation of Luke 16: 22 – to no effect save that of violating authority.

'The Room in the Dragon Volant' is told in the first person by the principal actor in the drama, a young man travelling in France in 1815. The editor's prologue speaks of *Mortis Imago*, an essay of two-volume length written by Hesselius on the subject of powerful drugs but apparently unpublished. 'Carmilla' is prefaced with remarks about an essay 'on the strange subject which the MS. illuminates'. This has particularly interested the editor who concludes:

I was anxious, on discovering this paper, to re-open the corres-pondence commenced by Doctor Hesselius, so many years before, with a person so clever and careful as his informant seems to have been. Much to my regret, however, I found that she had died in the interval.[6]

From all of this it might seem that the editorial dimension of the book is seriously flawed, but this would be a mistaken view. It is a collection rigorously organised in its very appearance of inconsistency and decentredness. The dates of the various events naturally differ, but they point steadily towards the late eighteenth century ('The Familiar') and the close of the Napoleonic Wars ('The Room in the Dragon Volant') as inclusive. It is true that the action of 'Mr Justice Harbottle' reaches back to the period of Jacobite rebellion, but the document presented to the reader is more prominently dated to 1805. The years 1795–1815 appear to have been Hesselius's *floruit* – as the editors of reference books have it – the years of virtually uninterrupted war in Europe.

Location proliferates on a similar scale – England, Ireland, France and Austria, with the Low Countries, Germany and Hungary implicated, and Poland and Turkey alluded to in the closing pages. Le Fanu's fiction does not create a unified landscape, any rounded solid world either British or Irish, urban or rural; instead it spins elliptically on a trajectory which demolishes the notion of a controlling centre. Nor does it project an orderly or stratified hierarchy, either of class or of value. Thus, the displacements of Le Fanu's fiction are only part of its comprehensive rejection of all notions of fixed centrality, reliable identity and social stability.

Action ranges wide but not without symmetry. The immobilised consciousness of young Beckett in 'The Room in the Dragon Volant' should be read as the counterpart of a lascivious and protean immortality in 'Carmilla'. Sexuality doubles up for religion – but that's hardly rare. What is more curious is that the narrator of 'Carmilla' addresses herself to a woman ('a town lady like you') while we are officially led to believe that Martin Hesselius is her correspondent. At the structural or narrative level this reproduction of transferred gender ('what if a boyish lover had found his way into the house ...?') echoes the narrated substance of the tale. But whether it echoes by way of confirmation or mockery is less clear. 'Boyish' still implies the lover's femaleness even as it insinuates the word 'boy'.[7]

It is with a sense of shock, then, that one notices that the ghost stories of *In a Glass Darkly* are keenly attentive to cash-flow and investment, as if indeed Balzac had returned from the dead to add a few details to the vague treatment of wealth usual in Le Fanu's fiction. 'The Rev. Mr. Jennings ... has, they say, sixty thousand pounds in the funds.' Less precisely, the discreet Thomas Herbert tells us that the unfortunate Captain Barton was 'in affluent circumstances'. 'Mr Justice Harbottle' derives an income from the narrator's financial deals – 'a small annuity charged on some property of mine' – with an informant who further distances the reader from the action. The foolish Beckett open his narration of his adventures in 'The Room in the Dragon Volant' with the sentence 'In the eventful year, 1815, I was exactly three-and-twenty, and had just succeeded to a very large sum in consols, and other securities.'[8] Even the remarkable narrator of 'Carmilla' is careful to establish herself financially in two opening paragraphs riddled with credit worthiness:

> In Styria we, though by no means magnificent people, inhabit a castle, or schloss. A small income, in that part of the world, goes a great way. Eight or nine hundred a year does wonders. Scantily enough ours would have answered among wealthy people at home. My father is English, and I bear an English name, although I never saw England. But, here, in this lonely and primitive place, where everything is so marvellously cheap, I really don't see how ever so much more money would at all materially add to our comforts, or even luxuries.
>
> My father was in the Austrian service, and retired upon a pension and his patrimony, and purchased this feudal residence, and the small estate on which it stands, a bargain.[9]

Marx, who read E. T. A. Hoffmann avidly and loved Balzac's bizarre stories, might have thought this an oddly materialist way to begin a tale of smouldering female homosexuality, vampirism and picture-jumping. The systematic initiation of each story in *In a Glass Darkly* might be read as simply underlining the pious maxim that the rich are not privileged in matters of suffering or folly. The concentration of the action within the years of great imperialist conflict – 'the time of the breaking of nations' – gives some support to this interpretation of the stories as social criticism.

Yet the references to money and inheritance serve also to underline other kinds of debt in the fiction itself. One would note the regularity of their disposal at the commencement of each story; they constitute a series of unverifiable measurements of a character's 'position' in the world. 'The Room in the Dragon Volant' tells how a romantic-minded young man, travelling shortly after Bonaparte's first defeat, is trapped in an inn called The Dragon Volant. Actively, his enemies are an alluring woman and a drug called *imago mortis* (the illusion of death), but in more strictly textual terms the inn's very name signifies the continuance or resumption of hostilities – *le dragon volant* was a particularly awesome cannon used in the Napoleonic Wars. The double reference in the story's title constitutes a kind of plagiarism between idiom and action. Its anti-hero exemplifies the dangers of literary unselfconsciousness.

Remembering the pendulous Miss Pitt of 'The Vampire Lovers', you may find such claims dully academic. 'Carmilla' is after all the classic story of vampires in which aberrant sexuality, and not precocious textuality, threatens to steal the show. Sexuality in Le Fanu's fiction generally lacks energy when it is running in the conventional and heterosexual channels. Only when two women become close do the barometers of feeling begin to rise. To date, this has been seen as somehow a biographical trace, indicating perhaps some latent homosexual tendency in the author. And in this, as in the matter of the Protestant Ascendancy, *Sheridan Le Fanu and Victorian Ireland* was careless.

For there is a more strictly textual view to be taken of those pairs of women – Dorcas and Rachel in *Wylder's Hand*, Carmilla and Laura – who project a male-excluding intimacy. Seen in the light of Balzac's hermaphrodite angel, they are so to speak the survivors of a once ideal disposition of sex/gender in which each finds a complementary Other. Expressed in the terms of *Séraphita*, it is as if Le Fanu's women are brought together just as Minna and Séraphita are on the dangerous ice-field. But in the case of Le Fanu's women, each sees the other as a replication of her own gender, and there is no Wilfrid nearby who may intervene between the two. This is not simply a matter of psychological divergence between Balzac and Le Fanu. As the contrast of spring and autumn suggested, Le Fanu's fiction explores a terminal spirituality not an imminent one. Thus, in 'Carmilla', the two women are not only drawn into a degree of biological intimacy which both excites and disgusts the narrator, they are also extinct at the point where the narrative commences its contact with the reader. I say 'extinct' rather than 'dead', because something of generic conclusion is signalled in the story; a kind of figure (melodramatically presented as a vampire) is eliminated just as a family line (the narrator's) is also (less explicitly) brought to a conclusion. This latter death comes as a surprise to the nameless editor of the surviving narrative, and the prominence of a variety of textual mediations compensates for the ultimate extinction of the two women. These two might be seen also as signifying aspects of temporal and religious continuity no longer viable in a world where cash is constantly cited as a measure of all things.

What is audacious in Le Fanu's fiction is its own handling of the act of literary borrowing. 'The Room in the Dragon Volant' had begun with a carriage nearly overturned, from which a beautiful woman may be rescued by the (male) narrator; in 'Carmilla' a similar accident befalls the (female) narrator into whose company the alluring stranger is thus introduced. As a child the narrator had experienced a sensation 'as if two needles ran into my breast'. Later, after Carmilla has taken up temporary residence in the castle, the narrator dreams of a 'sooty-black animal that resembled a monstrous cat' and then suddenly she felt 'a stinging pain as if two large needles darted, an inch or two apart, deep into my breast'. There is every opportunity to read this second phrase as confirmation of Carmilla's supernatural activities and (with the first phrase) as an indication that such forces have been playing on the narrator since her childhood or even – through shared ancestry – since an earlier time. The conventions of the vampire plot permit, indeed demand, such an interpretation. Yet one may read *In a Glass Darkly* more closely and less passively. It is from the upturned carriage borrowed from the previous tale that Carmilla emerges, and the double phrase about the needles enacts a further localisation of plagiarism within the text. We notice, but the narrative leaves unannotated, a sombre tapestry in the room where the new arrival recuperates 'representing Cleopatra with the asps to her bosom'. Her origins take place within the text as radically distinct from the narrative.

What the narrator of 'Carmilla' said of her Styrian home is true of the book generally, it is 'a Babel, at which strangers used to laugh'.[10] Amid the French and German of the governesses (one of them Lafontaine, a German!), the narrator and her father maintain English 'partly to prevents its becoming a lost language among us.' Lafontaine is not of course an impossible German name, but its significance here lies in its insinuation of literary names in a work of fiction which seems at first glance so different from the English stories of contemporary life where Marston and Wycherley nod and bow. The Great York Road of *Guy Deverell* is a less reflective place than Austro-Hungary. Yet amid such linguistic diversity, the narrator fails to notice that Carmilla (her ardent guest) is an anagram of Millarca who lived hundreds of years earlier, and whose name emerges with the renovation of a portrait. Like Beckett who fails to recognise artillery when he is 'seeking the bubble reputation / Even in the cannon's mouth', the narrator at this point is oblivious of her textual entrapment.

But the fiction 'Carmilla' overcomes this liability by being *two* interlocked tales, the one of seduction and the other (provided by General Spielsdorf) of blood-filled coffins and decapitation. Interpolation of the general's account of his own daughter's seduction and death by Millarca introduces a distinct inattention to names at least on the narrator's part. Perhaps it is not coincidental that her own Christian name (Laura) is casually revealed in the process; certainly she is careless of the near repetition of General Spielsdorf's name in Doctor Spielsberg's, just as she apparently ignores the obvious anagram of Carmilla/Millarca/Mircalla.

This oblivious attitude to names is counterpointed at an early point in the story where the narrator, telling of her gradual succumbing to the illness she associates with Carmilla's languorous embraces, writes the following very brief paragraph: 'The first change I experienced was rather agreeable. It was very near the turning point from which began the descent to Avernus.'[11] Avernus in itself poses no problems: it is a lake in the Campagna believed by the ancients to be the gateway to hell. Le Fanu echoes Virgil's lines from Book 6 of the *Aeneid*, 'Facilis descensus Averni …', a phrase assimilated to English by Milton and Dryden, suggesting how easy is the tempting path to damnation. We may think that the narrator is recalling how close her lapse into the world of the 'undead' had been, yet the perfect tense of the verb 'began' does not confirm that she escaped this descent. As with the master-narrator's account of himself as editor, the grammar of past and present shuffles these self-ordered categories as if they were cards in a pack. And Laura's description of the change as 'rather agreeable' maintains the ambiguous attitude towards Carmilla which colours the entire narrative. But if Avernus is admitted, then one looks closely again at the narrator's 'Styrian home' – it is but a minim away from being a Stygian home, a setting upon the banks of the River Styx in the Greek underworld. In a body of fiction where names so easily glide into each other, and where minuscule misquotation is the order of the day, a doubling of Stygian in Styrian cannot be wholly dismissed.

By her descent Laura (would have) abandoned conventional sexuality for the 'hot lips' of Carmilla on her cheek. John Marston, the dramatist whose name Le Fanu has used so many times in contexts of marital betrayal, has an oddly relevant line:

> Will I not turn a glorious bridal morn
> Unto a Stygian night ...?[12]

The violent deflection of this has its mollifying counterpart in 'Carmilla' where structural duality saves the narrator from any final participation in the vampiric climaxes. The general's story succeeds in transferring the decapitation necessary to eliminate vampirism from the narrator's beloved companion to another name who is – *ultimately* – identical with her. This double-helix structure, wherein the narrator is ultimately untainted and yet the vampire is glutted and dispatched, is a triumph of literary self-consciousness. This narrator (Laura) who has written to Martin Hesselius (yet has on one occasion referred to him as a 'town lady') throws in one further mediating authority with a final reference to Baron Vordenberg and his deep reading of John Christofer Herenberg's many impressive-sounding titles. Hesselius ... Vordenberg ... Herenberg ... these savants line up like expert witnesses, yet they never find a way into the text itself which is doomed to speak only to laymen.

Within this formal if remote elegance, visual imagery takes on greater coherence. Like the engraving of Belisarius and the picture of a wolf in *Uncle Silas*, the tapestry is a powerful association or merger of figures. Cleopatra is synonymous with seductive femininity, and in this role the vibrant Carmilla is reflected in the tapestry. But the depiction of asps on Cleopatra's bosom reflects the narrator's sensation of needles in her breast and the bite marks implanted by her nocturnal visitor. Both of the women of the fiction are thus present in the tapestry, which then surely signals some identification of the two. As in 'Borrhomeo' and 'Ultor De Lacy' the unsigned picture or other authorless depiction carries charges of sexual implication which are severely excluded from the Rembrandt poses of Austin Ruthyn. Both 'Date Obolum Belisario' (in *Uncle Silas*) and the Cleopatra tapestry here both allude to the downfall of a great military leader – Belisarius himself, allegedly at the hands of an ungrateful emperor, and Mark Antony of Shakespearean fame. One may feel that the asexuality of the dominant males in Le Fanu has to be read conversely, as the representation of repression.

Nevertheless, the power of the unsigned visual image is everywhere remarkable. 'Borrhomeo' offered an explanation of such power, an explanation in which property rights (or at least possession) played a central role. Early in 'The Room in the Dragon Volant' Richard Beckett and the mysterious countess are one-sidedly reunited through the medium of a mirror:

> I stood for a minute in fixed attention, gazing upon her, in the vague hope that she might turn about, and give me an opportunity of seeing her features. She did not; but with a step or two she placed herself before a little cabriole-table, which stood against the wall, from which rose a tall mirror, in a tarnished frame.
>
> I might, indeed, have mistaken it for a picture; for it now reflected a half-length portrait of a singularly beautiful woman ... The face was oval, melancholy, sweet ... I never saw a living form so motionless – I gazed on a tinted statue.[13]

If this is a calculated manoeuvre on the adventuress's part, she achieves it by allowing herself to be absorbed into an art-lover's perception, indicating yet again the power which the picture exercises over its viewer. The notion is taken to far greater extremes in 'Carmilla' where in the fifth chapter 'the grave, dark-faced son of the picture-cleaner' delivers several crates of refurbished portraits to the castle. As in the little scene with Beckett and his countess, art is tied to dirt and to antiquity, a tarnished frame in one and a dark-faced deliverer in the other. Indeed, the boy's status is gradually upgraded as he produces a particular portrait formerly thought to have borne the inscription 'Marcia Karnstein' and the date 1698: 'The artist now produced it, with evident pride. It was quite beautiful; it was startling; it seemed to live. It was the effigy of Carmilla!'[14]

Nevertheless, this 'absolute miracle' fails to impress the narrator's father who 'went on talking to the picture-cleaner, who was also something of an artist, and discoursed with intelligence about the portraits or other works, which his art had just brought into light and colour'. The indifference of the males to Carmilla's age-old portrait is reciprocated when she fails to acknowledge a compliment offered by her host a moment or two later. The non-reciprocal utterances between the sexes consolidate the bond between the two women, and lead on to Carmilla's most explicit declaration of love for her young hostess. It is of course a declaration verging on soliloquy or self-communing, 'I live in you; and you would die for me, I love you so.'[15]

Laura (as we now know her name to be) had early responded to her guest's ardour, but with verbal nuances which redirect the grammar from verbs, nouns and pronouns on to more elusively relational items: 'Now the truth is, I felt rather unaccountably towards the beautiful stranger. I did feel, as she said, "drawn towards her, ..."'[16]

Where does the emphasis fall in that first sentence? Is there any personal inflection in it? Or has not the dissolution of individuality (which is what vampirism as a theme anxiously debates) already set to work in the near-absence of a imprinting personal rhythm. In place of what one might idly suspect to be a missing past participle in the first sentence, the repeated preposition 'towards' looms larger. It is a characteristic of Le Fanu's style throughout the collection. When we say that ghosts, ghouls and spectres are insubstantial, we imply that some element of grammar apart from nouns best signifies them. Le Fanu's world, even in the more mundane novels, is prepositional: relation holds it together *and* haunts it. A universe of nouns and verbs is replaced by a multiverse of prepositions, conjunctions, disjunctions. Marx said so in relation to class, and soon Freud and Einstein were to say things even more revolutionary.

We have already seen that no single perspective is sustained throughout the five narratives. As for narrators, their role is highly questionable. When the prologue to 'Green Tea' informs us that the editor/narrator disqualified himself from surgical practice with 'a very trifling scratch by a dissecting knife' are we to read this as a foreshadowing of the Reverend Jennings's cutting his own throat in the story which immediately follows? Interpreters of a Lacanian disposition might see the editor's trifling accident as an act of self-mutilation, symbolic of castration perhaps, and certainly as damaging to the scribal capacity as to the incisive one. An even more pathological reading would inquire if the apprentice-surgeon's recourse to a *dissecting* knife did not foreshadow his own, if not Jennings's death. If there is any merit in any of these suggestions, what kind of relationship (between Hesselius's secretary and the subject of the paper by the Reverend Herbert, submitted to Hesselius) can we possibly imagine? Instead of seeking to link up these mutually remote characters in some pattern of behaviour, perhaps attention should rather focus on the objects named – dissecting knife, razor and so on.

The great enchantment

For we have to contend with the unnecessary and inert reference to a servant's razors in 'The Room in the Dragon Volant'. These may shadow the instrument by which Jennings inflicts his own death, or the knife which cut the editor's fingers off, but they do so without any participation in narrative, any attachment to character. Instead, they constitute part of a serial process in the collection of stories. No object and no source of light has 'caused' these shadow-allusions, they exist solely at a verbal level and are projected by a narrative quite distinct from the official documents of the Reverend Herbert and the Anglo-Hungarian lady. The stories, so to speak, leak into each other – as the two overturned carriages have already shown – at a level again quite distinct from those of a German physician's papers, his English secretary's translation, the depositions of first-person narrators and so forth. Perhaps this is implicit in the diversity and decentredness of the book as a whole in which Hesselius appears merely to annotate the work of others. But the implication for an understanding of Le Fanu's fiction generally is striking, as the serial objects link up with the serial names (Marston, Scarsdale etc.) to challenge all presuppositions about mimetic literary practice.

The implications of such a reading of 'Carmilla' are worth pursuing for they affect *In a Glass Darkly* in its peculiar entirety. We begin with a pious clergyman and end with lesbianism, the offence Queen Victoria found unbelievable. The vampire theme had of course been sounded by John Polidori, Lord Byron's travelling companion and physician, with 'The Vampyre: a Tale' (1819). This precursor sets up a specific tension of demand and autonomy in Le Fanu's story – there is as it were an obligation to custom, to literary convention, but there is also remarkably little *weight* of precedent to be acknowledged. The first-time imitator is obliged to make original (unprecedented) decisions in avoiding orginality. To appreciate the complexity of this dilemma, we should look briefly at Polidori's inaugurating vampire story.

The circumstances of its composition are well known. When Byron and his associates were staying in the Villa Diodati, a competition in story-telling was organised, with the poet himself delivering fragments of a tale (quite similar to the one Polidori ultimately published) on 17 June 1816. In the succeeding years, the latter worked on his own contribution and, in the words of Patricia Skarda 'fashioned a version of a vampire tale more remarkable for its echoes than for its originality'. Polidori's sources were predominantly Byronic – *The Giaour* and *Childe Harold*. For whatever reasons, 'The Vampyre: a Tale', though actually written by Polidori, was published (April 1819) as though it had been Byron's work. One may see this illusion as an attempt to disguise or cancel plagiarism by the illicit association of the plagiarised author's name, or one may see it as a further level of plagiarism in which the 'victim' author is obliged to carry a reading of his own words and tropes assembled by another hand.[17]

The complexities do not end here. 'The Vampyre' appears to be a plagiarism – of Polidori by Byron – but its narrative is also a disguised account of Polidori's attempt 'to clear an imaginative field for himself', to resist Byron's mastery by an act of emulation or overcompensation. Skarda marshals the evidence for this view at some length, but we can virtually reduce the problem to one of names and in doing so implicate Le Fanu's debt to this precursor fiction. Polidori's use of the name Ruthven derives from Lady Caroline Lamb's novel *Glenarvon* (1816, written after the rupture between herself and Byron) while Polidori's Lady Mercer is a fictionalised version of Lady Caroline herself. 'Ruthven' is almost indistinguishable from the 'Ruthyn' in Le Fanu's *Uncle Silas*, and he later assumes the title earl of Marsden (which Skarda obligingly relates to John Marston). This latter assumption of a literary source for Ruthven/Marsden's second name is facilitated by the fact that his travelling companion (based on Polidori himself) is surnamed Aubrey. At the level of plot, 'The Vampyre' concludes with a summary of its own which might serve for *Guy Deverell* and other of Le Fanu's fictions. It tells how of two men travelling together one should die, and the other returning home 'should be startled at perceiving his former companion moving about in society ...'[18]

Incestuous elements also surface in 'The Vampyre' and here too there is room to speculate as to Le Fanu's anxieties. For the moment, however we note that the fictional exchange of energies between Ruthven/Marsden and Aubrey reveals actual identification, while the former's vampiric appetites are reserved for the latter's sister. (This might be considered an instance of having your Kate and eating it.) 'Carmilla' compresses much of this plot by eliminating the male altogether, and just as Rose Velderkaust had evidenced no *suitable* resistance to going with her demon lover so Laura shows remarkably little awareness of the monstrous nature of the embraces she chronicles. We expect her to conclude with a horrified recollection of her near-initiation into the ranks of the undead; instead her final words suggest a degree of longing for her 'boyish' lover:

> to this hour the image of Carmilla returns to memory with ambiguous alternations – sometimes the playful, languid, beautiful girl; sometimes the writhing fiend I saw in the ruined church; and often from a reverie I have started, fancying I heard the light step of Carmilla at the drawing-room door.[19]

Given that the reader already knowns that Hesselius's nameless editor has established that Laura is dead, the formal requirements for interpreting these last words as a yearning which has been fulfilled have been provided. This is not a matter of plot but of technique. Concentrate for a moment on the phrase *the body of the text*, and one can see how vampirism is just a gluttonous synonym for plagiarism and 'Carmilla' a summary in fiction of Le Fanu's fictional practice. In turn, *In a Glass Darkly* could be approached not so much for its thrills – spectral monkey and premature burial – but as a late-romantic anatomy of literature. The radical achievement of Le Fanu's last stories lies in their treatment of language as being, not the purpose-designed playground (*Das Spielsdorf?*) of an integral Self, but an autonomous, arbitrary and necessarily ambiguous medium in which self itself is repeatedly translated, rewritten, silenced, disengendered and disinterred.

Having noted the sophisticated way in which the collection of stories reflects upon its own literary status, we should not conclude that the problems of a cruder ideology simply disappear. Le Fanu's recourse to non-Irish settings was prompted by real economic circumstances and not by any reaction against realism in fiction or against local feeling. Examined in this light, even 'Carmilla' refuses to live wholly in exile. The story's placenames veer away from recognisable Styria and Gratz, beyond the seemingly allusive Avernus, to the more local Dranfeld and Drunstall – the last being almost a passable attempt at an Irish townland name. If this seems excessive – but would not Drumstall be perfectly fitting? – then we must note the very curious manner in which topographical detail (direction especially) is indicated in the fiction. Vampires enjoy certain privileges in this regard, of course, but leaving aside loco-motion from coffin to cradle we still find evidence that jeopardises the conventional movements of conventional characters. Early on we are told that General Spielsdorf's schloss is 'nearly twenty miles away to the right'.[20] As the narrator is writing to someone (Hesselius ... the town lady?) living elsewhere, this use of the right/left axis (which depends on a shared bodily orientation) indicates nothing. In an explicitly distanced narrative structure of this kind, citation of left and right introduces a dimension which is at once intimate and unfixed. Le Fanu's novels occasionally disclose a moment in which the topographical is somehow compacted into the temporal: in *Checkmate* the process is so extreme as to implicate a simultaneity of all events in the present. More familiarly, the early moment in Maud Ruthyn's narration of her encounter with Hans Emmanuel Bryerly calls for comparison. Walking 'in deep shadow' in the garden at Knowl, the two undergo a radical change of mood and surroundings when 'suddenly we turned to the left, and there we stood in rich sunlight, among the many objects he had described'.[21] But beyond issues of plausibility, we must note how a change in direction is treated as a change of location – 'and *there* we stood ...'. These unmediated movements echo the very strange lay-out of the future world (Heaven or Hell) provided by Emanuel Swedenborg and obliquely cited in *Uncle Silas* as when Maud notes that Bryerly's prayer sounded more like 'farewell'.

If the General lives over to the right, Carmilla herself resolutely refuses to specify her home, saying only that it 'lay in the direction of the west'.[22] This refusal to provide a verifiable account of her origins is of course familiar to readers of the literature and folklore of supernatural visitations. More particularly in Irish folklore, the west has certain fatal connotations, and perhaps these may do to explain Carmilla's orientation. But if we avoid an exact locating of Carmilla west of Styria by invoking folklore, the Irish implication has returned by the back door – Carmilla gives cause for further scrutiny in terms of sectarian difference, when she demands of the narrator, 'How can you tell that your religion and mine are the same[?]'[23] No allegorical equation of fictional setting and social origin will work. Instead one is confronted again by the instability of what appears for the moment as a fixed point of reference. Like the carriage, or like the razors and dissecting knife, setting or provenance ripples below the narrative like sharks in a placid sea.

Were one to pursue such isolated and yet striking details as Avernus and location by left and right, then an illuminating context in which to conduct the exercise would be the discontinuous sequence of Irish literary texts that suggest, assume, posit or debate that *this*, the here and now, is Hell. *Uncle Silas*, at least as it has been interpreted in *Sheridan Le Fanu and Victorian Ireland*, fits the bill. If Ireland is to be identified as 'the here and now', then it is the anomalous metropolitan colony which was Victorian Ireland that can be read as Hell. Don Juan, in Bernard Shaw's *Man and Superman* (1903), provides a pithy description of the condition, 'Nothing is real here. That is the horror of damnation.'[24] Keegan, in *John Bull's Other Island* (1906), is no less explicit, 'I wondher what you and me did when we were alive to get sent here.'[25] It is tempting to conclude that only the peculiar status of Victorian and Edwardian Ireland within the United Kingdom justifies the hyperbole. However, Yeats in *Purgatory* (1938) and Flann O'Brien in *The Third Policeman* (pub. 1967) resurrect the theme in the years immediately before and after the commencement of the Second World War. Le Fanu's fiction may lack the wit of Shavian drama and the concentration of the later texts cited. Nevertheless, the imagery of a ruined house in Yeats's play and the rhetoric of history employed by Yeats's Old Man is at one with Le Fanu's central concerns. However incompetent or self-decomposing his novels may come to seem, the short stories of *In a Glass Darkly* constitute a sophisticated anatomy of romanticism.

Notes

1　J. Sheridan Le Fanu *Uncle Silas; a Tale of Bartram-Haugh* Oxford: World's Classics, 1981 p. 220.

2　'German Ghosts and Ghost Seers' *Dublin University Magazine* vol. 17 (January 1841) pp. 42–3.

3　Neil Cornwell *The Literary Fantastic* Hemel Hempstead: Harvester Wheatsheaf, 1990 pp. 90–2.

4　J. Sheridan Le Fanu *In a Glass Darkly* Dublin: Gill and Macmillan, 1990 p. 4.

5　Ibid. p. 39.

6　Ibid. p. 241.

7　Ibid. p. 262.

8　Ibid. pp. 5, 41, 84, 119–20.

9　Ibid. pp. 241–2.

10　Ibid. p. 243.

11　Ibid. p. 278.

12　John Marston 'Antonio's Revenge', I, i, 89–90: see *The Selected Plays of John Marston* (ed. Jackson and Neill) Cambridge: Cambridge University Press, 1986 pp. 103–4.

13　*In a Glass Darkly* p. 122.

14　Ibid. p. 269.

15 Ibid. p. 270.
16 Ibid. p. 258.
17 Patricia Skarda 'Vampirism and Plagiarism: Byron's Influence and Polidori's Practice' *Studies in Romanticism* vol. 28 no. 2 (summer 1989) p. 250.
18 Ibid. p. 257
19 *In a Glass Darkly* p. 314.
20 Ibid. p. 242.
21 *Uncle Silas* p. 12.
22 *In a Glass Darkly* p. 260.
23 Ibid. p. 263.
24 Bernard Shaw *Man and Superman* in *Collected Plays with their Prefaces* vol. 2 London: Reinhardt, 1971 p. 637. (Act III).
25 *John Bull's Other Island.* Ibid. p. 923. (Act II).

12

Serialism?

In quality of writing, the contrast between novels and tales in Le Fanu's last years was stark. The only notable innovation in the longer work was the introduction of a Welsh setting in *The Tenants of Malory* (1867), a novel which kept up the nominalist pressure by incorporating another author's name (Sir Thomas Malory) into its title and reintroducing the ever-recurring (Richard) Marston. Beaumaris, Angelsey and the North Wales coast were utilised in the fiction right up to the last novel, *Willing to Die*. But in terms of what the world calls *style* and *organisation* few of these novels – few even of their chapters – deserve attention on their own account.

Not the substance of texts but their restless interrelationships generate interest. When the basic plot of 'A Chapter in the History of a Tyrone Family' (1838) was adapted for *The Wyvern Mystery* (1869) Le Fanu did more than just plagiarise himself. One of his few surviving notebooks contains a fragment also based on 'The Tyrone Family' and bearing close resemblance to a passage in another novel serialised alongside *The Wyvern Mystery*: this is *Loved and Lost*. We have then the unparalleled exploitation of an early story in the writing of *two* later serial fictions, both of which were *anonymously* published in *The Dublin University Magazine*. In both rewritings, setting is transferred from Ireland to England of course, but arguably not for the first time. A case has been made in the *Cambridge History of English Literature* that Le Fanu's earlier story had been read by the Bronte sisters and that Charlotte Brontë drew on it for elements of *Jane Eyre*.[1]

Strangely enough, North Wales rarely features in the shorter work, in connection with which there is the persistent problem of Irish traces hallmarking fiction apparently set elsewhere. These traces may appear to be of little or no consequence, the product

quite simply of the author's background. It has been claimed that
'Mr Justice Harbottle' draws on the careers of two Irish rogues, the
banker John Sadleir and the judge William Keogh, together known
during their brief political eminence as 'the pope's brass band'.
Keogh was a friend of Le Fanu's, one of his few dining companions
in late years; Sadleir committed suicide on Hampstead Heath in
1856, following the collapse of a Tipperary bank which he had used
to fraudulent ends. (Dickens's Mr Merdle in *Little Dorrit* (1856–7) is
said to be based on Sadleir.) Such alleged sources are less significant
in Le Fanu's fiction than the odd detail of the judge's drowsy
thoughts as he waits for his cronies: 'with another yawn, he laid his
cocked hat on his knees ... and began to think of pretty Mrs.
Abington'.[2] That was first published in *Belgravia* in 1872. Back in the
1820s and 1830s, Abington (County Limerick) had been the Le Fanu
family's home (a few miles south of Cappercullen), and in 'The
Child Who Went with the Fairies' (1870) the parish churchyard is
named as the victim's burial-place.

Such wholly external links with Charlotte Brontë and Charles
Dickens may yet be read internally. That is, they should be
recognised as intrusions into an exceedingly tender psychic domain
which Le Fanu had fenced around with signals – elusive and allusive
– of an autobiographical kind. Dickens indeed went so far as to
advise him on plot and character, suggesting 'an Irish youth who is
incapable of his own happiness or anybody elses, and attributes that
incapacity – not to his own faults, but to his country's real or
supposed wrongs'.[3] It is hardly surprising that Le Fanu did not act
on the advice. No novel of his deals with a contemporary Irish
character. But if Ireland and contemporaneity are mutually exclusive
in Le Fanu's fiction, the fact may be of wider significance also.
The permanent immediacy built up through the interaction of
Maturin's Irish footnotes with Spanish episodes of *Melmoth the
Wanderer* is not sustained in any manifest tradition of Hiberno-
gothic, and we may have to look in other quarters for evidence of its
transformation. The literary revival, combining a refined appreciation of folk material with a sense of apocalypse deriving both
from Irish political crisis and English 'decadence', will overshadow
Le Fanu just as surely as it will draw on his pioneer work. The
man himself, if such there was, remains inscrutable. And if we
cannot look into Le Fanu's psychology for an explanation of
his obsessive patterns in naming, altering names and re-writing

generally, nor find an explanation in some retrospectively conceived tradition, where do we look? Two complex webs of intertextuality suggest themselves, one constituted solely of work by Le Fanu himself, and the other involving Balzac once again, and the art of painting.

'Le Chef d'oeuvre inconnu' has been mentioned as an available source for 'A Strange Event'. First published in 1831, it was steadily revised and expanded by its author before appearing in more or less final form in 1837 – still two years earlier than Le Fanu's story. Much debate has been engendered on the topic of Balzac's sources for the theories expounded by his invented artist Frenhofer, and several commentators have identified Diderot's 'Essais sur la peinture' as one such.[4] But even if one assembles an argument whereby Diderot fathers both the term *genre* and Frenhofer the imaginary painter, the relationship between Balzac and Le Fanu requires further exploration. Swedenborgianism, which Le Fanu first incorporates into fiction with 'The Mysterious Lodger' (1850), and first exploits systematically in *Uncle Silas* (1863) is already at work in Balzac's *Séraphita* (1834–5). This is still prior to Le Fanu's commencement to write and publish, and so one might argue in terms of influence. But what are we to make of the relationship between 'A Strange Event' (1839) and the story 'Pierre Grassou' which was not published until the following year?

Like his use of Swedenborg, Balzac's allusions to Gerard Dou in the last-named story exemplify an area of literary activity in which painting and spiritualism are discussed or dramatised – an area wider than that in which Le Fanu is usually considered. It is possible that he read some of these Balzac stories – 'The Red Inn' (1831) should be seriously considered – but quite impossible that 'Pierre Grassou' influenced 'A Strange Event'. Once that point is conceded, influence scarcely matters. For example, the English poet William Blake had initially embraced Swedenborgian ideas and it is reasonable to conclude that Blake influenced Yeats in this regard. Yet Blake rejected Swedenborgianism, and so the influence must be characterised as deeply ironic. The *symbolistes* also fell under the spell of the northern mystic, and Yeats was not unversed in late-nineteenth-century French literature. Against such instances of influence-as-sequence, one should recall the synchronism of Yeats's interest in the 1930s in Swedenborg, Balzac and authoritarianism, with the suppressed Le Fanu of *The Words Upon the Window-pane* as the significant absence ironising the official Yeatsian tradition commencing with Swift, the absent but official hero of the play.

Nevertheless, if one were in search of a model for Le Fanu's treacherous Marston, then Balzac's Vautrin deserves attention. Like Marston – or at least the name Marston – this master criminal moves through several of the novels in the *Comédie humaine*, befriending and betraying in turn, but ultimately forsaking crime and becoming head of the Sûreté under the name Saint-Estève. The crucial difference between Vautrin and Marston is precisely that the French character has a traceable career and that, while he may pass under adopted names, there is no question of his being appropriated to or by other characters. In the end a comparative study of Le Fanu and Balzac is likely to founder on – paradoxically – the rock of Marston's insubstantiality.

Le Fanu's most sustained exercise in rewriting commenced with his first novel. *The Cock and Anchor* had first appeared anonymously in three volumes in Dublin in 1845: it remains one of his most readable works, yet seemingly isolated from the other readable novels of the 1860s. (Few will have noticed that the name of Mr Audley, Mary Ashwoode's elderly attendant in her flight to safety in Ardgillagh, will be abbreviated and extended in *The House by the Church-yard* when Lord Dunoran's son introduces himself as A. Mervyn.) But Le Fanu did not wait until 1861 to resume adjustments of his first novel. There had followed a little noticed third edition – still anonymous – under the altered title *Sir Henry Ashwoode, the Forger* published by Parry of London in 1851, using sheets from a Dublin one-volume second edition of 1845.[5] Twenty years then elapse before a Victorianised version with an English setting appears under the name *Checkmate* (1871) and – hard on its heels – *Morley Court* (1873), a 'Yellow Back' edition of what is virtually (but not exactly) the text of 1845, as if *Checkmate* in turn required rewriting in order to redirect it towards its original form. This is as close to a contemporary Irish novel as Le Fanu ever came.

Names and portraits recur in this complicated and extended act of rewriting – itself employing four names, should one decide that it constitutes a single text and not some less controllable plural textuality. The villain of *The Cock and Anchor* was named Blarden, the heroine Mary Ashwoode. In *Checkmate*, Walter Longcluse is 'a refined and polished edition of Nicholas Blarden, but because of this smooth finish, he is infinitely more sinister than the coarse ruffian described in *The Cock and Anchor*'.[6] Now, Longcluse turns out to have been Yelland Mace of old – within the terms of the 1871 novel – and the realisation that he also used to be Nicholas Blarden merely extends this. But while Proteus wriggles, what has happened to Mary Ashwoode? In changing her family name to Arden she has reintroduced (or has devoured) all but the first two letters of Blarden's. Here, in the innocent business of textual revision, the fiction enacts the same plastic manipulation of names which is elsewhere the supernatural basis of Carmilla/Millarca's elusive identity.

Plastic manipulation was precisely the means of disguise adopted by Yelland Mace after he had murdered Henry Arden long years ago, the pioneering surgeon being a Paris-based German baron named Emmanuel Vanboeren. Thus *Checkmate* begins with a remarkably synchronised double inspection of manufactured faces. Longcluse is inspecting an Arden family heirloom, a portrait by Van Dyck in urgent need of repair. Unbacked and with the paint lifting off the decayed canvas, it is mute evidence of the extent to which a simulated or artificially created face can break down under the pressure of years. While Longcluse eloquently admires the painting, an Arden family servant recognises his voice (despite the plastic surgery) as that of young Harry Arden's attacker.

The disguised villain does not – as one expects – wholly insulate himself from all reference to the name he bore at the period of the murder. Audaciously, Longcluse has alluded directly to his former self, claiming to have had his purse stolen by Yelland Mace before he fled. The unforced parallel of painted image and altered visage in the novel's opening pages is no less striking than the ironic presentation of *theft* as the relationship between a man and his former identity. Longcluse pursues this line of thinking when he flatters Alice Arden's talents as an artist with chalks – 'Your copy will be a finer thing than the original.'[7]

Crime, whether in the form of murder, purse-snatching or counterfeiting, plays a substantial part in *Checkmate* even to the point where it seems that Le Fanu is determined to follow in Wilkie Collins's footsteps. After a gambler has been murdered in, or close to, Longcluse's presence, the police seize one of his boots with the assistance of a servant. Readers of *The Moonstone* and *The Hound of the Baskervilles* feel confident that this is part of some forensic investigation – measurement of heel markings etc. But the issue of the boot is quietly laid aside, and the scientific inquiry deflected into very different areas, ultimately resurrecting the business of Mace's having undergone plastic surgery.

Meanwhile names have directly substituted themselves for the persons whom one might reasonably suppose to be the subject of the novel. Not only does Alice Arden bear the remains of Blarden's name from the 1845 novel, she is herself occasionally referred to in the new text as Halice Harden, this mimicking the accent of a cockney servant. So much is perhaps just comic stage-business. But when her Uncle David visits France to establish the real relationship between Longcluse and Mace of old, the cockney version of her name is quite unreasonably transposed also. Not only does Baron Vanboeren's pronunciation reintroduce Harden, but a Parisian secretary renders the visitor as d'Ardennes. Arden-d'Ardennes– Harden, the name Arden is still fluid and refuses to settle into a wholly singular form. One may glance at *Arden of Feversham*, thinking that an author who cites Walsingham, Marlowe and Marston is once again drawing on Elizabethan literary sources. The play, sometimes attributed to Shakespeare, was based on a real-life murder also treated dramatically by George Lillo (1693–1739) in a posthumously published work. Such an echo of a title rather than an author's name would be a rare innovation in Le Fanu's obsessional patterning. But in fact *Checkmate* has passed beyond such superficial devices, and internalises the name Arden as an alterable microtext which none the less seems to identify some stable personality.

Personality undergoes new sea-changes also. Mace has not simply disguised himself by means of plastic surgery; the physical reshaping has brought a psychic alteration also. Longcluse seeks to marry Alice Arden, flatters her as a copyist superior to her subject material, and evidently feels positively towards her. But the frangibility of the new man is ironically exposed by his creator, Baron Vanboeren. When David Arden confronts him in his Paris studio, and inquires 'Was there any correspondence between Yelland Mace and Walter Longcluse?' the baron produces two plaster casts (the 'before' and 'after' of the same face), and smashes them vindictively when Arden refuses his price.[8] Despite this set-back, Arden unexpectedly meets a Frenchman who strikingly resembles Longcluse but who definitively is not Longcluse. This stranger and Arden go through an elaborate misunderstanding in which the Longcluse double suspects that his purse has been stolen

– as Longcluse's allegedly was by Mace at the time of the original crime. The question now perhaps is – to what extent has the notion of personality survived the nominalist surgery to which it has been subjected?

Checkmate is a bagatelle of duplications, and character is evidently as much subject to this process as a picture, a plaster-cast, a purse or a plot. If, in undergoing plastic surgery, Longcluse has somehow also effaced to a slight degree his criminality, then the agent of the change is himself presented as a grasping scoundrel. Emmanuel Vanboeren bears the Christian name of Swedenborg whose doctrines had so enthralled the Ruthyn family. The question put to him by David Arden – 'whether there was any correspondence ...?' – unwittingly adopts Swedenborgian jargon, and leads the baron into some playful talk which sustains for a moment longer the separate identities of Mace and Longcluse. The physical impossibility of sustaining this is enacted in the breaking of the moulds which is then itself counterbalanced by David Arden's uncanny encounter with *another* figure who not only resembles Mace/Longcluse but is epitomised in the business of a stolen purse.

The novel is now closing round upon itself, revealing the villain of old and even echoing incidents from the opening pages. Then a decaying picture had played its part, so it is fitting now that Baron Vanboeren's Paris house should be replete with paintings. No fewer than twelve Watteau panels decorate the study doors; these together with other artistic treasures have come down intact from the days of the French Revolution, despite the fact that all had belonged to Madame Du Barry, the king's mistress who was guillotined during the Terror. The Ardens' decayed Van Dyck, showing an ancestor of the Civil War period, is thus counterbalanced by miraculously preserved relics of the *ancien régime*.

All in all *Checkmate* appears to be a brave attempt to eschew the renowned names which had punctuated the previous novels. Yet the result is a novel even more thoroughly introverted than *Uncle Silas*. It was possible to argue in favour of the latter as a parable worked out according to the elaborate symmetries and correspondences of Swedenborgianism. All that survives of Swedenborg in *Checkmate* is his Christian name. The named characters are still pushed through their paces as villains, heroines, lovers and servants, but it is an unconvincing performance. A new movement is already under way alongside the conventional plot, a movement not of the characters but purely of their names. It is not extensively developed, to be sure, but it has gone further than the three-dimensional grid structure of – (1) dramatists's names; (2) names beginning with M; and (3) Marston. In *Checkmate* (Bl)Arden–d'Ardennes–Harden retains something of the Marston phenomenon, but it is altogether more fluid, capable of metamorphosing itself like an element in *Finnegans Wake*. One explanation of this might speak of an autistic quality in the writing, a non-communicative repetitive broadcasting of a single item in a series of elementary permutations. The title of a short story, 'Wicked Captain Walshawe, of Wauling' (1864), has something of the same quality. The result certainly is that *Checkmate* lives up to its name – otherwise inexplicable – in that no external coherence can make sense of its circlings and echoings. Like the would-be Christian's vision of God, meaning has become trapped within the medium through which one had trusted to receive it.

The foregoing approach to *Checkmate* gave every indication of respecting relevance of plot, centrality of character and verifiability of mimetic realism. In the event, these concepts were scarcely ever truly engaged in that odd fiction. Le Fanu's rewriting of *The Cock and Anchor* as a contemporary story of English life effectively eliminated the two fundamental categories – story and life – upon which character and plot depend in the mimetic mode. Naturally Jonathan Swift, the pre-eminent if marginal figure of authority within the first novel, is expunged. By a disturbing corollory, so is that breezily amusing villain, the earl of Wharton, sometime lord-lieutenant of Ireland. Authority, both the moral kind and the merely institutional, has dissolved. In place of historical reference, the present tense thrives in the new novel, whole chapters are dictated in it or (rather) it dictates whole chapters of an action which never really acts or is acted. The point could be demonstrated in a dozen curious versions, as when a sentence switches arbitrarily from one tense to another – 'Alice sighs, and looked wearily through the window' – or, more ponderously, when the narrator (misidentifying Marx misquoting Hegel) announces in a sentence of remarkable oscillations, 'the well-worn aphorism of the Frenchman, "History repeats itself," was about to assert itself'.[9]

Nothing asserts itself. Instead we have a demonstration of how absolutely contemporary the action is/was, yet by its nature 'contemporary' is shot through with the most relativised implications, and action acquires the name of passivity. The young in particular, and more especially young lovers, are suspended in narratives of the utmost limpidity, gazing rather than seeing. In other words the novel, while at first resembling third-rate Dickens, has taken on something of the quality of an Anglo-Irish Mallarmé – third-rate again, no doubt, but far more unexpected than Dickens. While pretending to summarise the plot and delineate the characters of *Checkmate*, one was actually focusing on intensely local issues within the text.

Checkmate so ostentatiously fails as a work of fiction that it threatens to become a metafiction, a primitive demonstration of the truth (or *some* truth) about fiction as such. The curious procedure which a reading of *Checkmate* entails bears a certain resemblance to the progressive reductions of Edmund Husserl's phenomenology by which the entire world of nature, history and empirical fact is eliminated from an increasingly pure contemplation. If this sounds pompous one should recognise something very similar in V. S. Pritchett's observation that, as readers of Le Fanu, 'we pause when we recognize that those other hands on the wardrobe ... are our own'.[10] What the fiction drastically investigates is the possibility, even suspicion, that 'the other' does not exist. Yet the other is a necessary precondition for coherent thought of the self; in the absence of an other, self is everything and nothing. Hence the proliferation of secondary existences in Le Fanu's fiction generally, for these act as buttresses shoring up a mansion of uncertain ontological status. Of course what one is left with after reading *Checkmate* is not the philosopher's pure transcendental ego but the primitive and ceaseless questionability of character itself encoded in the act of naming and occasionally projected in the internal fiction of portrait-description. That this was a disturbing business for Le Fanu is obvious – and irrelevant for all but biographical purposes. W. B. Yeats's *John Sherman* (1891) would suggest that Le Fanu's case was not unique in this area.

But then we have to take *Morley Court* into account. Though the circumstances of publication are obscure, it is undeniable that Le Fanu looked steadily past *Checkmate* to discern the text of the original *Cock and Anchor* which reappears under a fourth title, posthumously like Lillo's version of the Arden plot. The elimination of history, of politics, and of authority, which *Checkmate* recorded in its highly interiorised simultaneity, is again questioned, and a nearly unaltered text of its original form issued. It is as if Yelland Mace had survived Longcluse's suicide.

Serialism?

Let us prepare to complete – or abandon – the close examination of Le Fanu's fiction. His career ends with the publication of his first novel, under another name – recurrence could hardly be better instanced. When incidents recurred within an individual novel, we had been initially inclined to put this down simply to jaded imagination on the author's part. However, more closely examined, some of these turn out to be incidents of recurrence which recur. To take the simple case first, Charke in *Uncle Silas* is said to have cut his own throat with his razor; in fact he was murdered, and it was a second crime which revealed the way in which the first had been possible. Throat-cutting recurs in 'Green Tea', but within *In a Glass Darkly* the death of Jennings has already been foreshadowed in the editor's accidental mutilation of himself and will be echoed in 'The Dragon Volant' when Beckett's servant departs pointlessly for the razors. The recurrence of doubled or doubling events proceeds in the masked balls of 'The Dragon Volant' and Spielsdorf's interpolated story in 'Carmilla'. In the latter, not only do the masked figures have, so to speak, doubled identities, but Carmilla/Millarca is an extensive exercise in such identification.

In anticipation of this, 'The Fatal Bride' of two decades earlier had introduced the unlucky duellist, adding a curious phrase about 'the afterwards too-celebrated Captain Jennings'.[11] Given that Jennings dies in the duel, his later fame already is couched in terms of the posthumous, a circumstance further complicated by the anonymous narrator's promise for further instalments from 'the reminiscences of a bachelor'. The abrupt curtailment of Le Fanu's intended series of stories, and its replacement by the story of Richard Marston, may be explicable in terms of 1848 and the events culminating in the rebellion and the state trials. Yet the Jennings of twenty and more years later uncannily keeps faith with the broken promise of January 1848.

We should take stock at this point, summarising the evidence before us in the manner of Sherlock Holmes. The case indeed is an intriguing one. For a start, the evidence itself displays considerable instability. We have a suspect called Marston who crops up in quite a number of contexts – 'Some Account of the Last Days of the Hon. Richard Marston of Dunoran' (1848), its renamed and exported version called 'The Evil Guest' (1851), *Wylder's Hand* (1863) where the Marston in question is a female housekeeper and apparently blameless, *The Rose and the Key* (1871) where his Christian name is Charles, and *Willing to Die* (1873) where he arrives by way of ship-wreck and reintroduces the theme of bigamy. Amid these reported sightings, we have to take into account the dog that did not bark in the night – 'Some Account of the Last Days' is Victorianised as *A Lost Name* (1868) but instead of Richard Marston's name we get Mark Shadwell's. This Marston is clearly a slippery character, living in two centuries, personating both sexes, having at least two Christian names. Is he a character at all?

The problem of names follows automatically. Marston's name is lost to the three-decker novel (*A Lost Name*) deriving from the original story of his last days, but the role of master-of-the-house is occupied by another character who bears a dramatist's name, [Thomas] Shadwell. This leads us to consult two lists of associates – one, the many dramatists, writers and historical figures already amply specified; and two, the many names clustered after the initial letter M. For it is time to consider as a structuring energy the lists of names in which he features within Le Fanu's work. One of these is ostentatiously referential – to George Berkeley, to Adam Loftus, Christopher Marlowe, John Marston, and so forth. That it is *the list* which points to history and to literary history in particular, and not the individual name or character, should be stressed. No particular figure in the past is denoted, just as no possible name (e.g. Ben Jonson or even Ben Shakespeare) is absolutely excluded. The list is serial, neither specific nor complete, but referential in that the reader can devise the basis upon which it is constructed. Protean as ever, Marston has a place in it – several places, given changes in forename and gender.

The second list is serial also but wholly non-referential. This is the list of names commencing with M. Here the determining source is not history in any form, but the arbitrary internal arrangements of language itself, especially the alphabet. Between Marlyn and Mordaunt, any number of additional names could be devised. Quite a number of these do occur – including Merton and Mervyn and Marston – but the series again is open. In *A Lost Name* an enigmatic historical feature of the nominalism at work in *The House by the Church-yard* is extended – Charlie Mordaunt is the nephew of old Mr Mervyn, and thus the two Peterborough antagonists of Civil War days have their familiar Victorian reconcilation. One particular restraint appears to operate – all of the names cited so far consist in two syllables – but this serves only to indicate the arbitrary yet systematic manner in which the list organises itself. For it is not too much to say that an autonomous process is at work. Names shape-change ever so slightly so as to avoid the responsibilities of reference while maintaining its appearance. Thus we read Berkely, not Berkeley; Richard, not John, Marston. Or, to be more thorough, names shape-change so as to conceal the impossibility of reference.

To explain these odd interchanges, we have within reach a startling theory consisting in two propositions. (For the sake of brevity, the titles of individual books will be used but the implications extend well beyond these.) Let us display them clearly:

Proposition One: *In a Glass Darkly* narrates the process of literary plagiarism in terms of an imagined cannibalism (more specifically, vampirism).

Proposition Two: the rewriting of *The Cock and Anchor* enacts a cannibalism of names.

Both propositions depend on the seriality of the fiction, in its treatment of incident, character and even object (cutting device, razor, dissecting knife etc.) and especially in its tacit acceptance of language as anonymous, arbitrary and autonomous. Both propositions advance a woman (Mary Ashwoode, Carmilla) as the locus of possible transformation. Yet if this suggests that women may provide stability of character (where the men slither out from under their names and insinuate themselves into half a dozen temporary disguises), the promise is not borne out by the evidence. Ethel Ware, narrator of Le Fanu's last novel, lapses into unconsciousness to a degree fatal both to her own presentation and to the novel's elementary credibility.

If Fredric Jameson's radical reinterpretation of Max Weber shed light on the significance of Dutch painting for Sheridan Le Fanu, perhaps his reading of so ferociously intellectual a novelist as Jean-Paul Sartre can be of assistance here. Writing of a distinctive feature in modernism, Jameson observes that

> It is not so much a question of literary space ... as it is of false space: a kind of confusion pointed out by Bergson, in which the old habits of purely visual, spatial perception, grind on in a situation in which space in the ordinary sense is no longer present. It is a little like watching something through glass, and slowly coming to the realization that it is at the glass itself that we are staring.[12]

This accidental echo of Le Fanu's title of 1872 went some way towards confirming the analysis of a ' prepositional world' glimpsed through *In a Glass Darkly*. That the Hegelian–Marxist proceeds in the next paragraph to illustrate his point by reference to *Ulysses* should not redirect us into the abandoned programme of tradition-building. On the contrary, it is still in the critical area of character that the application of Jameson's insight can most usefully be pursued, though not to the exclusion of larger innovations in the political domain. In making the leap between text and social world, we violate no absolute frontiers. The final irony may be however that, instead of demonstrating how fictional character is mimetically founded upon 'real life', the world of marriage and money and mortgage turns out to be itself pervasively textured in a way which Le Fanu's problematic characterisation renders more legible than does the classic practice of an Eliot or a Thackeray. This is not to argue for his superiority as a novelist, but it is certainly to insist on the distinctive features of the Irish interaction of fiction and society, which in turn must have implications for the several ways in which this interaction functioned within the actuality of the United Kingdom of Great Britain and Ireland. This in turns raises questions as to the price paid – and by whom – when Eliot achieves her English realism.[13]

At first sight, the demonstration of seriality provided by Jean-Paul Sartre looks strikingly ill-suited to the needs of Le Fanu's readers. The setting is a busy metropolis, the particular moment a rush-hour and the behaviour of a Parisian bus queue. 'The travellers waiting for the bus take tickets indicating the order of their arrival', but from this seemingly innocuous piece of regulation the notion (reciprocity) of separate and comparable existences is systematically excluded until – in suitably abstract language – 'every Other is both Other than himself and Other than Others ...'[14] This radical degree of self-alienation is not necessarily special to the modern city, but it would be characteristic of modernising cultures and would give rise to acute anxiety in sectors of the society where modernisation was especially feared or resisted. At the end of his life, Yeats tried to distinguish England from Ireland in this regard as if to prove an exemption from the condition of being modern. Gilding the lily, he attributed part of his observation to his 'best-informed relative', once again insinuating the merit of closely bound communities and kinship groups:

Serialism?

My best-informed relative says: 'Because Ireland is a backward country everybody is unique and knows that if he tumbles down somebody will pick him up. But an Englishman must be terrified, for there is a man exactly like him at every street corner.' . . . The hero Finn, wishing for a son not less strong of body, stood on the top of a hill and said he would marry the first woman that reached him. According to the tale, two thousand started level; but why should Jones of Twickenham bother?[15]

This is from *On the Boiler*, Yeats's last essays deeply committed to an authoritarian politics: the recourse to heroic saga is thus a fitting response to urban alienation, though in doing so the poet perhaps concedes that Willy of Rathfarnham is no less immune to the force of starndardisation than Brother Jones – he merely has more exotic conpensations. Joyce, writing at the same late date, jokingly conceded the serial and secondary aspect of modern experience in referring to 'the reel world'.[16]

Dublin in Le Fanu's early days had seemed coherent, fully adequate, in good hands. God, after all, was in his heaven. Precisely when the change came about cannot be tabulated. If Archbishop Ussher in the seventeenth century calculated the date of the Creation, even down to the time of day, his Victorian successors had a far more urgent and much revised timetable for the Fall. It occurred with the dissolution of the Irish parliament in 1800, or with Catholic Emancipation thirty years later. But then the Famine made its claim, and then the 1848 rebellion ... Fenianism ... Disestablishment ... The Fall itself was a serial occasion, experienced in ever more immediate terms by tenacious members of the 'Establishment'.

In the late nineteenth century, writers sought to protect literature from the effect of seriality by a kind of pure writing, which would 'reflect back to each isolated reader, each solipsistic consciousness, what it best suited him to project into it'. However, this pursuit of the irreducibly and unmistakably personal experience ends in a contrary realisation that descriptive language really leaves us in cruel suspension:

the chair itself is clear enough, but we do not know who is sitting in it ... Even the chair itself is less described than it is simply *named*, so that if there happened to be *several* ... chairs in this book, one in the murder room, say, the other in the narrator's study, the word itself in its isolation would furnish us no way of determining the reference ... All words are general words. No matter how lavishly we pile concrete detail on detail, no matter how painstakingly we enumerate the properties of the unique object before us, we will never find ourselves doing anything but combining abstractions: the word *desk*, the word *brown* ...[17]

Le Fanu's fiction oddly prefigures much of the fiction – Robbe-Grillet's – upon which this analysis is based. Certain narrators or woman characters apart, Le Fanu's characters do not live in the way that Jane Austen's, Thackeray's, George Eliot's (etc.) are reputed to live. Instead 'the absolutely unique, the absolutely personal, is abandoned to its fate, repressed, driven back into the content where it reemerges as a last, meaningless, unanalyzable *datum* about the main character himself: his obsession (torture, jealousy, *idée fixe*)'.[18] Le Fanu's novels in the 1860s progressively displayed more and more of this tendency, until even the titles themselves (of published or projected novels) trumpet their own obsession – *Haunted Lives* (1868), *Willing to Die* (1873), *The House of Bondage* and *Premature Sepulture* (advertised at Christmas 1872 in *London Society*).

A whiff of sadomasochism is no skin off the nose of a *nouveau romancier*. Le Fanu's particular instance of serial displacement from one character on to another lies not so much on the axis of pain/pleasure but rather in the ethical domain of guilt/innocence. Once again Marston is implicated, but it is by his absence from *A Lost Name* that he reveals something like a central, irreducible concern in Le Fanu's fiction as a whole. Carmel Sherlock plots the murder of his master's guest. Why he should do so is never clearly indicated; he is a reader of arcane literature, a dreamer who holds views about the significance of certain letters in the alphabet:

> My father died of fever at Easterbroke; my poor mother at Rochester, and my dear sister at Wyden – all great losses – dreadful, sir, dreadful – one at Christmas, that's yule – the next on Easter Monday, and the last on the Royal Oak day, we used to call it – the anniversary, you know, and the villain who robbed me was Robert Eyre Yardley .. So I have reason to hate those letters E. Y. and R. and they are doubled in [Roke Wycherly's] name, and the rest – ay, here's the account deducted – Sandford's – and the rest are O, K, W, C, H, L – and they are your unlucky letters, sir ...'[19]

Here narrative and character on the one hand, system and superstition on the other, are passing in the night. Sherlock lists sombre items from his biography (based mainly on proper names) which give credence to his fear of Sir Roke Wycherly – recurring letters being the rationale of this. Meanwhile, his master is writing a letter to Sir Roke and Sherlock himself is officially engaged on calculating figures – estate accounts. Both letters and figures become deeply ambiguous terms – the surface plot revolves round a royal mail of misdirected, carelessly mislaid letters, and the 'figure' of Carmel Sherlock frequently stands out in profile. In its textual decomposition, *A Lost Name* confuses letters (of the alphabet) with letters (in the mail bag, 'hated letters. They never had a pleasant tale to tell'), figures (in the accounts) with figures (against the skyline). In addition, the world of *belles lettres* is endlessly inscribed in a novel already nominally given over to such minor figures as Shadwell, Sherlock and Wycherly – in pp. 90–125 of the second volume, we encounter Chaucer, Cervantes, the earl of Buckingham, George Herbert, De Quincey, Virgil, Dryden and Dante. The novel's titular loss of name results in such literal chaos, and the narrative drives the point home when, in the guest-room, Sherlock discovers the murder already committed and Sir Roke already dead. The master of the house, Mark Shadwell, is in fact the guilty party. Intention and commission have shifted their relative positions, and done so around so little a word, so big a preposition, as 'before' or 'after'.[20]

Some notion of stable, integral and responsible character can hardly be guessed in the alphabetical space between Shadwell and Sherlock; a quasi-identity between the two is all too often hinted, something which has been slipped out or otherwise repressed. Instead of designing the missing element along ideal lines, however, we should rather inquire into the historical context in which this extraordinary body of writing emerges. After all, Le Fanu himself had a reputation as *persona abscondita*. But if he was dubbed the Invisible Prince during these years, the reality was that Dublin, his principality, was invisible. The city changed, yet change eluded literary representation. Shy of contemporaneity, Irish fiction found even the railways difficult to absorb.[21]

A crucial demarcation line between the previous and the coming age was the Census of 1861. Famously, this is the census whose pages – like Seán Mac Reamoinn – were broken down by age, sex and religion. For the first time statistics of denominational allegiance are recorded and published: in Ireland as a whole Catholics account for 77.69 per cent, a statistic which includes higher concentrations in the south and west, lower in the north-eastern counties. What perhaps disturbed adherents of the Establishment was the virtually identical proportion of Catholics in the capital city (77.1 per cent). Twenty years after municipal reform in 1840, Dublin – centre of British administration and long the bastion of Protestant monopoly in local government – is just a representative statistic and nothing more. The figures themselves startled no one, but their import and the symbolism of their public circulation sounded the knell of a presumptive authority.

The city's shifts and rifts were tabulated in its almanacs and yearbooks. Back in the 1820s, when the Le Fanus were quitting Dublin for Abington, *Wilson's Dublin Directory* respectfully listed in separate sections – (1) the Nobility and Gentry, – (2) Merchants and Traders, – (3) Barristers, and – (4) Attornies. The man who would become Sheridan Le Fanu's father-in-law (the unbending tory lawyer, George Bennett of 7 Fitzwilliam-street) appeared in both the first and the third of these lists. A sub-note to the first assured readers – 'The private Residents of the Professional and Trading Classes will be found under their respective heads.' All's right with the world.

By twenty years later, Bennett had moved. Pettigrew and Oulton's *Dublin Directory* for 1845 has him safely recorded in 18 Merrion Square, South. But the same list puts the leading barrister of the Munster circuit on the same page with James Behan, undertaker and proprietor of job coaches living at 8 Camden Street, Lower. Such listings were promiscuous, though barristers were half-rescued by having (in addition to their place in the main alphabet) a separate section. Unfortunately Le Fanu's father-in-law is bi-located at *12* (not 18) Merrion Square, South. To mitigate against this arbitrary mistake, the same directory provides a Street Directory by means of which confirming double checks can be mounted on any footloose ratepayer.

In 1865 the appropriate control is *Thom's Irish Almanac*, in its twenty-second year of annual publication. Grandly and lavishly it presents elaborately abstract 'Statistics of the United Kingdom'. This it follows in its Irish section with a single list of 'Nobility, Gentry, Merchants and Traders'. Bennett had died, and J. S. Le Fanu, barrister, replaced him as the occupant of 18 Merrion Square, South. On the same page, and within six entries of each other, one finds 'Leinster, his grace the duke of ... *Leishman*, Abraham, copper merchant ... *Leman*, Sarah, vestment manufacturer ... *Lemass*, Joseph, city tavern and concert hall, 126 and 127 Capel Street ...'.

That's how Le Fanu's fictional characters relate to each other, by linguistic proximity rather than social or familial intercourse. Even pathetic Carmel Sherlock's superstition operates by a systematised linguistic tic – the Easterbroke where his father died is replicated in the Easter Monday when his mother did. Compared to this immobilisation, the social hugger-mugger generated by alphabet-ising names constitutes a peculiarly potent form of seriality in which class is simultaneously elided and inscribed – the duke and the copper merchant exist in parity but they are also differentiated in a manner which secretes innuendo into seemingly factual data like the names of streets and so forth. *Thom's* compensates for the egalitarianism of one section with another. A rigorously classified, and still alphabetised, list of tradesmen etc. makes manifest the number of one's fellow (i.e. rival) nail makers, while other occupations are shuttled about by means of relentless cross-referencing – 'Looking-glass Manufacturers (see Carvers and Gilders)'. This is an organisational procedure quite different from the 1825 directory's listing of professions and trades 'under their respective heads'; deference was still a motivating principle then, even if it was not the only one at work.

Having commenced his career as novelist with an historical account of Dublin, *The Cock and Anchor* (1845), and then finding himself obliged to adopt settings in modern times which however were also English, Le Fanu rewrote his first novel largely in the present tense and with central Parisian scenes. It is in these latter renegotiations between the historical and the mimetic that the fiction most effectively reveals the structure of contemporary experience. When elderly David Arden betakes himself to Baron Vanboeren's Watteau-preserving shambles in Paris, he discovers that the plastic surgeon has preserved records of his work in a collection of plaster casts alphabetically arranged. This is the obverse of Carmel Sherlock's belief in the arcane significance of a few isolated letters: now letters provide a comprehensive guide to erased identities, synthetic replacements – the baron alludes sardonically to his 'resurrections'.

But there is more. The alphabet does not simply provide a means of filing data, even when the data are as physical, as literal, as Vanboeren's plaster of Paris. Arden is escorted through a necropolis of representionality, at once recalling Victorian bank vaults and anticipating twentieth-century extermination camps: 'Along both walls of the narrow apartment were iron doors, in deep recesses, that looked like the huge ovens of an ogre, sunk deep in the wall ...'[22]

While the implication of this is *unheimlich* in Freud's sense, the surface continues its relentless replications – 'wall' and 'deep' both recur as if to enclose the space and ensure its apart-ment seclusion as a heremitic system. But the sentence continues: 'and the Baron looked himself not an unworthy proprietor. The Baron had the General's faculty of remembering names and faces.'[23] The insistent repetition of 'the Baron' across successive phrases amounting to fewer than a dozen words is eloquent testimony to the uncertainty underlying identity. By way of Newtonian reaction, 'the General' appears from nowhere, generated by an unknown idiom, his hopeless function being to confirm all that is left of identity – names and (plastic) faces. This moment of personalised irreferentiality soon passes as Arden is led further into the box-within-box vaults of the plastic surgeon from where the ciphers and multi-linguistic codes on each container are transmitted back to the reader in a rhythmic phrase ironically preserving at the level of systematised chalk marks 'characters in red, some, and some in black, and others in blue'.[24] That first 'some' is the last relic of living human utterance in this necro-narrative.

Accounts of the background to the Anglo-Irish literary revival may be criticised precisely for settling for background. The structure of feeling – the term of Raymond Williams, of course – to be disinterred from Le Fanu's late fiction can have its large impact on interpretations of individual authors and texts, or on the complexities of ideological mud-wrestling. For the moment, however, the more directly personal register of the alphabetised directory as *memento mori* may be in order. The principle of the truly commercial directory is advertised competition, and the incorporation of Society (via lists of the Nobility, Gentry etc.) only extends that ruthless principle. The expansion of explicit, purchased advertising in the back pages of *Thom's* underlines the anxieties of such a society – by the 1860s, it is almost entirely taken over by life assurance companies. Le Fanu himself features in these directories, and successive entries over the years amount to a dossier of pretence and invaded privacy. Listed as Tip Staff in the courts from 1842 to 1852, he derived no more than £10 a year from what was wholly a sinecure. The later directory's public recording the rateable valuation (£130 p.a.) of 18 Merrion Square, South mocked and concealed financial insecurity, mounting debts to his brother William and encumbrances on a property which was never really his own. There is surely a discernible degree of personal, authorial feeling in the late novels' repeated complaints about money-lenders. Indeed, the figures of Levi and Goldshed occur in *The Tenants of Malory, Haunted Lives* and *Checkmate*; in the first of these Levi plots with Larkin who has been taken over from *Wylder's Hand*. Compared to Charles/Richard Marston and the [Bl]ardens, these are rather more conventional instances of serial character of a kind which will become commonplace in the detective novel.[25]

Whether one turns to Jürgen Habermas and his theory of 'the bourgeois social sphere' or to Sartre's idea of urban alienation as 'serial unity', a radicalised view of the modern city is wholly compatible with this reading of Le Fanu's late fiction. Joyce's Dublin is not without its pre-texts after all. What is disturbing in Le Fanu *read in this fashion* is the degree to which compatibility veers off into formal nihilism. The characters of *Checkmate* are not indeed mimetically constructed in accord with the self-image of Victorian city-dwellers: on the contrary, they mimic entries in almanacs and thus perform acts of negative revelation. It remained for Joyce in *Ulyssess* to radicalise this melancholic complacency into a political form, a formal writing of the modern *polis*.

Notes

1 *Cambridge History of English Literature* Cambridge: Cambridge University Press, 1964 vol 13 pp. 407–8, 414–16.

2 'Mr Justice Harbottle' in *Best Ghost Stories of J. S. Le Fanu* (ed. E. F. Bleiler) New York: Dover, 1964 p. 262. This story deserves extensive analysis in its own right. The judge of the title is approached in 1746 (*sic*, the year of Culloden) by one Hugh Peters ('That should be a Whig name') who informs him of a quasi-Jacobite conspiracy. Though the plot allows for the possibility of imposture, the historical Hugh Peters was executed in 1660 on a charge of concerting the death of Charles I. Peters had his own renown as a chaplain in the parliamentary army during the Civil War, but his more recent fame stemmed from Edmund Burke's rhetorical use of him in *Reflections on the Revlution in France* (1790). The judge dies a suicide, and the official plot concerns a wrongful execution so that the judge may secure the victim's wife.

3 For Dickens's advice of April 1870 see W. J. Mc Cormack *Sheridan Le Fanu and Victorian Ireland* (2nd ed.) Dublin: Lilliput Press, 1991 p. 216.

4 The crucial edition/text for Anglophone readers is Honoré de Balzac *Gillette; or The Unknown Masterpiece* (trans., with an essay by Anthony Rudolf) London: Menard Press, 1988.

5 *Sir Henry Ashwoode, the Forger: a Chronicle of Old Dublin City* London: Parry & Co., 1851, 3 vols.

6 Nelson Brown *Sheridan Le Fanu* London: Arthur Barker, 1951 p. 62.

7 J. S. Le Fanu *Checkmate* London: Hurst and Blackett, 1871 vol. 1 p. 145.

8 Ibid. vol. 3 pp. 248, 261.

9 Ibid. vol. 3 pp. 33, 194.

10 V. S. Pritchett *The Living Novel* London: Chatto & Windus, 1946. p. 96.

11 *Dublin University Magazine* vol. 31 (January 1848) p. 18.

12 F. R. Jameson 'Seriality in Modern Literature' *Bucknell Review* vol. 18 (1970) pp. 64–5.

13 For a critique of Eliot in a related context, see Edward Said *Orientalism* New York: Pantheon Books, 1978.

14 Jean-Paul Sartre *Critique of Dialectical Reason* (trans. Alan Sheridan-Smith) London: Verso, 1982 p. 261 etc.

15 W. B. Yeats *On the Boiler* Dublin: Cuala Press, 1939 p. 24.

16 James Joyce *Finnegans Wake*. London: Faber, 1939 p. 64.

17 Jameson loc. cit. pp. 72–3.

18 Ibid. p. 74.

19 J. S. Le Fanu *A Lost Name* London: Bentley, 1868 vol. 1 pp. 32–3.

20 *A Lost Name* vol. 1 p. 22. On morality and temporal sequence see T. W. Adorno *Minima Moralia* (trans. E. F. N. Jephcott) London: Verso, 1974 pp. 78–80.

21 Other developments may have registered more intimately. Numerous schools for the middle classes were opened in Dublin – Blackrock College in 1860, Synge Street in 1864 and Alexandra College in 1866. Sectarian difference doubtless kept the Synge Street boys and Alexandra girls out of each other's mind (if not sight, for the two were only half a mile apart). But the extension of education to Catholics and to women was only one sign of accelerating social change. Alexandra came too late to be of use to Sheridan Le Fanu as the financially troubled father of two daughters: he was of the previous age, when privacy characterised woman's upbringing. Madame de la Rougierre, tutor to Maud in *Uncle Silas* (1864), might be read as the last word in private education. George Moore's *A Drama in Muslin* (1886) takes up the theme of women's education but is conditioned throughout by the author's embrace of naturalism. Le Fanu's exposure of the inadequacy of fictional narratives and styles based on a tacit representationalism was passed over in favour of Zola's doctrinaire remodelling of the same.

22 *Checkmate* vol. 3 p. 236.

23 Idem.

24 Ibid. vol. 3 p. 239.

25 There is reason to believe that Le Fanu had second thoughts about the characterisation of Levi; see Paul Hopkins 'The Author's Annotated Copy of *The Tenants of Malory*: J. Sheridan Le Fanu Regrets Some Anti-Semitic Expressions' *Long Room* no. 30 (1985) pp. 32–5.

13

Gladstone and Ascendancy:
or, Here we go round the upas tree

It is fitting that Sheridan Le Fanu died as the spectral world of his fiction debouched into the streets around him. Naturally it was the poor who first evidenced the systematic degradation resulting from implementation of what Marx had seen as the ghost story of reality. The new middle classes, variously constructed, saw to it that they did not see. The architecture of a new Dublin, spreading beyond the canal boundaries into former villages and townships such as Ranelagh and Rathmines, relocated the Georgian squares in the historical imagination. The process had begun long before his death on 1 February 1873, and the lost middle decades following the Famine have assisted in the suppression of Victorian Ireland. It was in these years of quiet, painful adjustment that a complementary process of re-enchantment or mystification began to take place. Two new concepts entered the vocabulary of social description in search of acceptance as normative, even as self-evident truths, later to combine as 'the Anglo-Irish Protestant Ascendancy'.

'The Anglo-Irish' emerged slowly as a quasi-ethnic category. Initially it had denoted no such *group* but rather indicated more vaguely an area of tension between the Establishment and the people. (By the first of these latter terms is indicated both church and state at least until the disestablishment of the Church of Ireland in 1869, and by the second is meant an ever more confident alliance of nationalism and ultramontane Catholicism.) Something of the double-sided vulnerability of Le Fanu's social constituency can be gauged from the angry declaration of *The Dublin University Magazine* in November 1849 that it would not 'suffer Anglican dictation' – i. e. instruction from England, or rather Great Britain, or rather the imperial parliament of the United Kingdom.[1] But as such pejorative usage of 'Anglo-' and 'Anglican' petered out, the narrative of nineteenth-century Irish history was all too often presented as the clash of rival groups at home – Unionists, Protestants, Catholics and Nationalists. These last four descriptions still retain an ideological prescription whereas 'Anglo-Irish' will effect its ideology programme by imposing a seemingly timeless ethnic identity which at the same time is double (English and Irish) in its proclaimed origins. Yeats will appear curiously well-placed to be first heroically to disinherit himself from a cultural legacy on which the forger's ink is scarcely dry. A generation later, Elizabeth Bowen will be eloquent on the ambiguity of such an identity, by then imposed and decomposing.

Earlier, more than one commentator observed that, in his youth, 'the people' were the Protestants of Ireland whereas the phrase later came to be identified with a distinctively Catholic nationalism. Ethnogenesis, it is fair to suggest, rarely if ever occurs in isolation, and the making of 'the Anglo-Irish' was only one effect of the mid-nineteenth-century crises. The development of a nineteenth-century Catholic Irish democracy was matched by fundamental ideological realignments among Protestants, and this in two vitally important sectors. Extension of the ballot, together with rapid if late industrialisation in east Ulster, created a new social force centred on Belfast; in response to Parnellism and the Land League, the older middle class which had variously been whig or tory came to fall in behind a united conservative programme. Despite the apparently consolidating effect which this second alignment might be thought to have had, by the end of the nineteenth century the Anglo-Irish were only 'in' Ireland, no longer proprietorially or confidently 'of' it. It is hardly too much to say that the adjective-cum-noun 'Anglo-Irish' was called into currency to exemplify in a specific way the relation of those prepositions – 'in' and 'of' – one to the other. Le Fanu's precarious financial hold on no. 18 Merrion Square, South had a symptomatic value, even a prophetic one.

It was a starkly exposed position. Anglican dictation loomed even larger in the late 1860s than it did in the wake of the Famine. Gladstonian liberalism quickly replaced an exhausted whiggery, and Gladstone's programme placed the Irish landlord system, education, and the established church at the head of its list of demons. The moral earnestness of the new Prime Minister threw some of his Irish opponents into confusion, as did his habit of encouraging the submission of opinions, ideas and proposals from anyone and everyone of influence. From the intellectual and emotional ferment of his study in Hawarden, North Wales, there emerged the second and far more potent agent of Irish enchantment. Wigan, Lancashire, can claim to be – if not the birthplace – then certainly the launching pad of Protestant Ascendancy as a social élite.

We have obtained an illicit or privileged glimpse into the alchemist's cauldron of nineteenth-century ideological transformation. With the breakdown of certain elements thought to be irreducible – in this case, fictional character, notably – the imminent release of sub-atomic elements or the fusion of previously incompatible ones is revealed. The convergence here of prophetic and chemical vocabularies is deliberate, for the closing decades of the nineteenth century brought a plethora of disruptive and revolutionary projects into action. The names of Nietzsche and Einstein, Freud and Blavatsky, Weber and Bergson may be unfamiliar in Anglo-Irish critical discourse but they serve here as shorthand for a global alteration in the philosophical status of the individual. Yeats might conveniently be considered as an Irish negotiator among these figures.

Three specific stages of an historical epoch characterised by shattering insights and by comprehensive schema of repression can be briefly investigated here. In their Irish aspects, these are the efflorescence of Protestant Ascendancy, the demonising of Charles Stewart Parnell and the later (but far from unrelated) interest of W. B. Yeats in fascism. But Sheridan Le Fanu has served to make these visible to the naked intelligence, and it is only reasonable that he should be fitted into a genealogy or prolegomenon.

The Anglo-Irish literary tradition – or more accurately, *critical* tradition – constantly seeks a fixed moment of inauguration. It may be Maria Edgeworth's *Castle Rackrent* or Yeats's *The Wanderings of Oisin*, but each instance throws up a tally of prior influences and debts, acknowledged or otherwise. The very notion of a canon is predicated on a comprehensive plagiarism which it then seeks to banish by rules of admission and exclusion. Writing when no one claimed to be inaugurating anything, and standing at the head of no intimidating or legitimising literary pedigree, Le Fanu was free (so to speak) to feel the anxiety of influence. If he belonged to an unheroic generation, knowing neither the excitement of the Edgeworths' radicalism nor that of the Yeatses' nationalism, by the same token he lived through a mid-Victorian phase where the plurality of all origins and beginnings could be discerned – nervously. Le Fanu's fiction allows one to see that originality and imitation are mutually dependent.

Consequently, Sheridan Le Fanu should not be regarded as the inheritor (from Edgeworth or whomever) of an entailed literary tradition, or the harbinger of a greater tradition in Yeats, Synge and the other 'Anglo-Irish' revivalists. If placement of him must be effected by reference to individual careers, then the emphasis might fall on other figures. John Kells Ingram (1823–1907), the author of 'Who Fears to Speak of '98 ...', and later a proclaimed positivist and disciple of Auguste Comte, became president of the Irish Statistical Society in 1878. Another such neglected contemporary – though younger than Le Fanu, of course – was George Sigerson (1836–1925), an Ulsterman by birth and a graduate of the Royal University (through its constituent college in Cork) who was the first to translate Jean-Martin Charcot's work on neuropsychology into English. Younger still, but active at a precocious age, was W. E. H. Lecky (1838–1903) whose essay 'The Declining Sense of the Miraculous' (1863) soberly and lucidly announced themes which Le Fanu's generation still found disturbing. Ingram as professor of Greek and author of a much translated *History of Political Economy*, Sigerson as antiquarian and pioneering physician, Lecky as historian *and* M.P. demonstrated a buoyant Victorian confidence in the world which Le Fanu never reached. A rupture of religious belief, together with the institutional ruptures of disestablishment, had causes and effects which were not immediately evident. Far beyond any topicality, Le Fanu's fiction in the late 1860s contributes to a new psychic diversity in which the old solidities of Church and society, nation and individual, mind and body are dissolved and dispersed.

If one were to single out an individual as Le Fanu's inheritor, the choice must fall on someone of diametrically opposed temperament. Standish James O'Grady's polemical writing is gripped by a extremity of commitment before which the cautious editor of *The Dublin University Magazine* would have quaked. In 1901 he published a two-part essay on the decay of the Irish aristocracy under the title 'The Great Enchantment'. Drawing on material as diverse as the heroic saga tale 'The Stupefaction of the Ultonians' and H. C. E. Childers's report on the over-taxing of Ireland under the Union, O'Grady denounced politicians of every hue, excoriated the rising middle class, and repeatedly emphasised the magical powers by which this 'farce-tragedy' was consumated. Spells, poisonous fogs, illusions and delusions, were penetrated and exposed. The figure of Blue Beard, metamorphosed as a demented Master of Fox Hounds for the democratic era, rides through these essays, adding a gruesome imagery to the trenchant arguments and exhortive rhythms. O'Grady, for all his reading of Marx, was an arch conservative in whose mordant view the labouring classes might yet produce statesmen and prime ministers – 'yes, as the boiler sends up scum'. In addition to the sub-gothic rhetoric of Blue Beard cutting off his own limbs to satisfy the hounds allegedly under his own command, two more particularised features of O'Grady's polemic link him antithetically to Le Fanu's curious fiction of thirty years earlier. First, he defines the essential quality required of any possible leader in the depraved conditions of Edwardian Ireland as 'a martyr-like suppression of self'; secondly, he nowhere refers to the Protestant Ascendancy, evidently finding it an irrelevant notion in his sweeping survey of Irish society, politics and history.[2] Le Fanu's contribution to the Anglo-Irish critical discourse was to be a lost name. Recovery of the writing attached to that name must jeopardise some of the treasured pieties of that tradition.

In the run up to his epochal speech in the election campaign which finally brought him to power, Gladstone consulted the Reverend Orlando T. Dobbin (a cousin of Le Fanu's and a regular contributor to *The Dublin University Magazine*), Dr Sigerson, and Archdeacon Stopford and others either by direct correspondence or through their pamphlets. The speech at Wigan was particularly notable for one magnificent rhetorical trope. Lining up his targets he conjured behind them one further image or chimaera and proceeded to characterise it in an extended and lurid simile:

> There is the Church of Ireland, there is the land of Ireland, there is the education of Ireland; there are many subjects, all of which depend upon one greater than them all; they are all so many branches from one trunk, and that trunk is the tree of what is called Protestant Ascendency. Gentlemen, I look, for one, to this Protestant people to put down Protestant Ascendency which pretends to seek its objects by doing homage to religious truth, and instead of consecrating politics desecrates religion ... We therefore aim at the destruction of that system of ascendency which, though it has been crippled and curtailed by former measures, yet must be allowed by all to exist. It is still there, like a tall

tree of noxious growth, lifting his head to heaven and darkening and poisoning the land as far as its shadow can extend; it is still there, gentlemen, and now at length the day has come when, as we hope, the axe has been laid to the root of that tree, and it nods and quivers from its top to its base... [3]

Prior to 23 October 1868, one would have been hard tested to find as lengthy and orotund an invocation of Protestant Ascendancy. The phrase had little idiomatic acceptance in the vocabulary of political debate, and certainly it did not name any readily identified social group or 'class'. That was to come, for the moment there is 'a system of ascendency'. The process is launched precisely through Gladstone's ambiguity, reiteration and colourful hostility, for it is not entirely clear from the speech whether the speaker believed Protestant Ascendancy to name a social group or not – a gap for interpretation was willy-nilly left open. The insistence that it 'must be allowed to exist ... is still there' carries a semantic ambiguity. The interpretation 'allowed that it does exist' must have priority though there is room also for 'permitted to exist' – while a nervous repetition is also sustained.

Gladstone re-baptised the Protestant Ascendancy by reading an order of anathema over its head. The paradox of this is less remarkable than appearance might suggest. The Quakers had taken as their familiar name a term used initially in contempt, and the grouchy old Junkers of East Prussia bore as their name an age-corrupted German phrase meaning, simply, young men. So the metamorphosis of Gladstone's denunciation into a programme for self-enhanced dignity and cultural re-orientation follows a certain pattern in the naming of social groups. Gradually marginalised in politics, challenged in the learned professions and undermined in land-ownership, a really diverse body of middle-class Protestants (with a small aristocratic topping) coalesced in the years after Wigan as *the* Protestant Ascendancy. If the financial and social pressures producing erosion constituted an instance of Weberian disenchantment or even desacralisation, then suddenly venerable and unitary Ascendancy admirably countered with an ideological spell.

The unnamed but recognisable upas tree by which Gladstone introduced the notion of poisonous growth, unfamiliar now, had a long history as a romantic metaphor. Running back through Coleridge and Francis Danby (and even Pushkin) to Robert Southey and Erasmus Darwin, this legendary object sublimely combined the natural and supernatural for a generation of poets. Behind Darwin's *The Love of the Plants* lay a *mélange* of travellers' tales, journalistic imposture, and serious botanical inquiry where the upas tree and the actual *Antiaris toxicaria* intertwine. If the Protestant Ascendancy was a upas tree, its roots lay in very disturbed soil.[4]

Paradox, irony of the most cruel kind, characterises this anomaly of nature. According to reports, prisoners condemned to death in Java were offered a chance of escape if they would undertake to collect the upas tree's poison for use by the authorities in the execution of other prisoners. But as the tree was believed to strike dead all those who approached it, the journey merely postponed the moment of execution and re-ascribed the fatal act from human agency to Nature itself. Yet John Danby's vastly gloomy picture of the barren valley and the obelisk-like upas tree at its centre looks more like an allegory of urban life than a scene – even a grotesque one – from Nature. It radiates a sense of comprehensive desolation, as the one hopeless hope which the individual, condemned by society, has of re-entering society. The upas tree was, it seems, singular, unique and fatal to all other forms of life. As an parable of alienation it rivals William Blake's myriad images of the industrial city.[5]

It has been said before that, even as a rallying-point or -cry in the 1790s, Protestant Ascendancy did not exist until it was threatened by reform.[6] Enchantment lent distance to the view. This complex aetiology, according to which a seemingly prior condition or entity is caused by a later one, characterises even more intimately the emergence of Protestant Ascendancy as a 'class' in the late nineteenth century. Before that point in its development, the term had been closely linked to the corporate towns of Ireland, to their (pre-1840) exclusively Protestant charters, and to the anti-reform zeal of the Dublin guilds in the 1790s. It is important none the less to note how a rural gentry shaken and in some cases displaced by the Famine, and an urban professional middle class perturbed by the expansion of its privileges to a rising Catholic component, coalesce under the banner of the Protestant Ascendancy, and even admit rather different class elements to affiliate by virtue of a shared 'history'.

A few immediate features of this momentous process, culminating in Yeats's sublime invocations of Swift, Grattan, Burke, Parnell and others, require attention. One quite simply is the elusive lineage of this ideology, the difficulty in tracing precisely where the authoritative citations are to be found. Swift of course is silent, not least because the concept had not been coined even forty years after his death. Burke is savagely ironic about an upstart 'junto of jobbers', Grattan mischievously bewildered, and so forth.[7] Protestant Ascendancy as an ideological force is an infinite regression, by which everyone presumed to be implicated projects on to everybody else an optical illusion of the concept's unchallengeable reality. All origin involves plagiarism, imitation or travesty, sometimes after the event and in sinister disguise. In other words, ascendancy is another serial factor in the culture emergent in the last days of Sheridan Le Fanu.

What's more, as a narrative of history involving irruption, consolidation and imminent fall, it particularly resembles a fiction by Sheridan Le Fanu in that it invokes historical and literary names – 'the people of Burke, and of Grattan' – without limiting itself to verifiable aspects of these careers. These citations attach themselves more to rhetoric than to semantics. The new and bourgeois war-cry of 1792 is subterraneously deployed throughout the early and middle years of the nineteenth century to resurface in Wigan as a badge of long-standing privilege. In turn, Gladstone's upas tree becomes the totem pole of the Anglo-Irish (who require such a central organising device in order to achieve their quasi-ethnic quasi-integrity). The objective correlative is then ritually forgotten, purged from the memory, and the liberated value of Ascendancy is celebrated in Yeats's 'Commentary on "A Parnellite at Parnell's Funeral"' (1934), scrutinised in Bowen's *Bowen's Court* (1942) and indulged elsewhere.

Alternatively, one can turn to Le Fanu's fiction and find there a complementary structure. The lists of dramatists and Elizabethans possess a rhythmical quality, punctuating the flaccid prose of the weaker novels with their regular trochees – Berkely, Marlowe, Marston – so that they approximate to the semantic aspect of rhyme as analysed by Roman Jakobson. Attached to doomed or lethal characters, these irretrievably isolated names constitute a proto-ascendancy, modelling in fictional guise for the Swift, Goldsmith, Grattan, Burke, Gregory, Yeats, Synge etc. etc. of the imminent Protestant Ascendancy.[8]

When the discovery of a sophisticated anatomy of romanticism in *In a Glass Darkly* threatened to sever Le Fanu from the traditionally conceived body of Irish literature, we noted instead how the relation between nationalism and colonialism was implicated in the very texture of imagery and allusion. Ireland, as a consequence, could no longer be regarded as the uncomplicated sovereign entity enshrined in nationalist ideology nor the wholly passive field of an externally prompted power. This shift towards a more dynamic and mutual relationship in his political unconscious was replicated in our criticism of Le Fanu's writing. The attempt to establish a formal link between his early fiction and the stories of Balzac may have come to no firmer conclusion than the subsequent inquiry into *Checkmate*. Yet if Le Fanu's career reformulates unexpected questions rather than confirming reliable answers, the benefits may be substantial.

One such benefit might emerge under the heading Comparative Literature, a term coined and a discipline founded by another of those Irish successors of Le Fanu's whom the nationalist/colonialist alliance in criticism have suppressed. Hutchinson Macaulay Posnett (born 1854 or 1855) shook the dust of Trinity College off his heels in the 1880s, departing to teach classics in New Zealand. But before he left, he had published short works on the historical method in studies of jurisprudence (London, 1882), on the Ricardian theory of rent (London, 1884), and the pioneering *Comparative Literature* (New York, 1886) which was his Dublin swansong.[9] Though Posnett had read Marx, these details function more as signal than substance. German dominance in the historical and social sciences deserves to be noticed, principally so that the overwhelmingly Anglocentric perspective of the Irish critical tradition may be overcome. For example, with its displaced aristocracies, radicalised proletariat and bohemianised gentry, parts of the Habsburg Empire (rather than England, or even Great Britain) would accommodate a comparative study of late Victorian and Edwardian Ireland. Le Fanu's 'Carmilla', in that sense, is exemplary. By way of establishing Irish credentials, its Stygian setting needs no gothic tradition.

With the political crisis of 1880–91, a new fractured and spectral 'class' came to monopolise the term 'Anglo-Irish'. By this exercise in ethnogenesis another item is added to the crane-bag of Irish cultures, traditions and tribes. Ulster Unionism, and with it a new sense of political Protestantism, followed suit. Meanwhile the complex, quivering web of social and economic realities beneath the ideological rhetoric lay un- or under-noticed, unless it was noted by attentive readers of Le Fanu's novels. It is to this political dimension that we must now turn, and German perspectives can shed unexpected light even on that uniquely *sui generis* Anglo-Irish phenomenon, Charles Stewart Parnell.

Although Karl Marx and Max Weber are often thought of as rival interpreters of the modern world, their accounts of capitalist society should not be regarded as incompatible. Weber's emphasis on bureaucracy rather than class conflict would seem to render his sociology more directly applicable to the enigma of Irish conditions, given – (1) the apparently unique nature of class structures and terminologies, and (2) the highly developed state of bureaucratic administration. No such application has been attempted, at least in relation to Victorian and Edwardian Ireland. In approaching the dramatic episode of Parnell's fall, one should note a particular feature of Weber's argument. As societies develop economically and organisationally, a complementary process of de-sacralisation or disenchantment (*Entzauberung*) occurs. Rationalisation, with its emphasis on long-range guarantees of ends, becomes incompatible with inherited practices of a ritual or non-utilitarian nature. In critical situations, the impasse is resolved through the agency of a *charismatic* leader who, while attending to the ordinary affairs of his society, is seen to possess extraordinary powers. Seen in these terms, Parnell is suddenly more a textbook instance of Weberian categories than a hero of the Anglo-Irish tradition. In this connection, what is significant is not his Protestant background or gentry status, but rather the exfoliation of Irish bureaucracy in policing, poor law, ecclesiastical salaries, education, encumbered landownership and – critically – the extension of tenant participation in economic and political activity. Should surviving patriots feel affronted by the late incorporation of Parnell into German sociology, let it be noted that the charismatic status of Cuchulainn was noted by the Webers while honeymooning in Scotland in 1893.[10]

In Weberian terms, Parnell was a transitional leader whose charisma functions to establish continuity between a traditional authority in the past and a rational order as yet to come. The decisive feature of Parnell's career was of course the sudden collapse of that attempted continuity, in political scandal and subsequent death. The very term 'fall' implicates an irreversible occurrence, at once beyond the comprehension of the individual and yet accountable to him as an offence. The theological and the commonplace usages coincide – the fall is what befell Parnell – just as in his prelapsarian state he combined ordinary efficacy and extraordinary authority. Yeats, in his *Autobiographies*, confirmed a German literary analogue in his interpretation of the politician's end – 'During the quarrel over Parnell's grave a quotation from Goethe ran through the papers, describing our Irish jealousy: "The Irish seem to me like a pack of hounds, always dragging down some noble stag."'[11] That Goethe's remark (of 7 April 1829) related to matters quite different from the death of a hero in no way invalidates Yeats's insistence on a romantic juxtaposition of lonely hero and cowardly mob. In 1903, Thomas Mann published 'Tonio Kröger', the short story which most poetically summarises the dichotomy between the demands of day-to-day normality and the artistic vocation. The concluding paragraphs are cast in the form of a letter which is also a manifesto:

> I admire those proud, cold spirits who venture out along the paths of grandiose, demonic beauty and despise 'humanity' – but I do not envy them. For if there is anything that can turn a *littérateur* into a true writer, then it is this bourgeois love of mine for the human and the living and the ordinary. It is the source of all warmth, of all kind-heartedness and of all humour, and I am almost persuaded it is that very love without which, as we are told, one may speak with the tongues of men and of angels and yet be a sounding brass and a tinkling cymbal.[12]

Perhaps the one word recessed in the process of translating this passage is that rendered here as 'demonic'. Tonio's reference is not simply to a psychological type nor even to a certain familiar attitude of dedication to a calling. Through him, Mann invokes a long established German concept of the *Dämonisch* to which Goethe had given eloquent testimony in the last book of his autobiography. Originally, demons existed somewhere between gods and men, but in their romantic assimilation a deindividualised power is substituted. 'It was not godlike, for it seemed unreasonable; not human, for it had no understanding; nor devilish, for it was beneficent; nor angelic, for it often betrayed a malicious pleasure.'[13] The demonic, therefore, intervened in human history or manifested itself in the career of some extraordinary figure, but was itself without continuity or character. In conversation, Goethe is said to have associated Peter the Great and Napoleon with this power; in the autobiography he more circumspectly links it to his own play *Egmont*, which deals with a noble opponent of the counter reformation whose political fate is tragically intertwined in his love of a woman of the burger class. Commenting on the plot, Goethe remarked that, though men may triumph over a host of enemies 'the meshes of state policy are harder to break through.'[14] These meshes become the cages, files, dossiers and alphabetised lists of the bureaucratic world diagnosed by Weber. The demonic is translated into the charismatic also, being regulated and systematised even as it is eliminated in the process.

Notes

1 *The Dublin University Magazine* (November 1849).
2 Standish O'Grady *Selected Essays and Passages* Dublin: Talbot Press, [n.d.] p. 168 etc.
3 *Speeches of the Right Hon. W. E. Gladstone Delivered at Warrington, Ormskirk, Liverpool, Southport, Newtown, Leigh, and Wigan in October 1868* London, [c. 1868] pp. 97–8.
4 See Geoffgrey Grigson *The Aeolian Harp and Other Essays* London: 1947. pp. 56–65.
5 Francis Greeacre *Francis Danby 1793–1861* London: Tate Gallery, 1988. pp. 89–91.
6 See W. J. Mc Cormack 'Vision and Revision in the Study of Eighteenth-Century Irish Political Rhetoric' *Eighteenth-Century Ireland* 2 (1987) p. 33.
7 Ibid. p. 231 etc.
8 See 'Yeats's "Sorrow of Love" Through the Years' by Ramon Jakobson and Stephen Rudy in Jakobson *Verbal Art, Verbal Sign, Verbal Time* (ed. Krystyna Pomorska and Stephen Rudy) Oxford: Blackwell, 1985. pp. 79–107. More generally see 'Retrospect' (1961) in Jakobson *Selected Writings* I (2nd ed.) The Hague: Mouton, 1971 esp. pp. 657–8.
9 See Joseph Th. Leerssen *Komparatistik in Grossbritannien 1800–1950* Bonn: Bouvier, 1984 pp. 60–3 and notes.
10 See Max Weber *On Charisma and Institution Building; Selected Papers* (ed. S. N. Eisenstadt) Chicago: University of Chicago Press, 1968. On Lecky's influence see the introduction by H. H. Gerth and C. Wright Mills in *From Max Weber; Essays in Sociology* London: Routledge, 1948 esp. pp. 53–4.
11 See J. Oxenford (trans.) *Conversations of Goethe with Eckermann* London: Dent, 1930 p. 314. The comment, prompted by imminent Catholic emancipation, related to the harassment of Protestant farmers by Catholic neighbours, of a minority by a majority – 'The Catholics do not agree among themselves, but they always unite against a Protestant. They are like a pack of hounds; which bite one another, but, when a stag comes in view, all unite immediately to run it down.' Goethe, who had been reading English newspapers, was suspicious of papal ambitions in the political sphere.
12 Thomas Mann *Death in Venice and Other Stories* (trans. David Luke) London: Secker & Warburg, 1990 p. 194. (ellipsis in the original).
13 J. W. von Goethe *Autobiography* (trans. John Oxenford) London: University of Chicago Press, 1974. vol 2 p. 423.
14 Ibid vol. 2 p. 424.

14

Yeats
and gothic politics

The literary formulation of Parnell's last year – the divorce scandal, the conflict with party, prime minister and church, the by-elections, and the death in Brighton – is a construct in which romantic notions of the demonic figure if not prominently then at least powerfully. Post-mortem sightings of the Chief included an unscheduled appearance at Bayreuth, during the interval of a Wagner opera, and this despite his notorious philistinism and indifference to all 'cultural' pursuits. When Yeats, pretending to abjure politics, wrote that after Parnell 'Ireland was to be like soft wax for years to come' he was elevating the literary into the role previously occupied by a rather crudely defined notion of politics. Literature did not replace politics; it promoted politics to become a more sophisticated and pervasive cultural mode than had been available to the lobbyists at Westminister.[1]

Parnell died in 1891 and the great concentration of Yeats's writing about Parnell dates from the 1930s. To be sure, there are early instances, but 'To a Shade' (written in September 1913) adopts an attitude which is essentially prospective. In Richard Ellmann's words, the poem 'addresses Parnell as "thin shade", not only because a ghost has no body but because Parnell's desires for the future have been so starved ...'. Thus the dead politician not only joins 'a jury of ghosts and legended heroes' of whom Homer, Duke Ercole and Swift are three notable instances, but he is also positioned as a watchman interrogating the present in order to discern what the future may bring by way of improvement upon the contemporary.[2] Yeats advances Parnell in a series of such positionings. For example, speaking to the Royal Academy of Sweden at the time of his Nobel Prize celebrations, Yeats declared that the modern literature of Ireland, and indeed all that stir of thought which prepared for the Anglo-Irish war, began when Parnell fell from power in 1891. A disillusioned and embittered Ireland turned from parliamentary politics; an event was conceived; the race began, as I think, to be troubled by that event's long gestation.[3]

More than a decade later, in 1936, he sharpened the attitude towards Parnell and parliamentary politics in the first of his *Essays 1931 to 1936*. Insincerity is now diagnosed as having discredited democracy in 1891, and the next sentence announces as a logical *sequitur* – 'All over the world men are turning to Dictators, Communist or Fascist'.[4] Between these two placid endorsements of the consequences stemming from Parnell's fall – note that Yeats avoids the term death – there are others no less remarkable, the most extensive and concentrated being the prose and verse surrounding 'Parnell's Funeral', a poem written forty years after the event commemorated. Again Ellmann astutely identifies the motive force behind the work, 'the death of Parnell is described as if it were the death of some pagan god, and the ancient rite of eating the hero's heart to obtain his qualities is introduced metaphorically to explain the course of Irish history after Parnell's death'.[5] Thus, Parnell's death is something more cataclysmic than ordinary death because Parnell possessed charismatic if not indeed semi-divine status; simultaneously, it is hardly death at all – and for the same reasons.

A pattern at once serial and binary also operates in Yeats's placings of Parnell. We have already noted the first of these characteristics; the second treats Parnell and Daniel O'Connell in much the same way as it treats Swift and Goldsmith, linking the first of each pair with a tragic value, the second with something lighter or lesser. Speaking at a meeting in Trinity College shortly after the outbreak of the First World War, Yeats paid tribute to Thomas Davis and in doing so denigrated the genius of O'Connell, with his 'appeal – as of a tumbler at a fair – to the commoner ear, a grin through a horse-collar'.[6] During the Civil War he published passages from the volume of autobiography which later became the second book of *The Trembling of the Veil*, wherein we read of a specific episode in Parnell's tumultuous career: 'Once he had seemed callous and indifferent to the House of Commons – Forster had accused him of abetting assassination – but when he came among his followers his hands were full of blood, because he had torn them with his nails.'[7] Twenty years after the first of these remarks, and twelve years after the second, the 'Commentary on "A Parnellite at Parnell's Funeral"' reworks both of them: 'When we talked of his pride; of his apparent impassivity when his hands were full of blood because he had torn them with his nails, the proceeding [*sic*] epoch with its democratic bonhomie, seemed to grin through a horse collar.'[8]

Several accounts could be offered of these variations and repetitions. The horse collar image of 1914 is closely integrated to the figure of O'Connell who doubtless attended many a fair and pulled the vote of many a tumbler; that of 1934 has a surreal power not unconnected with its unconnectedness to any human figure. We may chalk this up as an enhanced poetic use of the recycled image, or we may note the elimination of the contextual, the human, the historical. Something along these latter lines must be recorded in response to the two employments of Parnell's hands torn with his own nails: in the first instance, specific provocation, sufficient evidence of an appropriate self-control is provided; in the second, the hands have a stigmatic aura, linked only to pride and 'apparent passivity'. Perhaps it is unremarkable that the poet engages in self-quotation, with a resultant truncation of phrase. But, emphatically, Yeats was not a writer of exhausted imagination. Indeed, the quality of the repetition lies precisely in the augmented imaginative force.

I wish to argue that Parnell appears serially and not repetitively in Yeats's writing, that this very curious feature is initially made possible by the uncertainty as to whether Parnell was/is such a being as merely dies, and that the Weberian charisma of the historical Parnell is translated serially into what Ellmann calls 'some pagan god'. Certainly, a quick glance at the list of titles at the back of a *Collected Poems* will prove an accelerated rate of the hero's name – 'Parnell's Funeral' (1932–3), 'Come Gather Round Me, Parnellites' (1936) and 'Parnell' (1937). The earlier 'To a Shade' (1913) and the distinctly premature 'Mourn – and Then Onwards' (1891) strikingly fail to name Parnell, despite the excited political conditions of their day. As a named person (or persona) in the verse – and the name occurs twelve times in the three late poems mentioned – Parnell belongs to the 1930s. There are other Yeatsian heroes less frequently invoked – Jonathan Swift and Roger Casement, for example. But there are also those contemporary dictators to whom Yeats can make such nimble reference in recording the discrediting of democracy.

It is fair to say that, given the lapse of time since the death of that individual, these names relate to poetic *persona* as distinct from historical person. Part of that transition is imaged in Yeats's phrase 'soft as wax for years to come'; another part of it in the resultant absolute integrity of the finished *persona*. From the fluidity (in the last analysis, disintegration) of the person buffeted in history's ebb and flow there emerges the hard, heroic figure of the poems. The process is far from smooth or easy. Not only the passage of time but the hiatus, largely detectable through dates linked to major violent upheavals – the First World War, the Civil War, the 1930s – between death and celebration characterises the transformation of Parnell, just as the litany of names constituting Yeats's augustan Ireland is also the consequence of a juncture between the age of Jonathan Swift and the propagation of that rhetoric ironically enveloping him in a synthetic tradition of Protestant Ascendancy.

In *The Literary Fantastic*, Neil Cornwell has adapted the approach of Tzvetan Todorov to redefine what gothic literature was and how it worked. Central to this approach is the insistence that such fiction offers two (conflicting, perhaps irreconcilable) interpretations of events, and maintains as fully as possible, or for as long as possible, a neutral attitude towards them. These interpretations involve, fundamentally, supernatural or natural agencies. Dark deeds in the belfry may be the work of ghosts or, alternatively, disgruntled gravediggers. Preferring terms like 'the pure fantastic' to ambiguous ones such as 'the gothic', Cornwell locates the fantastic on 'a frontier between two adjacent realms'.[9] Or, in the words of Christine Brooke-Rose:

> If the supernatural *eventually* receives a natural explanation, we are in the fantastic-uncanny; if the events are not supernatural but strange, horrific, incredible, we are in the uncanny (with the accent on the reader's fear, not on his hesitation). On the other side of the line, if the supernatural has to be *eventually* accepted as supernatural, we are in the fantastic-marvellous (with the accent on wonder). Presumably, then, on the left of the line, in the fantastic-uncanny, not only is the reader's hesitation resolved but his fear is purged; whereas on the right of the line, in fantastic-marvellous, this fear is turned to wonder.[10]

Cornwell reminds us that the aesthetics of gothicism begin with Edmund Burke, not only through his *Philosophical Inquiry into the Origins of Our Ideas of the Sublime and Beautiful* (1757) but by practical application in his *Reflections on the Revolution in France* (1791) also. It is timely to have the generic categorisations of the fantastic/gothic re-historicised even to this limited degree. The shifts in Yeats's several presentations of Parnell with his bleeding hands do constitute a movement from the uncanny to the marvellous, from contexts which are strange and even horrific (yet naturally accounted for, in the setting of the House of Commons, an accusation of abetting murder) to others which are marvellous in the sense that the death of a god inspires wonder, awe and even worship. However, these shifts also occur in a historic framework of their own, with November 1914 and the rise of fascism acting as rudimentary markers on the field of action.

Burke plays a part in Yeats's mythological Protestant Ascendancy but, given his Catholic origins and his own excoriating comments on emergent ascendancy, his role is less flamboyant than Parnell's. Reference to the essay *On the Sublime and Beautiful* suggests that Yeats drew from the eighteenth century more than a vocabulary of augustan balance and public service; there was an irrational side to the period, to be personified not only in Blake but in such earlier figures as Burke the aesthetician and Goldsmith the sentimentalist. If Yeats revered Swift for his service to human liberty, Swift also detested free thought. (Swedenborg also must be accounted among these eighteenth-century influences, even if he lacked Irish credentials; and we should note the absence of Sheridan, too radical by half for inclusion in the honours list.) The young Yeats discounted eighteenth-century writing, and his rediscovery of its value for him broadly coincides with the final emergence of Parnell the *persona* from a silent chrysalis. In addition to poems already listed as incorporating Parnell's name, there are also the controversial 'marching songs' or 'Three Songs to the One Tune', in the commentary on which Yeats deftly links the Ascendancy to problems of contemporary politics. Though he denies that any political movement exists (in April 1934) willing to undertake the task of making the world knowable 'in the concrete', it is far from clear that he is looking beyond Ireland. What is clear is the violent, irrational nature of the mission to which he would commit himself:

> If any Government or party undertake this work it will need force, marching men; (the logic of fanaticism, whether in a woman or a mob is drawn from a premise protected by ignorance and therefore irrefutable); it will promise not this or that measure but a discipline, a way of life; that sacred drama must to all native eyes and ears become the greatest of all parables. There is no such government or party to-day;

should either appear I offer it these trivial songs and what remains to me of life.[11]

The argument about Yeats's attitude towards fascism has been long and inconclusive, and little is to be gained by rehearsing again the contributions of Conor Cruise O'Brien, Patrick Cosgrave, Elizabeth Cullingford, Grattan Freyer and the others. Both sides of the dispute have overlooked highly revealing evidence, and publication of a greater body of Yeats's private writings must be awaited before any final verdict is passed – if verdict there must be. Yet we can establish an interim judgement, in which gothic features of his politics are identified. What confuses the issue initially may be the assumption that gothic literature is or was confined to fiction, especially the novel, and especially that of the late eighteenth century. Yet consideration of architecture must indicate exactly how widespread, if also how ill-defined, the gothic fashion was. And gothic, in keeping with its intricate deaths, revenants and post-mortem excitements, was constantly in a state of revival – the parliament at Westminister dates from 1840. Further confusion has been added to the local debate by the assumption that Ireland, like every other nation or proto-nation, must have had a gothic tradition, whereas it is the pervasiveness of these patterns everywhere which is noteworthy. Yeats's gothic, as evidenced in his demonic transformation of Parnell, is implicated in his sense of international politics from the First World War onwards.

On this question Michael North appears to follow the line established by Elizabeth Cullingford, which is to assign the undoubted authoritarianism and unmistakably violent rhetoric to a restricted Irish sphere. In fact Yeats himself had dextrously used the same strategy to defend Parnell, 'then at the height of his career' for whom he declared a preference over the radical Michael Daviit, the latter having 'wrecked his Irish influence by international politics'.[12] This assumption that a categorical distinction divides the Irish from the non-Irish spheres is here revealed in all its *a priori* conservativism, for Davitt's foreign campaigns (in Africa and the Middle East) did not begin until years after Parnell's death. Consequently, it is natural that, while Pound is linked to fascism and Eliot to conservatism, Yeats partners 'cultural nationalism'.[13] However, North enters the debate at a sufficiently late date as to be able to bring together the charge of fascism and aspects of the recent historical argument about the origins of Protestant Ascendancy. He reads 'The Statues', for example, as an attempt 'to close the gap between sect and nation, part and whole, while simultaneously insisting on forcing it farther open'. A larger and less hysterical attempt at the same undertaking occurs in Yeats's elaboration of the Protestant Ascendancy which

> is as much a logical solution to this discord as an actual class. It resolves the tension between liberal individualism and nationalism by making the nation synonymous with certain isolated individuals, just as it resolves the conflict of one class with the rest of the state by making that class into the state . . . If the Ascendancy represented true Irishness and the fledgling democracy some false imposition, then action taken in the name of the Ascendancy served Ireland.[14]

North's argument brings us to the central puzzle of Yeats's politics. How could one fearful that his dreams might be trodden upon provide marching songs for the Blue Shirts, how could the upholder of divorce rights champion indissoluble family bonds as the very basis of social organisation, how could the pupil of John O'Leary and the lover of Maud Gonne refuse aid to a concentration camp prisoner? How – in short – could beauty and the beast exist in such close spiritual, intellectual and emotional proximity one to the other?

The gothic element in Yeats's poetic strategies involves one crucial assumption relevant to these paradoxes – death, in that schema, is less than absolute. Parnell may fall, but resurrection can be relied on. Swift, though invisible, absent, long dead, may trumpet his authority above the shabby chatter of séance-goers in *The Words Upon the Window-pane*. Everywhere names – MacDonagh and MacBride and Connolly and Pearse – not only list but re-enlist the dead. In a related connection, North proceeds more abstractly:

> At almost all times in his life, whatever his immediate political allegiances, Yeats thought in terms of a paradoxical figure whereby a part distinguished by its difference from the whole came to represent that whole. Thus the same figure could stand for difference, division, heterogeneity and also for identity, unity, and a tyranny of the same . . . By the logic of Yeats's paradoxical figure, the more his class met with opposition the more truly in the right it was, because it represented by virtue of difference. This force and violence finally become their own justification.
>
> The movement offering the most violent reconciliation of part and whole was, of course, fascism . . . [15]

The great enchantment

It would be wrong to suggest that the worthies who constituted the social constituency gradually becoming known as the Protestant Ascendancy were adherents of fascism, consciously or otherwise. However, Yeats's characteristic re-creation of a high simulacrum bearing the same name as that constituency is not thereby exempted from suspicion. Guido de Ruggiero may be quoted to the effect that 'aristocracy was the general class *par excellence*' and the precedent applied sympathetically to the Protestant Ascendancy as presented by Yeats.[16] But the import of recent debates on the historical origins of ascendancy has been to stress the essentially middle-class, even bourgeois, base of an ideology arising from anti-revolutionary alarm in the 1780s and 1790s.[17] Thus, if Yeats advances the assumption that his Ascendancy is both isolated and embodies Ireland in its chief persons, then the result is not some miraculously surviving ancient aristocracy but a hegemonic bourgeoisie of unusual contours. Not de Ruggiero but Marx and Engels are the commentators required here:

> each new class which puts itself in the place of one ruling before it, is compelled, merely in order to carry through its aim, to represent its interest as the common interest of all the members of society, that is, expressed in ideal form: it has to give its ideas the form of universality, and represent them as the only rational, universally valid ones. The class making a revolution appears from the very start, if only because it is opposed to a *class*, not as a class but as the representative of the whole of society ...[19]

Dating from 1846, this looks back to 1789 while also anticipating 1848. While they speak of 'each class' (as if the law promulgated applied to every conceivable instance), in practice Marx and Engels are concerned with the triumph first of the bourgeoisie and (later, perhaps) of the proletariat. No satisfactory Marxist account of late eighteenth-century Irish society has been devised, but it can be readily agreed that the advocates of Protestant Ascendancy in the early 1790s were privileged and yet nervous members of the middle class (urban and rural) alarmed at the prospect of revolutionary politics catching hold among the disenfranchised or disadvanced in their own stratum of society. By the twentieth century, Protestant Ascendancy as a class description conjured up notions of a dispossessed former landowning elite, eminent culturally, marginalised politically, and of economic importance principally through relocation into the professions and management and the more respectable branches of trade. To see this ascendancy as synecdoche, as a part standing for the whole of Irish society, is to invert the history of late-eighteenth-century Ireland in order to create (retrospectively) a heroic middle class. Yet Yeats cannot admit that his ascendancy is fundamentally bourgeois, and so is for doubled reasons compelled to cast its role as the vanguard of an anti-democratic politics, the few against the many, not the part for the whole.

The argument about his right-wing politics has concentrated largely on the 1930s when, with the accession of Hitler, the issue became urgent everywhere in Europe. However, as early as 1923, Odon Por's *Fascism* (issued in English translation by the Labour Publishing Company in London) had advanced even the saintly George William Russell's *The National Being* (1916) as 'a virtual blueprint for Italian fascism', linking AE with no less a co-operativist than Machiavelli. Still, North lets AE off lightly enough, declining to note that he had contributed to a further publication of Por's on the guilds of pre-Mussolinian Italy, also published in 1923.[19] Nothing could more clearly demonstrate the vulnerability of an agriculturist, regionalist or visionary politics to peremptory appropriation by emerging fascism. Yet 'From Democracy to Authority', Yeats's *Irish Times* statement of 16 February 1924, parading the names of Paul Claudel and Benito Mussolini for approval, cannot be explained away in terms of external appropriation.

We can return to the several utterances about Parnell, for they are counterpointed with observations about democracy. In Stockholm late in 1923, Yeats had attributed 'the modern literature of Ireland, and indeed all that stir of thought which prepared for the Anglo-Irish war' to the disillusion and bitterness resulting from Parnell's fall – 'Ireland turned from parliamentary politics'.[20] Later, in 1934, disillusion with democracy is justified for what seems at first glance a much earlier period than Parnell's: 'When we talked of his pride . . . the proceeding [*sic*] epoch with its democratic bonhomie, seemed to grin through a horse collar.'[21] But the unexpected 'proceeding' (where 'preceding' might seem more likely) is in keeping with the expunging of the historical O'Connell (however travestied as 'a tumbler at a fair') from the image; now Parnell as *persona* interrogates the future from the grave. 'Bonhomie' seems too sophisticated for the beggar-on-horseback high spirits of O'Connell, and we need a further passage to have that noun more plausibly anchored. For, two years later still, in 1936, Yeats is inclined to reverse the order of events surrounding the fall; now he sets them in a garden landscape with formally dressed spectators, and in doing so completes the passage from the failure of democracy, through democracy as failure, into the *Realpolitik* of the 1930s:

> They were all tolerant men of the world except the peasant-born Irish members; tolerance is most often found beside ornamental waters, upon smooth lawns, amid conversations that have no object but pleasure. But all were caught in that public insincerity which was about to bring such discredit upon democracy. All over the world men are turning to Dictators, Communist or Fascist. [22]

The succession of the last sentence here upon its predecessor is breath-taking, but wholly at one with the ambiguity of preceding/proceeding, for an objective reality of time in history is the chief victim of Yeats's fluency. The oddly phrased *bonhmie* previously associated with O'Connell would surely be more at home among these rich, late-Victorian flowering lawns, and not at the fair with the horse-collared tumbler. None of these three passages about Parnell is complete in itself: to understand the commentary of 1934, one needs to look back to 1923 and forward to 1936. In similar fashion, the Swift of the history books is amalgamated into the Swift of Yeats's Protestant Ascendancy, an exercise which is the undeclared agenda of *The Words upon the Window-pane*, the play which effectively inaugurated the *annus horribilis* (1934) of Yeats's gothicism. Central to its dramatic impact is the decision, lying outside the text in the drafts and preliminaries, to exclude the name of Le Fanu and hence to suppress the mid-Victorian mediations by which eighteenth-century concerns turn into twentieth-century obsessions. Perhaps the Le Fanu traces in the manuscripts are slight in themselves – slight but, given the unusual name, unmistakable. Yet it is in these touchingly honest, guiltily suppressed, details that Yeats gives evidence that a truly full account of his politics might obviate the need for a verdict and make possible a more humane response to the denial of human variety.

To the end Yeats obstructed such mitigation, thirsting always for accusation. Posthumously published and diplomatically edited by the widow, *On the Boiler* (1939) proclaims a revolutionary/counter-revolutionary politics distinguished by verbs in the imperative mood. 'Desire some just war ...' smacks of an ethical residue were it not for the author's proclaimed contempt for justice and such trifles

– 'A government is legitimate because some instinct has compelled us to give it the right to take life in defence of its laws and its shores.' The grammar of the pamphlet is ferociouly at odds with its *lex* (or form of words). Nouns, especially proper nouns or names, swagger through the argument. 'Berkeley, Swift, Burke, Grattan, Parnell, Augusta Gregory, Synge, Kevin O'Higgins, are the true Irish people, and there is nothing too hard for such as these.'[23] It is not suprising to find a Yeatsian *reprise*, 'I say to those that shall rule here: if ever Ireland again seems molten wax, reverse the process of revolution.'[24] The politicians are the writers, once Yeats has finished with them, and they are an ascendancy.

In the end, it is not possible simply to enter a *nolle prosequi* against Yeats's name on the matter of his fascist leanings. First, the evidence is so highly *suggestive*, as in the passage where he declares that no government or party exists (in 1934) capable of imposing the discipline, inspiring the fanaticism necessary to the achieving of a way of life, a sacred drama. A glance suggests that Mussolini and the Nazis are alike dismissed in this sweeping disavowal. Yet the curious phrase about 'all native eyes and ears' suggsests that it is perhaps a disavowal of only local application, uttered after he had become tired of the Blue Shirts whose General O'Duffy had failed to eat of Parnell's heart. By late 1938 and even in his last days, Yeats was less guarded in distinguishing clinically between the Irish and European spheres. To Maud Gonne he had written in June 1938 that 'for the first time' he was expressing what he believed about Irish and European politics.[25] In August a speech at the Abbey Theatre and an interview in the *Irish Independent* left no one in any doubt as to his approval of Nazi legislation in its disinheriting of Jews and its commitment to a eugenical programme.[26] Conor Cruise O'Brien has gone so far as to suggest that 'there was something in [Yeats] that would have taken considerable pleasure ... in seeing England occupied by the Nazis, the Royal Family exiled, and the Mother of Parliaments torn down. Meanwhile in Ireland one would have expected to see him at least a cautious participant, or ornament, in a collaborationist regime'.[27] Those remarks gave offence, but neither the offender nor offended took in the significance of Dorothy Wellesley's post-obituary in the London *Times* in which she indicated how politically active the poet was even in the last weeks of his life. Yeats died on 28 January 1939. Many, then as now, mark the occasion with sighs both of relief and of loss.[28]

The great enchantment

Notes

1 W. B. Yeats *Autobiographies* London: Macmillan, 1955 p. 199. See also Yeats's introduction to *Representative Irish Tales*.

2 Richard Ellmann *The Identity of Yeats* (2nd ed.) London: Faber, 1964 p. 114. It is worth noting that 'To a Shade', which does not name Parnell, dates from the month in which Yeats wrote the prolifically naming 'September 1913' in which his practice of invoking the noble (and relatively recent) dead commences. One could argue that a sequence of poems – 'September 1913', 'Easter 1916', 'The Tower' etc. – reaches its climax with the emergence of a resurrected demon in 'Parnell's Funeral'. No other such figure/name achieves incorporation into a poem's title before 1934.

3 Yeats *Autobiographies* p. 559.

4 Yeats *Essays and Introductions* London: Macmillan, 1961 p. 488.

5 Ellmann *Identity* p. 208.

6 Yeats *Tribute to Thomas Davis* Cork: Cork University Press, 1965 p. 15.

7 Yeats *Autobiographies* p. 232. The reference is to William Edward Forster, a veteran British politician who served as Chief Secretary for Ireland (1880–82) and resigned when the 'Kilmainham Treaty' was signed by the government and Parnell (negotiating from prison).

8 Yeats *The King of the Great Clock Tower, Commentaries and Poems* Dublin: Cuala Press, 1934 p. 29. See also Peter Allt and Russell K. Alspach *The Variorum Edition of the Poems of W. B. Yeats* New York: Macmillan, 1957 p. 835.

9 Neil Cornwell *The Literary Fantastic; from Gothic to Postmodernism* Hemel Hempstead: Harvester Wheatsheaf, 1990 p. 35. Cornwell devotes a good of space (esp. pp. 87–94) to the work of Le Fanu.

10 Christine Brooke-Rose *A Rhetoric of the Unreal; Studies in Narrative and Structure, Especially of the Fantastic* Cambridge: Cambridge University pPress, 1983 pp. 64–5. Quoted in Cornwell p. 36.

11 Yeats *The King of the Great Clock Tower* etc. p. 37.

12 Yeats *Autobiographies* p. 140.

13 Michael North *The Political Aesthetic of Yeats, Eliot, and Pound* Cambridge: Cambridge University Press, 1991 pp. 21–73.

14 Ibid. pp. 69–70.

15 Ibid. p. 70.

16 Idem.

17 This revaluation of the Protestant Ascendancy lies at the heart of the controversy initiated with my *Ascendancy and Tradition in Anglo-Irish Literary History from 1789 to 1939* Oxford: Clarendon Press, 1985, debated in several reviews (notably by Denis Donoghue in the *Times Literary Supplement*) and in the successive issues of *Eighteenth-Century Ireland*. I am preparing a bibliographical study of the 1786–7 'pamphlet war' in which the matter is further documented.

18 Karl Marx and Frederick Engels *The German Ideology* (ed. etc. C. J. Arthur) London: Lawrence & Wishart, 197. pp. 65–6.

19 North op. cit. p. 70. See also Odon Por *Guilds and Co-Operatives in Italy* and *Fascism* both trans. E. Townsend, both London: Labour Publishing Company, 1923. The sixth chapter of the former is 'Motives and Tendencies of the Dictatorship' (pp. 146–88).

20 See note 7 above.

21 See note 8 above.

22 See note 4 above

23 Yeats *On the Boiler* Dublin: Cuala Press, [1939] p. 30.

24 Ibid. p. 13.

25 Allan Wade (ed.) *The Letters of W. B. Yeats* London: Hart-Davis, 1954 pp. 909–10.

26 See Mc Cormack *Ascendancy and Tradition* pp. 393–4; also Mc Cormack 'Communicating with Prisoners' in Mc Cormack (ed.) *In the Prison of his Days; a Miscellany for Nelson Mandela on his Seventieth Birthday* Gigginstown: Lilliput Press, 1988 pp. 77–92.

27 Conor Cruise O'Brien 'Passion and Cunning: an Essay on the Politics of W. B. Yeats' in *Passion and Cunning and Other Essays* London: Weidenfeld and Nicolson, 1988 p. 50 (see also p. 2. This is an amended version of the essay first published in 1965 though the author protests (p. 2) that it is 'here reprinted exactly in its original form'.

28 Dorothy Wellesley's initialled post-obituary appeared in the *Times* on 9 February 1939.

PART FOUR

Elizabeth Bowen
and *The Heat of the Day*

15

Is the novel
properly entitled ...?

Collaborator, double-agent, fellow-traveller, fifth-columnist, mole ...
A new vocabulary sprang up in the middle decades of the twentieth
century pin-pointing specific forms of individual engagement in
exotic forms of politics. Though these may seem eternally attached
to such episodes as the Spanish Civil War ('fifth column') or isolated
figures like Vidkun Quisling and Anthony Blunt, the terms signify
particular intersections between privacy and the public domain.
Those more venerable villains – spies – have been with us since
biblical days, and even the lists of English literary heroes can throw
up a colourful instance – Christopher Marlowe. Tracked by police-
agents, Coleridge was suspected of being a spy. But the collaborator,
going further than the traditional role of traitor, attracts the most
intense odium. Or, to put it the other way round, extreme social
conditions which make possible the collaborator have much to tell
us about the nature of identity, of the self, of individual authority, of
the private/public distinction. The case of Paul de Man, wartime
antisemite in Belgium and late constructor of deconstruction, may
serve to suggest the threat to philosophical coherence implicit in
such conditions.

Different societies experience different conditions, and the most
revealing circumstances may well extend beyond the formal
boundaries of a given state or culture. A valuable and extensive
study could be written on the significance of the Second World War
in the development of Irish self-consciousness. By this latter term is
meant not only a consciousness of being Irish, or of Ireland as a
distinct entity, being also a consciousness of the Self as a problematic. Writing privately during the war years, Elizabeth Bowen remarked 'we are curiously self-made creatures' and proceeded to
characterise herself not only in Irish terms but also fugitive ones -

'cagey, recalcitrant, on the run, bristling with reservations and arrogances that one doesn't show'. In a published essay of 1937, the political analogy was already present. 'Complex people are never certain that they are not crooks, never certain their passports are quite in order …' This is more than another example of the low dishonest decade's recourse to international tension as a metaphor employed of the private life, even if Bowen proceeds to claim that her complex people are 'unobjective with regard to society; their standards are entirely personal.'[1]

One can point to work by Samuel Beckett, Dennis Johnston, Louis MacNeice, Flann O'Brien and Francis Stuart which, turning at some level upon the reality of the war, marked a turning point in their relationship with the social world. To be more precise, in each of these instances, a crisis of selfhood is discovered, and then either endured or evaded. Elizabeth Bowen, living in London but regularly returning to her native Cork (for reasons to be clarified shortly), responded as a writer by reactivating an aspect of her literary inheritance. An admirer of Sheridan Le Fanu's fiction, she adopted some of the stock-in-trade of the ghost story to investigate altered experiences of reality under the *blitz*. For present purposes, only her work of this period is considered, and within that *The Heat of the Day* (set in wartime but not published until 1949) is taken as her principal achievement in probing the mysteries of identity and the complexities of national and social origin. Her later novels, that is, *A World of Love* (1955) and *Eva Trout* (1969), may suggest a declension from this engagement. But, in the former, the empty seat maintained for the long dead Guy might be decoded as a suitably feeble attempt to repatriate Le Fanu's Guy Deverell from an English to an Irish 1950s setting: such simplified locations were not tolerated in the wartime writings.

It is a commonplace to say that Londoners of those days apprehended the passing moment, the endless night, in a manner which heightened time and yet almost abolished it. The ghost story offered conventions by which these drastic and alternating engagements in or out of time could be sensibly conveyed. Le Fanu's characters were usually haunted by the past, but some at least of Bowen's will be haunted in the present tense – and by it. But the ghost story also challenged the usual assumptions which readers of fiction make about personality – about its contours, its claim to uniqueness in each and every case, its blessed limitations as well as its sublimities.

Elizabeth Bowen and *The Heat of the Day*

Bowen's wartime *oeuvre* includes great variety. There are two collections of short stories, *Look at All Those Roses* (1941) and *The Demon Lover* (1945); two contrasting works of autobiography, *Seven Winters* (1942), which is slight and personal, and *Bowen's Court* (1942), which is massive and profoundly historical. To this must be added two works published well after the war ended – the novel already mentioned, *The Heat of the Day* (1949) and an incomplete miscellany of critical pieces, *Collected Impressions* (1950). This last-named volume opens with Bowen's introduction to an edition of Le Fanu's *Uncle Silas* (1864), an English-set novel developed from an earlier Irish-set short story by the same author. It is an objective of the present chapter to suggest that Le Fanu's kind of fiction – 'a romance of terror' was Bowen's description – has affinities with *The Heat of the Day*, and that consideration of these may aid us in appreciating Bowen's peculiar yet very substantial achievement. Some more recently collected wartime writings, notably an essay entitled 'Eire', serve to underline her preoccupation with the land of her birth. One has no desire to repatriate Elizabeth Bowen, but rather to explore her distinctive insight into the processes of dissolution, reformation and further dissolution which contribute to the seemingly solid notion of character. Identity is as much a will-o'-the-wisp in the discussion of fiction as it is in the seminar rooms of cultural politics.

One astute critic, writing of Bowen's work generally, says that 'she does not enclose the reader within one sensibility' but proceeds to link this with a questionable interpretation of her attitude towards time – 'she is interested in more than momentary, personal emotional sensations and responses.'[2] It is true that the critic in question, Hermione Lee, is keen to show how, in the fiction, 'personal dramas are related to the state of a civilization'.[3] Yet one may feel that something more thoroughly radical is at work in Bowen's fiction, and nowhere is a radical attitude towards character more evident than in *The Heat of the Day*. Published in February 1949, but written during the war, this novel constitutes not only an interrogation of fictional character as a realistic device but also an exposé of (Irish or English) identity as a fiction. Though the plot's exploitation of wartime dangers and the presence of a traitor among the English middle classes gives it a superficial claim to be regarded as a political novel, *The Heat of the Day* is a far more complex inquiry into the foundations of the relationship between Britain and Ireland than the Chekhovian *Last September* (1929). The very miminalism with which the later book admits Irish setting at once emphasises the importance of the theme and the rigorous pessimism with which the author addresses her diagnosis.

Perhaps one can usefully begin by considering the novel's title. In context, 'the heat of the day' may be taken to refer to the exposed condition of characters enduring German bombs and the deprivations imposed by rationing. One difficulty with this interpretation centres on the predominantly *nocturnal* timetable of the bombing. Then a biblical source might be considered also – 'These last have wrought but one hour, and thou hast made them equal unto us, which have borne the burden and heat of the day' (Matthew 20: 12). The context is a parable of Christ's in which he had told of a man hiring labourers to work in his vineyard. Though he hired men at day-break, and again at the third, sixth, ninth and even the eleventh hour, all were paid the same wages for their labour. The complaint just quoted is lodged by those who had laboured longest and directed against those who had for the same sum laboured for a mere hour.

The passage has perplexed even pious readers of the Bible and given hours of amusement to sceptics. If Heaven is 'like unto a man' who behaves as the employer has behaved, then Heaven manifestly does not give everybody their due. Moreover, the parable follows from an equally upsetting declaration that 'the last shall be first' and, in both regards, justice is seemingly reversed. Yet the underlying moral is partly psychological (those who have accepted that a penny a day is fair wages revise this view only when they see others receive the same reward for a lesser service) and partly theological (God's grace is given in fullest measure, even to those whose service has been tardy). While we may accept that the orthodox reading of the parable of the 'unjust steward' presents it as revealing how redemption or salvation is available to all even up the eleventh hour, there is a lower and yet wholly valid reading. For considering in psychological terms, resentment or disaffection is the topic upon which Christ had obliquely commented.

How does this shed light on the novel, on the affair between Stella Rodney and Robert Kelway, on the latter's treachery, on the mysterious Harrison's surveillance of the lovers, on young Roderick Rodney who inherits a house in Ireland, or pregnant Louie Lewis whose husband is away at war? To understand the relationship between the title and novel it is necessary to introduce the author herself into the debate, and then to remove her from it.

Born in Dublin in 1899 to a landed family from County Cork, Bowen first left Ireland in 1907 and, with remissions, spent the next thirty and more years living in England. During this time she acquired a reputation as novelist which linked her to such names as Rosamond Lehmann, Henry Green and Graham Greene rather than Liam O'Flaherty and Frank O'Connor. Bloomsbury and not Leopold Bloom was her point of reference. Apart from *The Last September* (1929), her pre-war fiction was solidly set in an English upper-middle-class world. Her evident disapproval of the way things were going in 1930s England might have been read by the astute as a latent interest in Ireland. Yet by background, class and education she had little in common with the makers of the new independent Irish state, not even with W. B. Yeats who might have been regarded as a mediating influence.

It was, oddly enough, the war which changed this relationship, or rather transformed its mere implications into a major theme. Bowen had been on the margin of political discussion through her friendship with Maurice Bowra who in turn had befriended Guy Burgess and Donald Maclean. She was also close, at least for a while, to Goronwy Rees whom Burgess tried to recruit as a Soviet spy. What was later called 'the climate of treason' was familiar to Bowen long before the war began. When it did begin, she found herself facing two ways: on the one side lay London and the milieu in which she had matured as an artist, on the other Ireland which she had first left at the age of eight. London was soon under bombardment; Ireland had promptly chosen to remain neutral. Its neutrality, coming under great diplomatic pressure after the fall of France in June 1940 and the intensification of the *blitz* in October, was the subject of Bowen's personal contribution to the war effort, her intelligence activities in Ireland in 1940–1. Here was material for further meditation on divided loyalties, the choice between continuity and safety, between immediate utility and a sense of origins. Yet these areas of innner conflict were to be augmented in the emotional and personal domain. Bowen had married Alan Cameron in 1923 but in 1941 she met a Canadian diplomat, Charles Ritchie, with whom she had a prolonged love-affair.

Throughout the period when *The Heat of the Day* was in ferment, the author was enmeshed in several overlapping webs of deceit and implicit treachery. Some of her acquaintances were engaged in espionage on behalf of a foreign power or at least had been approached as potential spies. Others were working in the British services; Harold Nicolson briefed Bowen on her 'activities' as she self-mockingly called them.[4] Even her lover was professionally involved, albeit on behalf of an allied state. Canadians, like the Irish, belonged to a very new state: in England they were at best 'insider-outsiders', linguistically integrated, emotionally and historically at odds. The congruence of international, local and even emotional crises was remarkable.

Her work in 1940–1 involved a return to Bowen's Court in Cork. Her commission was to test Irish opinion on the possibility of the British reclaiming the use of certain Irish ports, more broadly on questions of neutrality, and on attitudes at large towards the fascist enemy. Of these inquiries, that concerning the ports has captured the imagination of critics and commentators. But Bowen's cousin, Hubert Butler, helped her to seek out some Irish admirers of Mussolini so that she could gauge the extent of Irish sympathies with the Axis powers.[5] Through the illegal Irish Republican Army there were active links with Berlin; a Blue Shirt movement had volunteered to fight for Franco; and Mussolini's Italy naturally had admirers in a conservative and overwhelmingly Catholic society.

Nor did fascism solely attract adherents from the lumpen-majority: the Irish diplomat Charles Bewley was dismissed by De Valera early in 1939 because of his flamboyantly pro-fascist sympathies; Walter Starkey, a director of the Abbey Theatre, had been a founding member of a fascist think-tank in Paris; the novelist Francis Stuart took up a teaching post in Berlin right at the commencement of the war. All three were Catholics by birth (Starkey) or conversion (Bewley and Stuart), but they symbolised a cultural minority often thought of as Protestant in essence. King of the cats was Yeats himself, who had commended the radical right in Europe generally, and whose English friend Dorothy Wellesley intimated to him that she thought Hitler a better man than Mussolini.

The psychic condition Yeats found himself in at the beginning of 1937 deserves examination, for it constitutes part of the wider register of attitudes and obsessions which informed Bowen's world as novelist. Complaining to Wellesley in a letter answering her preference for the Führer, he wrote

You say I seem far away – I am far away from everybody & everything. Something happened to me in the darkness some weeks ago. It began with those damned forgeries – I have the old Fenian conscience – death & execution are in the day's work but not that. Everything seems exaggerated – I had not a symptom of illness yet I had to take to my bed. I kept repeating the sonnet of Shakespeare's about 'captain good' – I felt I was in an utter solitude. Perhaps I lost you then, for part of my sense of solitude was that I felt I would never know that supreme experience of life – that I think possible to the young – to share profound thought & then to touch. I have come out of that darkness a man you have never known – more man of genius, more gay, more miserable.[6]

The damned forgeries are the diaries of Roger Casement, used (but not forged) by the British authorities in 1916 to portray him as a homosexual and so discredit him in the eyes of all right-thinking Irish nationalists. Yeats is such a one; he has 'the old Fenian conscience' which accepts death and execution (murder, presumably, even if it is punished capitally). But not that. Whether 'that' is forgery or homosexuality is not quite clear, but the latter seems far more likely, despite Yeats's generous attitude to Wilde at the time of his public vilification. The ambiguity may, however, still have its point in that both forger and homosexual were/are conventionally thought to usurp or violate the place of a normative, original exchange. Concluding his letter, Yeats enclosed some draft poems. 'Ireland shall win her freedom & you still break stone' the 'Parnell' couplet ends in the letter to Wellesley. An accompanying lyric poem ends with the speaker asserting how his feet 'always beat upon the same small stone'. The sexual implications of citing the sonnets and of touching Wellesley (considered by some to have been lesbian) indicate a crisis of great profundity resulting both in a new personality ('a man you have never known') and in political poems emphasising changelessness. The stone's in the midst of all: fixity of character, evidently requiring assurance on questions of sexuality, is established through embracing a stone-like world. Here we witness in a literal sense Parnell the *persona* emerging from, also generating, that process of re-self-making.

The Heat of the Day, while it is blushingly modest compared to Yeats's correspondence, could be read in the same emotional context. Bowen's novel had a background of sexual irregularity (the Burgess/Bowra circle, as well as the author's heterosexual infidelity) but its eventual concentration on character largely excludes issues of 'gender-identity', opting instead for more thoroughly ontological questions. Nevertheless, concurrent imageries are to be traced in letter and novel. An underlying geological landscape of rocks and stones, extended through pulverised dust, baked asphalt paths and other arrid terrains, also informs the heroine's reflections on her love-affair.

Wellesley and Yeats in life, Stella Rodney and the house called Mount Morris in fiction – these act out the relationships, positions and ambiguities encoded in the very term 'Anglo-Irish'. Irish interest in fascism is relevant when certain objections to *The Heat of the Day* are considered. Rosamond Lehmann, for example, held that Robert Kelway ought to have been a Soviet, not a Nazi, spy. Yet if this might have fitted the immediate circumstances in which Bowen had lived and moved in the 1930s, it would have made no sense in relation to the other society which (literally) pre-occupies the novel – the society of Ireland. Had Bowen retreated permanently to the security and peace of Bowen's Court – just as MacNeice took off for America – her position would have made her (to some degree, however slight) complicit in that sympathy for fascism which she detected here and there in Ireland. Yet to remain in London, and then to *use* Bowen's Court for London purposes, was to be complicit against her birthplace and her ancestral home. (Thus Kelway's fascism is, amongst many other things, an Irish 'trace' in the novel.) In the now fashionable *argot*, Bowen was faced with 'an identity crisis' to add to all the other crises.

It is tempting to see Elizabeth Bowen in the character of Stella Rodney. But Hermione Lee is surely right in pointing rather to the 'disaffectedness' of the traitor Kelway as comparable to the author's own attitude towards English society. Nevertheless Kelway's work on behalf of the Nazis is never fully realised in the novel, whereas that of Harrison (who watches both Stella and her lover and pathetically hopes to replace the latter in her affections) is immediately comparable to Bowen's activities in Ireland. One interpretation of the biblical passage in the novel's title might operate on a political plane: those who qualify in some small degree qualify absolutely, whether their commitment is to treachery on behalf of a visionary future or to a resumed older loyalty. Bowen's attitude here is compatible with the emphasis placed by Thomas Mann on the *democratic* nature of German responsibility. His engagement was of course all the more striking for his own earlier disdain of politics and for his country's unspeakable brutality in suppressing every vestige of democracy through more than a decade of unparalleled slaughter.

Perhaps indeed, *The Heat of the Day* should be read outside the context of its English (and Irish) contemporaries. Starting with Mann's *Doktor Faustus*, or the New England tradition of Melville and Hawthorne as it descended to the 'conchie' Robert Lowell, one could assemble an alternative tradition to which Bowen's novel might more comfortably belong. Yet comfortable belonging is a feature this distinctly Protestant 'tradition' (merely hypothesised here) might on principle disavow, all the more so if Samuel Beckett's *Watt* or *Molloy* were to be considered for admission.

The allusion to Thomas Mann may serve to underline the extent to which the war, which forms the background to the doings of Stella Rodney and those who know her, was far from being exclusively a London matter. Raymond Williams has argued that the seemingly sequestered locations and actions of Jane Austen's novels are discernibly informed by the anti-revolutionary and anti-Napoleonic wars being waged by Britain at the time of their composition. In the distinctly more threatening situation of 1941, Bowen's fiction quite naturally admits more of the invasionary danger facing England. But even beyond these obvious references to the blackout and to air-raids, there may be in the act of entitling her novel of wartime London an allusion to the infinitely greater violence visited upon other populations.

On 15 April 1945, the British army liberated the concentration camp at Bergen–Belsen. There were in all some 55,000 survivors. Though it had not been the first camp to be liberated, Belsen was particularly well documented and illustrated in English newspapers and magazines. The *Illustrated London News* took the precaution of presenting photographs in a detachable four-page supplement, intended for adult readers only. In June, the British commanding officer decided on grounds of public health that the older part of the camp was to be burnt. In a speech delivered to the assembled troops and former prisoners, he concluded that the honour of igniting the first hut should be given to those who had 'borne the heat and burden of the day' (*sic*) during the liberation. It may seem that the phrase was oddly inadequate to the occasion, given what the onlooking former prisoners had borne and given the role of burning in the entire unspeakable catastrophe of the Nazi system. However that may have struck people at the time, the speech was incorporated into a book published in 1946, Derek Sington's *Belsen Uncovered*, almost three years before the publication of Bowen's novel of wartime loyalties and the transvaluation of all values. Does Bowen's title then bitterly comment on the relatively easy burden endured by British civilians; does it, therefore, cast a strong noontide shadow over Stella Rodney whose veritable curtain-line merely is 'I think I am going to be married'?[7]

Notes

1 See Hermione Lee *Elizabeth Bowen: an Estimation* London: Vision Press, 1981 p. 176. Also Elizabeth Bowen *Collected Impressions* London: Longmans, 1950 p. 68.
2 Lee p. 235.
3 Idem.
4 Victoria Glendinning *Elizabeth Bowen; Portrait of a Writer* London: Weidenfeld and Nicolson, 1977 p. 161.
5 Private information provided by Mr Butler in conversation on 12 April 1988 at his home in County Kilkenny.
6 See *Letters on Poetry from W. B. Yeats to Dorothy Wellesley* London: Oxford University Press, 1964 pp. 122–4. These letters were first published in 1940, when wartime readers' attitudes to Lady Wellesley's politics must have included some sense of outrage. Louis MacNeice's *The Poetry of W. B. Yeats* appeared the following year (1941) and Joseph Hone's biography early in 1943.
7 John Bridgman *The End of the Holocaust; the Liberation of the Camps* London: Batsford, 1990 pp. 56–7. Elizabeth Bowen *The Heat of the Day* London: Cape, 1949 p. 311.

16

Indefinite articles

Bowen's style has been the subject of frequent commentary, much of it reserved, even hostile. In part this results from the current disdain of Henry James's late novels as unfashionable. In part also, however, it stems from an unreasonable refusal to grant her something of the same licence granted to James Joyce whose manipulations of grammar, syntax, spelling and punctuation far exceed the gentilities of the Bowens and Jameses. Both James and Joyce incurred very minor debts to Sheridan Le Fanu, and Bowen's description of his style as 'nervous' recurs in her assessment of Mary Pakenham. At the risk of giving credence to notions of an unchanging Anglo-Irish identity, I would say that nervousness of style characterises Bowen's fiction also. Thematically, she may be further associated with Joyce through her obsession with betrayal. What Parnell individually was for Joyce, women are for Bowen – victims of systematic, callous betrayal. Yeats even managed to barter his emerging poem 'Parnell' in a fraught correspondence with Dorothy Wellesley. The world in which such systems operate requires a kind of vigilance in respect to language, a vigilance manifested in what some readers might regard as nervousness of style. In Bowen's novel of wartime, the point emerges from Robert Kelway's preposterous advocacy of 'the next thing', his uncanny euphemism for the fascist cause he has secretly assisted. To Stella's protests, he responds:

> If I said 'vision', inevitably you'd think me grandeur-mad: I'm not, but anyway vision is not what I mean. I mean sight in action: it's only now I act that I see. – What is repulsing you is the idea of 'betrayal', I suppose, isn't it? In you the hangover from the word? Don't you understand that all language is dead currency?[1]

Earlier, the impersonal narrative has established that, in the Kelway household (the monstrous country house with passages like swastika-arms), 'the dead language' is spoken: Kelway's declaration has, in effect, betrayed him. Betrayal and linguistic deadness cohabit, and certain repetitions in the novel indicate how far the rot has spread. It seemed to one character 'that Wisteria Lodge had weakened and faded inside the grip of the climbing plant' – perhaps because the act of naming has misspelt Wistaria. Yet Bowen is resolute in facing crises of betrayal and inadequate language, not merely stoical but positively heroic in the sacrificial response implicitly recommended. 'If thine eye offend thee, pluck it out' (Mark 9: 47).

More than any of Bowen's novels, *The Heat of the Day* has been subjected to severe censure as to the texture of writing, even by her admirers. Some lengthy quotation may be needed in order to demonstrate the complex effects she was engaged upon. Opacity features among the charges levelled, together with a wilful disordering of English sentence structure. It is necessary first to examine that 'opacity' itself, and to note how it is constructed from a myriad of extremely small details, like a wall built of a million outward projecting needles. For a novel dealing with potentially kinetic themes – war, treason, counter-surveillance – there is remarkably little action. Instead, much of the dialogue is concerned with the words which constitute dialogue; there are edgy repetitions, interrogations of a verb for aptness, an adjective for reliability. The vacuum caused by the absconding of action, or the abjuring of it by the author, is inundated with a language in which the least elements are likely to have greater weight than the ponderous ones.

When Kelway is obliged to announce or confess his real allegiance, Stella retorts 'you cannot say there is not a country'. This is less clear-cut than it seems. First, the courage to confront him had evidently come to her from her brief visit to Mount Morris, in Ireland. On the first occasion, he had lied and proposed marriage. Thus, when he finally initiates the confrontation, her response is distanced from the visit to Ireland but not emphatically located in here-and-now England. This is not to say that Stella was ghosting for her author, but the enveloping narrative remarks emphasise the complex synthesis which is 'country'. In addition, there is the obtrusive indefinite article preceding 'country', and that occurring not once but twice:

Instinctively she glanced first at the window, then at the window's reflection in the mirror: both were paler, it seemed to her eyes of dread. All fears shrank to this cold bare irrefutable moment: she shivered indifferently between the sheets. It had been terror of the alien, then, had it, all the time? – and here it was, breathing its expiring minutes, *his* expiring minutes, along the foot of her bed. He might have been right in saying she could not have loved him had there been in him no capacity other than love, but his denials of everything instinctive seemed now to seal up love at the source. Rolled round with rocks and stones and trees – what else is one? – was this not felt most strongly in the quietus of the embrace? 'No, but you cannot say there is not a country!' she cried aloud, starting up. She had trodden every inch of a country with him, not perhaps least when she was alone. Of that country, she did not know how much was place, how much was time. She thought of leaves of autumn crisply being swept up, that crystal ruined London morning when she had woken to his face; she saw street after street fading in evening after evening, the sheen of spring light running on the water towards bridges on which one stood, the vulnerable eyes of Louie stupidly carrying sky about in them, the raw earth lip of Cousin Francis's grave and the pink-stamened flowers of that day alight on the chestnuts in May gloom, the asphalt pathway near Roderick's camp thrust up and cracked by the swell of ground, mapped by seeded grass. She could remember nothing before everything had had this poign-ancy...[2]

The most unexpected detail of this is the quotation from Wordsworth's Lucy poems, 'rolled round with rocks ...'. Conven-tionally, these brief enigmatic pieces are read in connection with the poet's ilicit affair with Annette Vallon, a young French woman whom he met in the early years of the Revolution, that unavoidable, politicising cause-above-all-causes he had once espoused and later opposed. 'Lucy' is at once dead and perennially alive; the poems write her off even as they immortalise her. The relevance of the allusion can now hardly be missed in this fiction of sexual and political betrayal, even as the novel moves to insist that no single 'cause' can be identified for adoption. Robert's presence even when Stella had been alone mimes the element of time which contributes to 'country': each is potentially a delusion, and is actual delusion when Robert turns out to have deceived her. Yet the element of time, or a country's history, is not necessarily scuttled in the same revelation. For Stella has been considering a country, not the par-ticularised country of England or Ireland.

Indefinite articles

The very first word 'instinctively' had possessed logic, for the act had been to look at the window in response to the phrase 'beginning of a day'. The everything instinctive which Robert had denied is somehow diminished by this prior citation of the adverb 'instinctively', yet if the passage is to have positive force then the value of what had been denied must be demonstrated. The narrative enfolds elements of free indirect style which then fall back to permit Stella's direct utterance, after which a broader, less personally anchored movement takes over. The drastic shift is best exemplified in the clause which begins 'she saw' and nearly ends with 'light running ... towards the bridges on which one stood'; an interior vision of these places is overlaid with a previous sighting achieved from the point towards which 'she' now looks. Between those prepositions (from and towards) a new tension springs into being, replacing or at least obscuring noun, pronoun or what is conventionally thought to exist behind these. In keeping with this, 'she' has become 'one'. By the same token, the reflexivity of the opening sentences (window, window's reflection ... its expiring minutes, *his* expiring minutes) gives way to mere repetition connoting dulled attention (street after street ... evening after evening) even as the poignancy of this now realised as *having had been poignant* registers.

A frequent word in Bowen's writing of this period is 'nature'. Consider for example 'The Happy Autumn Fields', the story which achieves the same ineffable balance between those grossnesses known as England and Ireland as *The Heat of the Day* achieves in the longer form. A woman lingering in a bomb-damaged house asks, 'How are we to live without natures? We only know inconvenience now, not sorrow.' The long paragraph just quoted from the novel concludes with a related thought:

> Inside the ring of war, how peaceably little they had moved – never crossed the sea together, seldom left London – so, there had come to be the nature of Nature, thousands of fluctuations, in their own stone country. Impossible that the population, the other people, should at least be less to be honoured than trees walking.[3]

I confess this to be exceedingly difficult to comprehend – that 'peaceably little' is only the beginning. The first of the two sentences may suggest the augmenting richness of a relationship which had provided an ideal nature in the absence of that accessible in the countryside or at sea or abroad, nature raised to the power two, as it

were. But that sentence concludes by a transition from such pleni-
tude through 'thousands of fluctuations' (connoting movement,
energy, potentiality …?) into a 'stone country' which is the lovers'
own. The stone recalls Wordsworth and the paradox of the Lucy
poems:

> A slumber did my spirit seal;
> I had no human fears:
> She seemed a thing that could not feel
> The touch of earthly years.
>
> No motion has she now, no force;
> She neither hears nor sees;
> Rolled round in earth's diurnal course,
> With rocks, and stones, and trees.

Consideration of the poem in its entirety surely persuades us that
the 'trees walking' of the paragraph's conclusion are not just a
hallucinatory effect of intense feeling, whether of love or resulting
from the war. There is reason to believe that Bowen also had in
mind the story (Mark 8: 24) of the blind man cured by Christ: 'I see
men as trees, walking.' That Stella is, like the biblical figure, in the
process of recovering a faculty – in her case, of seeing Robert for
what he actually is, a traitor – remains undoubtedly true and apt.
Just as Lucy 'no motion has' yet is 'rolled round', so Stella recovers
her sight and cannot recognise what she had formerly seen. However, the remote presence of St Mark adds a further dimension to
this complex transaction, for he curiously records that Christ bid his
patient farewell with the word 'Neither go into the town, nor tell it
to any in the town'. This injunction too may have its part in the deep
structure of Bowen's compositional method, a method amounting
to a tacit belief in the value of suppressed or concealed merit, the
abjuring of a talent or faculty. But the Wordsworthian layer of
allusion is more likely to strike the average cultivated reader of the
day.

In keeping with the larger emotional *oeconomy* implicit in the
poem, according to which a dimunition of one or more of the senses
('neither hears nor sees') is counteracted by a paradoxical augmentation of energy, these walking trees are a violently re-formed image
of the central paradox. Wordsworth has illuminated the paragraph,
even if it still resists adequate comprehension. In terms of fictional
technique and structure, what is implicit is a character's realisation

(making real) of character's necessary cycle of resolution and dissolution. But the implication of recovery discernible in the paradox of
character is hardly encouraged in Bowen's writing, hardly moved
towards explication. The grammar, syntax and lexical iteration of
'impossible that the population ... should at least be less to be
honoured' frustrate what sense the phrase might convey, so that
'impossible' becomes wholly rhetorical. Lessness is precisely what is
possible, inevitable, necessary.

A sentence in *The Heat of the Day*, to which even her publisher's
reader objected, reads

'Absolutely,' he said with fervour, 'not.'[4]

Certainly the novel displays a range of syntactical dislocations unparalleled in her earlier work, though short stories of the same
period provide similar evidence of a general stylistic upheaval. Part
of this procedure conveys an oscillatory effect between speakers of
the dialogue:

Reaching up for the cups she said: 'Are you really dry?'
'I am drying off.'
'You are looking more like yourself.'
'More like myself, am I looking?' asked Roderick, with interest and
curiosity.[5]

Between Stella and her son, this may pass for warmth and intimacy in dialogue, but it soon invades the impersonal narrative
about them — 'he had to regret his mother's regretting the Army for
him.'[6] Yet the treacheries of language concern young Roderick also,
who can see the differences which even little bits of punctuation can
make:

His eyes ran down the typescript till they stopped at a line – 'look, this is
where I want to know what you think. When he's said about how he
bequeates Mount Morris, the lands, the etcetera, etcetera, to his cousin
Roderick Vernon Rodney, me, he goes on, *"In the hope that he may care in
his own way to carry on the old tradition."* – Why must lawyers always take
out commas?'
'Because what they write is meant to be clear without them.'
'Well, in this case it isn't. Which did Cousin Francis mean?'
Which what, darling?'
Did he mean, care in my own way, or, carry on the old tradition in
my own way?'
Uncomprehending, Stella returned her eyes to the cropped top of

Roderick's downbent head. 'In the end, I suppose,' she hazarded, 'it would come to the same thing.'[7]

Instability of language, sameness of meaning ... these haunt the pages of the novel more appallingly than any ghost. One word can link across time and space with the effect of abolishing them: when Stella is leaving for Ireland, she tells Robert that she had been there 'just about this time' of year 'twenty-one years ago'. Their final exchange and the next paragraph dealing with Mount Morris enact one such link:

'What a lot of water,' said Robert vaguely, 'has flowed under the bridges since then, or hasn't it? Floods enough to have washed most bridges away.'

There was no bridge for a mile up or down the river from Mount Morris ...[8]

But pervasively the highly distinctive language of *The Heat of the Day* is required to convey a quality of absence or negativity special to the novel and its theme: 'Not knowing who the dead were you could not know which might be the staircase somebody for the first time was not mounting that morning.'[9]

In this, the conventional ghost-story attention to footsteps on the staircase is inverted and intensified; the legacy of Sheridan Le Fanu is adapted to the spiritual conditions of systematic bereavement and impersonalised killing. The horror of the *blitz* was the absence of weapons: people fell down dead, killed either by explosions of air or by the components of their dwellings, just as in the ghost story some repression obliterates or temporarily conceals motive or opportunity. In *The Heat of the Day*, character is not immune to these pressures and evacuations. To keep in touch a sentence, together with and sometimes against the words which make it up, may have to turn round itself:

The block she lived in teetered its height up into the dangerous night. Inside, no porter was in the lodge: Harrison for himself set in motion the gothic lift. The halt of the hum and the rattle of gates on her floor gave her time to wonder before her bell rang: when it did, she came to the door, though promptly, with the air of one who had already decided this must be a mistake.[10]

The contrariness of anything teetering its height, the now familiar negative presence of 'no porter was in the lodge', the equation of sound (rattle of the gates) and non-sound (the halt of the hum), scarcely prepare the reader for 'Harrison for himself set in motion the gothic lift.'

If one were to hazard a normative rewriting of this, the result might look like 'Harrison set the gothic lift in motion for himself'. Gothic still looks unexplained as if the adjective qualified not just a mechanical contraption but, surreptitiously, style itself. 'Harrison for himself' comes close to inscribing one of those 'curiously self-made creatures' whom we contrast with the creatures of history the novel is concerned with. Yet 'Harrison for himself' as a notion is challenged, even stealthily assassinated elsewhere in the narrative. The occasion follows almost immediately after the Wordsworthian reprise, and here again lengthy quotation is advisable:

> The war-warmed impulse of people to be *a* people had been derisory; he had hated the bloodstream of the crowds, the curious animal psychic oneness, the human lava-flow. Even the leaden unenthusiasm, by its being so common, so deeply shared, had provoked him – and as for the impatiences, the hopes, the reiteration of unanswerable questions and the spurts of rumour, he must have been measuring them with a calculating eye. The half-sentence of the announcer's voice coming out of a window at News hour, the flopping rippling headlines of Late News Final at the newsvendor's corner – what nerve, what nerve in reverse, had they struck on in him? Knowing what he knew, doing what he did. Idly, more idly than all the others doing the same thing, in the streets with her he had thieved the headline out of the corner of his eye, without a break in their talk, with a hiatus in his long pitching step so slight as to be registered by her only through their being arm-in-arm in the falling evening. She now saw his smile as the smile of one who has the laugh.
>
> It seemed to her it was Robert who had been the Harrison.[11]

There is much to be said here, not least in associating the novel with George Orwell's *Nineteen-Eighty-Four*, that other disenchanted product of wartime austerity. The passage begins with close attention to the notion that, under the *blitz*, Londoners came together in an amalgamating way, people wishing to be a people in some tribal and bond-reinforcing way. The indefinite article attempts to inscribe this wish, but visibly relies on italic emphasis. Other images for the condition either reflect the earlier Wordsworthian allusion to earth's dense maintenance of the dead ('the human lava-flow') or repeat a feature of Stella and Robert's earlier union ('animal psychic oneness'). Yet central to all of this is the emphasis on Robert's unresting deployment of his power to see – an ability to thieve out of the corner of 'his calculating eye'. Foresight has translated nightfall into 'the falling evening', for Robert will shortly pitch from the roof of Stella's flat, and thus have (perhaps) that last laugh which others saw merely as a smile. Then, finally, it seemed to Stella 'it was Robert who had been the Harrison'.

The definite article here prevents an unabashed statement of identity. Yet what is 'the Harrison'? One interpretation would suggest that Stella is thinking of Harrison *as a type*, and indeed the appointment in February 1942 of a Nazi puppet-premier in Norway gave the English language just such a word. Yet while one might think of Robert as a Quisling, the part of speech employed in the sentence is the definite article. The difference is this – while Robert might be a Quisling or a Harrison (among all too many Quislings and Harrisons), Bowen's sentence goes further and strongly suggests that 'the Harrison' is unique, that by establishing Robert as the Harrison it would dissolve the possibility of any other person (Harrison) being the Harrison. It goes so far, but no further. The sentence retains an air of speculation, of rhetorical experiment. When Robert Kelway proposes to Stella, he has need to refer to 'what's-his-name': '"'What's-his-name'?" she said edgily. "You mean Harrison? It is an easy name to remember."'[12]

Everywhere in *The Heat of the Day* there is an ostentatious yet seemingly unproductive concern with names. This is neither a matter of psychologically revealing name-pairings (like Jaggers and Wemmick, Pip and Pumblechook, and Joe Orlick in Charles Dickens's great novel) nor of systematically deployed name-series deriving from literature (as in Le Fanu) or the Bible (as in Francis Stuart). Cousin Nettie is distressed to think that she may have called Roderick by his father's name. Louie and her friend Connie nearly quarrel over the unnamed father-to-be of Louie's child – '*Which* name wouldn't mean anything to me?'[13] These trivial and isolated details converge through their sharing a specific concern with the propriety of aligning names and fathers correctly.

Two scenes of recognition – or as close to recognition as the hidden mirrors of the novel admit – complicate these interlocking features of formal nomination, a dextrous use of grammar and the sense of the self-created self observed earlier. After Harrison's long conversation with Stella in the teetering block of flats, with Robert Kelway's falling to his death from the roof of her former flat as its principal topic, she calls him directly by his surname:

> 'That's the first time you've called me anything, I think.'
> 'I don't know your other, your Christian name.'
> 'I don't know that you'd care for that very much,' he said, shoulder-
> ing into the curtain behind the table.
> 'Why, what's wrong with it? – what is it?'
> 'Robert.'
> 'Oh, I see ... Well, I expect in any case I should have gone on thinking
> of you as Harrison.'[14]

This near-convergence of Robert Kelway and Robert Harrison, the traitor and the surveillance man, hunted and hunter, had been oddly reflected some pages earlier when Louie had read of Stella's evidence at the inquest on her former lover – 'for a moment she wondered whether it might not be Harrison who had fallen, under another name.'[15] The insidious symmetry of Stella's relationships with these two men undermines the reader's full confidence in their twoness, their separate identities. The language repeatedly jeopard-ises such confidence. To 'have fallen ... under another name' is to have found a separate and independent existence somehow fatal; of course, Louie only wonders this for a moment and may not even know Harrison's name which is supplied through the impersonal narrative. Here indeed is a case where the lawyers' attitude to commas is very particularly rebutted.

But Louie Lewis's own name echoes with a sinister lack of vari-ety, Christian- and sur-name being virtually the singlar and plural versions of the same sound. The first syllables of Christian- and sur-names of Roderick Rodney threaten a similar pattern. Robert, unal-tered but suppressed in one instance for most of the novel, serves both Kelway and Harrison, Finally remote Mount Morris reveals the alliterative echo to be pervasive. Indeed, at the conclusion of the chapter taking Stella to Ireland, we find 'that Mount Morris mirage' as if to extend the feature. As late as 1973 Rayner Heppenstall, who first came in contact with Bowen in 1939, recalled her bad stammer; the double initials of character- and place-name in the fiction might be even read as an involuntary inscribing of the author's own invol-untary speech.

Bowen's casual descriptions and metaphors in the fiction contrib-ute to the pattern. When 'a zip fastener all the way down one back made one woman seem to have a tin spine', there is one one too many for easy reading. Easy reading is not intended. Other repetitions are distinctly sinister: in a car outside Euston Station Ernestine Kelway is 'bundling around invisibly inside there like a ferret',[16] and later the grill-bar to which Harrison takes Stella is without shadows – 'every one had been ferretted out and killed.'[17] As with 'fallen, under another name', the avoidance of 'every shadow' allows the numerical pronoun to acquire a human implication (to become 'everyone'), as if to counter or complement reification in the tin spine further up the same paragraph.

Bowen's wartime London is a systematic *oeconomy* of interchanging times and places, the dead and the living, persons and things, persons and names. Her treatment of time in structuring the novel, together with many enigmatic utterances of the characters on the same topic, cannot be considered in any depth here, save to say that a suddenly admitted debt to the romanticism of Wordsworth and Blake deserves attention. On the question of character and its relation to the object, the affinity is Dickensian though with implications far more urgent than these nineteenth-century perspectives might suggest. What is conventionally thought to be discrete, multiple, separate veers towards a conglomerate identity; yet the individual also is subject to a species of disintegrating augmentation.

Stella, appalled by the danger to which Robert has exposed himself in coming to confess in her flat, suffers 'infestation by all ideas of delinquency'; moreover, she fears that their breach of the black-out regulations 'could be the signal moment for which Harrison had been waiting – posted as he could be, as she pictured him, by some multiplication of his personality all round the house.[18]

Following so quickly on the 'thousands of fluctuations' which she and Robert had experienced in that 'nature of Nature' to which they as lovers had access in avoiding the countryside, Harrison's multiplied personality goes some way towards confirming an identification of the two characters. Moreover, 'all round the house' officially denotes points externally surrounding the house while it also hints at an interior and more intimate 'infestation' within the house. Above all, Harrison longs simply to be 'around the house'. A modest interpretation of this emotional would-be dependence would see it as the obverse of Kelway's arrogant appropriation to himself of Stella's self. This would be in keeping with the familiar notion that hunter and hunted are intimately related, bound to each other, inconceivable apart. Such a fundamentally psychological interpretation does not, however, do justice to the formal complexity of *The*

Heat of the Day, nor to the radical evidence of character revealed as indeterminate in its supposed relation to discrete, separate, named human individuals. It is as if nouns and pronouns no longer dominate the grammar. Bowen's too is a prepositional world, its revelation made possible by the war over London, but its reality by no means limited to that period and place.

Reviewing Lady Mary Pakenham's autobiography, Bowen quotes a passage to the effect that the author 'was born knowing the difference between the Protestant Church and the Church of Rome', and glosses this with the remark that 'from living, or spending much time in Ireland, one learns that everything matters but nothing matters much', an observation uncannily close to T. W. Adorno's *Immer davon reden, nie daran denken*, an inversion of the pro-Anschluss slogan in 1930s Austria ('Never speak of it, always think of it'.) This instance of original sin – the knowledge possessed at birth – is a rare direct reference to matters of credal belief, on which Bowen is generally reticent. Yet Pakenham is applauded for her ironic immunity acquired 'no doubt from being Anglo-Irish, or having been Anglo-Irish at one period'. [19]

The notion of a temporary identity – and this without any ambiguous suggestion of apostasy or opportunism – fits uneasily into the assertive, stolid debates of the 1990s. Even among the litmus-paper-thin classifications of the 1930s it looks dangerously variable, even protean, though the correspondence of Edmund Burke could throw up passages where 'English' and 'Irish' are not mutually exclusive categories. What Bowen projects through her review of Pakenham's book is perhaps a desire for a renewal of, or a renewed access to, an eighteenth-century subtlety of mind such as Burke's. In one respect like Robert Kelway in *The Heat of the Day*, who was born wounded, Pakenham was born into the original sin of a political knowledge. Yet differentiating herself from the kind of ideological determination which was his and which demands singularity and permanence, she succeeded (at least in Bowen's view) in modifying an identity (Anglo-Irish) which happily lacked identicality with itself. In the light of this escape from the iron categories of race, nationality or determined function, we should read Bowen's specifically literary judgement of the autobiography – 'nothing is more telling than to under-write one's experiences.'

On the surface Pakenham appears to have 'automatically shut off [her] brain whenever politics turned up in the conversation'. Yet the admiring reviewer declares 'this book does so much to expose the débutante racket that one wonders why it has not been burned by the social columnist'. Undoubtedly Bowen's disenchantment with '1930s England' could take the form of blunt political preferences: reviewing A. S. J. Tessimond's admirably anti-capitalist drama she recommended it to readers of *Night and Day*[20] Whatever about Soviet conditions as reflected in these plays, debs and their dances were lesser concerns than the Irish Question. All of these, however, were subordinate to the issues underlying *The Heat of the Day* – these are unquestionably the war, and the questionable Self.

If Bowen's novel of 1949 is, in a phrase used by Dorothy Van Ghent in another connection, a 'thoroughly nervous world' then it jeopardises that show of unity which presented Louie Lewis as the lower-class counterpart of Stella Rodney. The superficial parallelism of Louie/Stella is lightly laid down upon a far more fractured and fracturing treatment of character, and can be put aside without difficulty. The resulting exposure is not simply a matter of fictional technique in relation to the novelist's reliable and well-attested material, character. The Self, as we have seen, is manifested to Bowen through the senses, through experience. But accounts of sensible deprivation also occur in the fiction. The wartime belief, or official demand, that social difference was dissolved under the common enemy's fire is one victim of Bowen's dialectical treatment of character, her double presentation of Kelway and Harrison as two and one. Her disaffection prevented her full incorporation of that myth of comradeship, yet it also stoked her determination to examine country and history as equally complex and unassimilable constructs, bit players only in the general failure of contemporary civilisation. This latter complaint can be instanced directly from her personal declarations, or more indirectly through the words of fictional characters to whom she was palpably sympathetic. What evidently cannot be located in contemporary civilisation is 'representative meaning', a responsiveness in one's circumstances to notions of value or significance.

Notes

1 Elizabeth Bowen *The Heat of the Day* London: Cape, 1949 p. 259.
2 Ibid. p. 265. For the reference to Wisteria Lodge, see ibid. p. 210 where an account of the graveyard in which Cousin Francis is buried veers into unacknowledged and not wholly accurate quotation of Keats's 'La Belle Dame sans

Merci' ('no bird sang' / 'no birds sing'). The issue of Bowen's recourse in this novel to poetry of the romantic period is touched on in particular relation to Wordsworth (see pp. 220 etc.) but deserves closer attention as evidence of allusion *and* divergence.

3 Ibid. p. 266.

4 Ibid. p. 213. See Hermione Lee *Elizabeth Bowen: an Estimation* London: Vision Press, 1981 p. 165.

5 *The Heat of the Day* p. 44.

6 Ibid. p. 47.

7 Ibid. p. 83.

8 Ibid. p. 155.

9 Ibid. pp. 86—7.

10 Ibid. p. 305.

11 Ibid. p. 266.

12 Ibid. p. 190.

13 Ibid. p. 314.

14 Ibid. p. 310.

15 Ibid. p. 265.

16 Ibid. p. 175.

17 Ibid. p. 217.

18 Ibid. p. 267.

19 For 'Blind Alleys' see Elizabeth Bowen *Collected Impressions* London: Longmans, 1950 pp. 106–7.

20 Norman Sherry *The Life of Graham Greene; Volume One 1904–1939* Harmondsworth: Penguin, 1990 p. 617.

17

'The neutral island in the heart of man'

In her 1939 preface to Rayner Heppenstall's now-forgotten novel about an oddly disabled masseur, she took the opportunity to commence with the announcement that '*The Blaze of Noon* is a story told in the first person by a man in whom one sense is suppressed: the "I" is a blind man.'[1] Beyond the initial word-play, the point is sustained – 'There is an absence of that *anxiety* directed upon the self, that sense of inexplicable inner disablement, of inefficacy for life that the "normal" – or five-sense – person feels, and for which he cannot account, and which ravages him *because* he cannot account for it.'[2] This should be brought into contact with another observation, already quoted, to the effect that 'complex people are never certain … that their passports are quite in order, and are, therefore, unnerved by the slightest thing'. To be complex, it is implied, is to be at some loss – unnerved, undocumented, lacking a sense. In writing of Heppenstall's hero, Bowen had oddly chosen to stress that his sense of sight had been 'suppressed', as if this might even have been a voluntary condition. That she read *The Blaze of Noon* carefully cannot be doubted. The author testified to her perceptiveness in a foreword to a second edition of his novel, and two additional factors link his work to hers. His title derives from Milton's *Samson Agonistes* who, blinded by the Philistines, is forced to labour in the blaze of noon: her vestigial allusion to the biblical account of the once blind man who sees 'men as trees, walking' had been explicit as an epigraph in Heppenstall's novel. Such contrasting references to sensory deprivation even penetrate Bowen's 1938 review of Pakenham's autobiography headed 'Blind Alleys': a key sentence reads, 'Much of the spleen that goes to make us so touchy and treacherous no doubt arises from the suppression of violence.'[3]

If *The Heat of the Day* is the major achievement of Elizabeth

'The neutral island in the heart of man'

Bowen's career during the war years and immediately after (1939–49), there is a substantial body of other work, both fiction and non-fiction, with an investigation of the intimate past occupying a prominent position in the latter category. In addition to the sustained writing of short stories, Bowen compiled and published the extensive, detailed and intelligently original family history to which she gave the name of her County Cork home, *Bowen's Court*. Introducing an American edition of her wartime stories, Bowen virtually appropriates a Le Fanuesque obsession with inherited guilt:

> The past, in all these cases, discharges its load of feeling into the anaesthetized and bewildered present. It is the 'I' that is sought – and retrieved at the cost of no little pain. And the ghosts ... what part do they play? They are the certainties. The bodiless foolish wanton, the puritan other presence, the tipsy cook with her religion of English fare, the ruthless young soldier lover unheard of since 1916: hostile or not, they rally, they fill the vacuum for the uncertain 'I'.[4]

What is not clear in this exposition is the nature or even status of the relationship between eruptions of the past and the uncertainty of the ego in her fiction. As always, grammar has much to tell the reader: the intransitive (or reflexive) verb 'to rally [?themselves]' has the appearance of governing a noun, 'vacuum', in the accusative case. If this were more than appearance, then the verbs to rally and to fill would be (so to speak) in apposition. As even ghosts cannot rally a vacuum, the phrase lacks any such unitary implication. Rally remains objectless, and the divergence between the plural 'they' and the singular, uncertain 'I' is increased, unfilled.

The story 'Summer Night' presents the problem in a distinctive way. It opens with a meticulous and loving account of an Irish rural landscape, through which Emma is driving at speed. She is embarked on an adulterous errand, however, and the apprehension of nature is gradually withdrawn from her vicinity within the narrative, noticeably after the reader learns that she has deceived her husband (a retired major, and so likely a First Wold War veteran) even as to her destination. She is expected in the house of one Robinson who is reluctantly entertaining unexpected guests. When one of these, Justin Cavey, declares loudly that 'there's been a stop in our senses and in our faculties that's made everything round us so much dead matter', we recognise the opinion as a familiar Bowen one. We recognise also that there is something excessive about it, revealed in the mode of its presentation.

Justin is a 'neutral Irishman' in whose heart 'indirect suffering pulled like a crooked knife'.[5] His sister, equally Irish in contemporary terms, is deaf. This deprivation ultimately leads her to experience an almost mysterical renewal of an old passion, at the hands (literally, for he guides her by the elbow as if she were blind, not deaf) of the stranger, Robinson, whom others discover to be shallow, loud and boorish. The particular victim of this boor is Emma who, having paused to phone her lover, overhears an Irish country-town hotel conversation about a wartime headline – '"What it says here," he said, shaking the paper with both hands, "is identically what I've been telling you."'[6]

The adverb is not just another of Bowen's foregrounded eccentricities of style. Justin, whose blend of neutrality and indirect suffering places him close to his author, can also sound at times uncannily like the traitor Kelway:

> 'I'm torn, here, by every single pang of annihilation. But that's what I look for; that's what I want completed; that's the whole of what I want to embrace. On the far side of the nothing – my new form. Scrap "me"; scrap my wretched identity and you'll bring to the open some bud of life. I not "I" – I'd be the world ... I might even love.[7]

Justin's nihilism is ensnared with a hyperaesthetic sensibility attuned to pangs, embraces, love, even though he suddenly breaks off to ask the boorish Robinson 'What's love like?' These exclamations uncannily echo the Yeats–Wellesley correspondence of January 1937, published in 1940 and thus (technically, at least) available to Bowen before the publication of 'Summer Night'. It would be vulgar to suggest that Bowen peeked, yet folly to ignore the coincidence of feeling in the two exchanges. Yeats is to have a 'new form' – Justin's phrase – with anxiety about Casement's sexuality evidently assuaged in the success of 'Parnell'. In turn, Justin's formulation rewrites, in apocalyptic terms, the crampt limitations of his political situation. Unable, or rather unwilling, to travel outside Ireland because of the war, he is a neutral who suffers on a crooked knife. His sister, whose apotheosis at the end of the story is otherwise a datum of her own or her author's sentimentality, is redeemed by a doubleness of perspective which recalls Stella Rodney's visionary look towards the bridge from which she looks. Near the close of the short story, deaf Queenie

> saw with joy in her own mind what she could not from her place in the

window see – the blue china house, with all its reflecting windows, perched on its knoll in the brilliant, fading air. They are too rare – visions of where we are.[8]

This little smack of Wordsworthian sententiousness on Queenie's behalf is balanced in the treatment of another female character, Emma's aged Aunt Fran, who suspects that sexual betrayal is at work in their household and who generally has given up on the modern world: 'All the more, her nature clung to these objects that moved with her slowly towards the dark.'[9] The preference for an earlier mode of living, even for a future definable exclusively in terms of darkness, silence and death, releases her into a present tense:

> The blood of the world is poisoned, feels Aunt Fran, with her forehead over the eiderdown. Not a pure drop comes out at any prick – yes, even the heroes shed black blood. The solitary watcher retreats step by step from his post – who shall stem the black tide coming in? There are no more children: the children are born knowing. The shadow rises up the cathedral tower, up the side of the pure hill. There is not even the past: our memories share with us the infected zone; not a memory does not lead up to this. Each moment is everywhere, it holds the war in its crystal; there is no elsewhere, no other place. Not a benediction falls on this apart house of the Major; the enemy is within it, creeping about. Each heart here falls to the enemy.[10]

The military terminology reflects a larger world than that of the major's household. Born knowing, the children of Aunt Fran's acquaintance replicate the condition attributed to Lady Mary Pakenham, that belle of the Anglo-Irish ball. Yet, writing in the *New Statesman* in 1941, Bowen went to great lengths to clarify, even perhaps justify, the independent Irish position in relation to belligerence and neutrality, to the bombing of English cities, and to the war generally. Neutrality did not find expression solely in Justin; there was an elsewhere, and she was prepared to emphasise the separateness of the Irish state by repeatedly referring to it by its official Gaelic title, Eire. On at least thirty occasions in the article, she repeated the distinctive bit of non-English nomenclature, as if it somehow enacted within her English-language narrative an integrity of its own. The Irish government's declaration of neutrality was

> Eire's first major independent act. As such it had, and keeps, a symbolic as well as moral significance – a significance that identifies, for the

people, Eire's neutrality with her integrity. Eire feels as strongly, one might say as religiously, about her neutrality as Britain feels about her part in the war. She has invested in it her natural consciousness. [11]

Virtually all the touchstone Bowen terms are employed here, together with the revealing description of wartime attitudes as religious. *The Heat of the Day* might now be seen as a religious work, even though its setting will have to be identified as the Garden of Gethsemane, its theme doubt, and its god decisively absent. The disaffection of the author, generally and as author of that particular fiction, is of a scale consistent with such a *via negativa*. Bowen's disaffection with 1930s England is a statement, necessarily and essentially negative, of her relation towards Ireland. Yet no positive assertion of an Irish identity is possible or desirable, for such a declaration would lack complexity of even the most elementary kind. Internally, in relation to the fiction, her attitude can be compared to the Nietzschean *ressentiment* of Robert Kelway. But in relation to Irish literary history, it stands in contrast to the politics of W. B. Yeats.

An unofficial, largely unconscious dialogue was conducted between Irish writers during the period revolving round the Second World War. For example, a sentence in *The Heat of the Day* reads like a direct riposte to Louis MacNeice. Of the lovers Stella and Robert Bowen had written, 'Their time sat in the third place at their table.'[12] MacNeice's celebrated poem 'Meeting Point' (written in April 1939 and collected in 1941, the year of Bowen's meeting Charles Ritchie and of her intelligence activities in Ireland) had opened 'Time was away and somewhere else' and preceeded to focus on a lovers' tryst. MacNeice's view of Ireland has been the subject of recent oversimplications, with Edna Longley writing curiously about independent Ireland's attitudes 'of the round tower standing aloof, of navel-gazing into the past at the expense of the present'. [13] These (om)phallic confusions do not wholly obscure MacNeice's irritation with Irish neutrality and isolationism, as indicated in the poem of his which supplies the present chapter with its title. Against such positions, Bowen replies with a subtle defence of the new state's politics while also working positively on behalf of the former colonial power. Neutrality, for her, involves issues larger than an alliance against fascism. It functions as a metaphor or projection of certain areas of personality; though Justin Cavey may resemble Robert Kelway, he is disqualified from self-destructive action. Emotional impotence, or immobility, has its advantages. His sister, however, is disqualified in a more benign sense and thus has renewed access to a world of love.

Hermione Lee has noted that Portia in *The Death of the Heart* (1938) reads *Great Expectations*, and that Bowen was fond of invoking Dickens in her later work: *Eva Trout* includes an important scene set in the house at Broadstairs where *Bleak House* was written. Yet the nominal connection between *The Heat of the Day* and *Great Expectations* – each has a [E]Stella who suffers from rival lovers – is of more importance than the simple registering of a great literary influence and debt. Dorothy van Ghent provides an account of *Great Expectations* which may yet prove valuable in classifying Bowen's wartime work more precisely. Central to van Ghent's analysis of Dickens's novel is her appreciation of literary montage as a technique intimately related to the processes of dreaming. But, she continues,

> This device, of doubling one image over another, is paralleled in the handling of character. In the sense that one implies the other, the glittering frosty girl Estella, and the decayed and false old woman [Miss Havisham] are not two characters but a single one, or a single essence with dual aspects, as if composed by montage – a spiritual continuum so to speak … The relationship between Joe Gargery, saintly simpleton of the folk, and Orlick, dark beast of the Teutonic marshes ('who comes from the ooze'), has a somewhat different dynamics, thorugh they too form a spiritual continuum. Joe and Orlick are related not as two aspects of a single moral identity, but as the opposed extremes of spiritual possibility – the one unqualified love, the other unqualified hate – and they form a frame within which the actions of the others have their ultimate meaning. [14]

While we note Estella, it is perhaps the treatment of Joe and Orlick which is most applicable to *The Heat of the Day*, not only because Harrison and Kelway are polar opposites in terms of both politics and sexual engagement, but because 'they form a frame within which the actions of the others have their ultimate meaning'. This is not to say that Harrison is a saint – say, of the common or garden anti-fascist variety. On the contrary, his dealings with Louie Lewis show him to be a callous if familiar monomaniac. Neither is Kelway the extremity of evil, for in some senses his mother and sister are the banality of that evil which he articulates in a more rarefied vocabulary – and banality, as Hannah Arendt memorably observed, is evil's trademark. No, van Ghent's account of Dickens's characters helps to show exactly how the actions of Bowen's other characters are thoroughly shaped – and it is shaped rather than framed – by the 'spiritual continuum' which is Harrison/Kelway. In the world of 1941, there are no saints, and evil cannot be limited to the doings even of a traitor.

If the corridors of Kellways' Holme Dene expand like a swastika, it is because such angularity is a violent reaction to the pathetic efforts of place-name elements now wholly sentimental (holm and dene) to make up a place. Yet Robert has been mounded by the same corridors in so far as they are an inheritance from a father declared inadequate. The less dramatic inability of Cousin Nettie to fit in to the landscape of Mount Norris (her husband's home in Ireland) led to a very mild derangement, yet the explanation she can offer sheds light on the grim English crucible of Kellway's fascism: 'Nature hated us; that was a most dangerous position to build a house in – once the fields noticed me with him, the harvests began failing; so I took to going nowhere but up and down stairs, till I met my own ghost.'[15]

At this point we should recall Bowen's classification of Sheridan Le Fanu's best known novel in her introduction to a post-war edition – '*Uncle Silas* is a romance of terror.' It is not the terror which links his novel to hers, for there is remarkably little action or feeling of that kind in *The Heat of the Day*. But the genre of fictional romance, long associated with disreputable areas such as the picaresque and the gothic and more recently rehabilitated to accommodate fiction by nineteenth-century American authors, might be shown to have claims on *Great Expectations* and *The Heat of the Day*.

In further describing *Uncle Silas*, she calls it 'sexless' and points to its 'sublimated infantilism'. Unfortunately she neglects to develop the second point which is certainly germane to her own late fiction. But if by 'infantilism' we mean the condition of being mentally or physically undeveloped, then her (self-) diagnosis relates generally to those characters of hers who are one way or another deprived of a sense or faculty (Queenie in 'Summer Night' is the most clear-cut instance) as well as those (cf. Miss Cuffe in 'Her Table Spread') who may be more genetically disadvantaged. Yet disadvantage is the reverse of Bowen's point. In the world of romance, the blind are seers and the crippled are saints. Somehow, their disability closes the gap between past and present, between knowledge and emotion.

This too reaches its apotheosis in her last novel, *Eva Trout* (1969), in which the voracious and 'unfinished' titular character is finished off by her own deaf and dumb child, armed with a gun.

For contrast, one might turn to the majesterial *Bowen's Court*, another wartime achievement but profoundly historical in its gradual approach to the author's self. At its close she describes her family as 'notably "unhistoric"'.[16] Given the care with which she compiled her chronicle, it is remarkable that Elizabeth Bowen never attempted a historical novel. Perhaps *The Heat of the Day* possesses qualities of a contemporary-historical novel, and in it the tension between a family disinclination to join in and a personal attention to epochal change finds some resolution. Yet the fiction as a whole is non-intellectual in its concerns even as it is resolutely so in its preoccupation with honesty in style. There are no election nights, general strikes, abdications or declarations of love and war. Of course, such omissions or grudging admissions are not to be measured on the surface of things. What Bowen symptomatically omitted was not just the race for Africa, but a profound historical movement of interpretation, of which Sigmund Freud and Max Weber may be taken as the symbolic leaders. In this she acts out an option taken in the mid and late Victorian decades on behalf of the academic and intellectual life of the United Kingdom as a whole, an option in favour of anthropology (consider the 1898 Torres Straits expedition, or James Frazer's *Golden Bough*, 1890–1915) and the study of so-called primitive cultures. The British option becomes all the more acute if it is considered in relation to contemporary developments on the continent – for example, Ferdinand Tonniess' elaborate distinction (in 1887) between *Gemeinschaft* and *Gesellschaft* as the basis for an examination of changing societies.

And yet she comes face to face with the consequences of such options taken. Bowen was not ignorant of pyschology or sociology, though she probably abhorred their terms; on the contrary she displayed very great insight into sexual matters and into the altering state of the society into which she had been born. But her desire was anti-intellectual while her talent was equally analytic. Like Freud, she appreciated the intensity with which minor details and unimportant objects could be infused with meaning. She knew that the self is less than it seems and is surrounded by powers of which it has little intimation. Like Weber, she experienced the dis-enchantment of the world, its loss of aura. Perhaps we can read her exposé of Robert

Kelway as a finally dismissive account of Weberian *charisma* in its last pathological stage, and this would be in keeping with her refusal to endorse a Yeatsian tradition of the past. She was the first and last figure in an alternative Irish 'tradition', postscript to something which was lesser than herself and yet essential to her.

Herein lies the unique contribution of *The Heat of the Day*, not to Irish or Anglo-Irish literature (for such classifications are presumptuous and coercive), but to literary history. Set largely in London and to a less extent in alliterative Mount Morris, it interrogates what 'a country' might be, without adding brochures of description disguised as chapters of fiction. Placing its central character between antagonists as differently accentuated as Kelway and Harrison, it challenges the very notion upon which their separateness continues to rely. The radical refusal to see 'a country' as one particular country states in other terms the radical refusal to see one character as not an other. Lucid with detail from the street and on the dressing-table, reliable as to rationing and blackout regulations, it turns away from realism into romance. This is no evasion of reality. It is the romance of irony which releases character from the iron cage of identification with the self.

Notes

1 Elizabeth Bowen *Collected Impressions* London: Longmans, 1950 p. 53.
2 Idem.
3 Ibid. p. 107.
4 Ibid. p. 51.
5 Elizabeth Bowen *The Collected Stories* London: Cape, 1980 p. 588.
6 Ibid. p. 585.
7 Ibid. p. 591.
8 Idem.
9 Ibid. p. 599.
10 Idem.
11 Elizabeth Bowen *The Mulberry Tree; Writings*. London: Virago, 1986 p. 31. This passage alone should be sufficient to dispel the conviction, announced recently by an Irish writer who also claimed to have read none of the novels, that Bowen was a British agent in Ireland.
12 Elizabeth Bowen *The Heat of the Day*. London: Cape, 1949 p. 187.
13 Edna Longley *Louis MacNeice: a Study* London: Faber, 1988 p. 25.
14 Dorothy van Ghent *The English Novel; Form and Function* XXXX p. 134.
15 *The Heat of the Day* p. 209.
16 Elizabeth Bowen *Bowen's Court* London: Longmans, 1942 p. 336.

EPILOGUE

The disinherited
of literary history

In 1934, the year in which Yeats received the Goethe Plakette from the Oberbürgermeister of Frankfurt, Elizabeth Bowen published a collection of short stories entitled *The Cat Jumps*.[1] The longest and best known of these tells of a bohemian house-party held in a country house near what is evidently Oxford. The young women go to the party, but are discommoded, even frightened by the proceedings. The owner of the house, negligently referred to as Lord Thingummy, is away; a dissolute young man, employed to catalogue the library, drinks too much; another takes one of the women on an aimless yet sinister tour of the upstairs rooms. The partygoers are bluntly declared by the narrative as enemies of society, each 'having been led to expect what he did not get.'[2] The story presents a familiar image of England in the inter-war years, adrift, pointless, teetering towards the brink which is more fully investigated in *The Death of the Heart* (1938) and (obliquely) in *The Heat of the Day* also. The story is entitled 'The Disinherited'.

There is no doubt that Nazi Germany courted Yeats, though the possiblity exists that a prime mover in the business was Charles Bewley, sometime Irish minister in the Berlin legation and ardent fascist. What is in doubt is the nature and extent of the poet's response. In an attempt to interrogate these disturbing implications I have raised a question which on first inspection may seem absurd – Did Yeats die in 1934? The evidence is not biological but psychological, or psycho-spiritual. A number of major crises in his life came to a head at the beginning of the decade – the death of Lady Gregory, his *altera mater*; the electoral triumph of Eamon De Valera (a former republican) and the rise of the Blue Shirt movement in reaction to De Valera's success; the Steinach operation to reinvigorate the poet's libido, and a growing number of sexual liaisons with younger women. Despite his veneration of country house living, Yeats would have found a niche among Bowen's disinherited. [3]

But by what means can one posit his *death*? Did not his liveliest poetry follow – the Crazy Jane poems, the late plays, copulation in the foam – on a floodtide of creativity lasting virtually to within hours of his actual death in January 1939? Basically, the death posited for 1934 is akin to the process described by Swedenborg to whom Yeats was once again turning. According to the Swede, after death the soul re-experienced the events of mortal life, now unable to repress knowledge of evil motivation and indeed increasingly exposed to the consequences of those events. Violence is no longer implicit but becomes active; greed and lust display themselves before the eyes of the soul. It is a revelation of the self in which no concealment, no delusion is possible. In more secular terms, we might call the Swedenborgian dreaming-back a *fantasia*, decasualised like Borrhomeo's nightmare immortality, locked conscious in the charnel house.

'The Disinherited' incorporates a subplot or retrospect, attached to a character called Prothero. He is chauffeur in a household where one of the two women lives as a semi-dependent, unconnected in the narrative with the low jinks at Lord Thingummy's. Some kind of sexual exploitation exists between him and the woman, but as she drives the car on the evening in question he is wholly and explicitly removed from the action. But Prothero is not all that he appears to be. To be precise, he may not be Prothero. Conversation between him and Davina bristles with suggestive bad jokes – 'You forget yourself,' she snaps. He answers 'I should like to.' Then, she demands to know 'Who are you?' and he merely replies 'My own man.' [4]

But alone in his room, Prothero is repeatedly composing a document, addressed evidently to a woman he has killed. A lengthy extract from one instalment of this private serial is inscribed more or less at the centre of Bowen's story. The introductory account of Prothero's nocturnal writing emphasises a kind of impersonal force at work: 'The pen rushed the hand along under some terrific compulsion ... Words sprang to their places with deadly complicity, knowing each other too well.' [5] Among the details offered in the inner narrative which follows is an account of a further murder, of a chauffeur called Prothero whose identity Prothero acquired in order to cover up the first murder – that is, of the woman to whom he is now writing. If this seems circular, worse is to come. Addressing his dead wife, he virtually quotes from the framing short-story, 'The Disinherited', in which he features as a minor character – 'whatever you did want you didn't seem to be getting.'[6] Prothero, or Not-Prothero, is an enemy of society also.

He is concerned with the moment of the woman's death, the wordless plea she made for her life. 'You tried with your eyes to say I should always see them but you were wrong. They are in a list, I can say them but I can't see them.' Prothero's mastery of language, his ability to control recollection of this traumatic moment by filing those eyes into a list of words, is also his mastery of guilt. To say is to repress seeing. Reflexively again, what are not seen are the organs of sight. Of course, he is not actually saying; he is writing. A fallacy in his defences may be detected in this distinction. In the last frenzied sentence of the main extract available to us, as readers of 'The Disinherited', Prothero declares that he will 'write loud' – I'll write so loud you will hear though you can't hear, *Anita* – '

The paragraph breaks off, with the articulation of the dead woman's name. Then, we read

> The pen charged in his hand. Dragging his hand down to the foot of the paper, in staggering characters it wrote – 'Anita, I love you Anita, Anita, *where are you? I didn't mean that, that was not me, I didn't, I can't bear you away. I see your eyes on my pillow, I can't lie alone, I cannot get through the night, come back, where are you, I won't hurt you, come back, come back, come back* –[7]

The dissolution of character, synchronised to the autonomous energy of language itself, has scarcely been more succintly written. Prothero may be mad, as Davina casually remarks. The murders may be figments of his imagination, but they are also figments of Bowen's. The surreal isolation of 'your eyes on my pillow' recalls the disembodied hand in Le Fanu's *House by the Church-yard*, but here it is linguistically contextualised among near phrases like 'hand to mouth' and 'I cannot lie' which haunt the demented narrative. A staggering character, Prothero writes staggering characters. The contamination which leaks across from character to context is brought to a climax when 'Prothero dropped the pen as though it were burning'. This is followed promptly by his burning the pages he has written in a stove. 'So his nights succeeded each other.'[8]

The difference between Bowen's imagination and Prothero's lies in the extent to which she is in control. Her fiction often enacts or

describes repression but it does so on the basis of conscious decisions. One knows what it is that is being repressed. Certain characters are considered special in that they lack a sense or faculty either
actually or metaphorically; for the most part such characters are
fortunate in that their condition of deprivation amounts to a renun-
ciation which in turn brings its own blessing. With Queenie Cavey –
the full name has its tone of playful release – 'the act of looking was
always reflective and slow', the two adjectives offering (first) a positive and complex feature, then (seemingly) a lesser and simpler
feature which is to be appreciated, however, at a higher level. For, as
she prepares for bed after her unexpected and ironical re-encounter
with emotion of the past, she is 'contemplative, wishless, almost
without an "I"'. [9] In the late work, this feature veers towards an
interest in what are virtually infantile states. But the war years
generated particular conditions in which the paradox of Queenie's
negative capabilities could be assessed and evaluated.

The ironic fantasia in 'The Disinherited' ultimately climaxes in an
excess of vision, a seeing of eyes on the pillow. Prothero, who
cannot escape from the identity he has purloined from the dead
chauffeur, cannot escape from the dead either. Fantasy, or the more
structured fantasia, does not constitute an evasion of reality, but a
placing of it, an establishment of primary relations. Thus, in *The
Heat of the Day*, Ireland is no bolt-hole for the enlisted Roderick; on
the contrary it is at Mount Morris that his mother hears news of
Montgomery's breakthrough and that Ireland has officially opted
out from the war. Ireland, if you will, is fantasia to England's reality;
but the proposition only holds as truly as its converse. In her London flat, Roderick calls the sofa a boat – 'The reality of the fancy was
better than the unreality of the room.' This is more than domestic
play, for the Mount Morris inheritance is said to stimulate feelings
that 'did not amount to desires, being without object; nor to halluci-
nations, for they neither deceived him nor set up tension'. [10] Thus
Kelway may be 'the Harrison', although that fantasia reverts to the
horrors of 'The Disinherited'.

Or, to borrow terms more appropriate to Le Fanu than the
subtler Bowen, the gluttonous immediacy of 'Prothero's' nocturnal
writing releases an equally insatiable past. In 'The Happy Autumn
Fields', the narrative is divided symmetrically (and almost serenely)
between the wartime present in London and a (probably Irish)
Victorian pastoral world: each of these settings intrudes into the

other. A Victorian girl has a visionary anticipation of some cataclysm lying ahead; a woman in a bomb-damaged room dreams from recollected photographs back to such a past. These negotiations between past and present also structure literary history itself. The contrast between Bowen and Yeats is peculiarly sharp in this regard.

Yet Le Fanu mediates between them. *The Cock and Anchor* had given Jonathan Swift his first outing as fictional character. Less comfortably, 'The Watcher' exposed the half-finished streets of late Georgian Dublin as a place of retribution. It seems therefore a pleasing symmetry that the novelist's name was at one point intended to feature in *The Words Upon the Window-pane*, Yeats's play about Swift. After all, this is set in a dilapidated house worthy of Le Fanu. But Swift does not appear in the play, he is detained among the dead, structurally related to the living characters by a Swedenborgian system in part derived from *Uncle Silas* and *In a Glass Darkly*.[11] After the early drafts, the Le Fanu name disappears from the dramatis personae. This repression of the massive reality which was Victorian Ireland is consequent on Yeats's indulgence of the Protestant Ascendancy as a quasi-aristocratic eighteenth-century cultural élite, for the elimination of Le Fanu effects the repression of that Victorian middle class from which Yeats himself came. Bowen, in contrast, constantly presses towards the admission (in both the intellectual and textual senses) of the embarrassing, difficult or wounding past. If on the haunted streets of Le Fanu's 'The Watcher', Yeats sought to built a great gazebo, an already ancient literary pedigree, it is fitting that he should both cite and suppress the papers of Martin Hesselius. Plagiarised at last, Sheridan Le Fanu could find peace as well as his modicum of literary immortality.

Plagiarism, when you come to think of it, was exactly the right literary mode for such a curiously structured social constituency as Le Fanu's, for it can pose as imitation and deference while carrying out acts of cheeky appropriation. Le Fanu's particular practice of the mode, involving both self-plagiarism and textually introvert tales of plagiarism, also acknowledged the non-social, the disconnected aspect of the culture he was tentatively encoding. It is a charge writers dread of course, yet it may lie at the heart of every inaugural act of writing: Prothero is only an extreme example of the case in which personal origination is overwhelmed by scribal forces.[12]

In this connection, the central paradox of *A Lost Name* takes on a representative force. The absence of the serial figure Marston, in a novel which trumpets the absence of a name in its own name, augments his status as outcast-and-delegate, as scapegoat, within a society sometimes located fictionally in Ireland, sometimes in Wales, sometimes in England. He is the representative Anglo-Irish Protestant Ascendant, exactly in so far as he is absent, incomplete, replicated and unpositioned. Ascendancy reproduces in social terms an evangelical message which also underpins much of what is – significantly – named the literary *revival*. One could return to the text from the Epistle to the Hebrews cited earlier: 'And this word … signifies the removing those things that are shaken, as of things that are made, that those which cannot be shaken may remain.'

The urge to accelerate the elimination of instability (whether social, intellectual or psychological) is a paradoxical one. On the one hand, the end in view is fixity, immutability, even (as an absolute end) immortality. On the other, the means necessarily involves vertiginous change. Ascendancy aims to eclipse history, yet the term itself implies a process of rising and falling eminence. It suggests exclusivity, yet it depends on the mongrel elements of an emergent ethnicity. It is these contradictions which the spasmodic characters of Le Fanu's stories and novels so vividly indicate. For to advance a case for Le Fanu's fiction as serialism is to run the risk of appearing to exaggerate it. In the history of early-twentieth-century music, serialism is a rigorously deliberate procedure, operating within mathematical permutations of exactly calculable values. Little of this applies to the work under examination, even if one still maintains that Le Fanu's characters anticipate much of the psychic fluidity explored in the modernist movement, Schoenberg included.

At all stages of such grand comparisons, one should seek to identify the mediating elements. Le Fanu has already served a purpose in comparing Bowen and Yeats. Relating Le Fanu to Bowen, the fiction of George Moore might reward further study. In the figure of Harding, who moves from novel to novel as an impotent mentor, advising the active characters and observing the general folly, Moore has perhaps redeemed the criminal aspect of Le Fanu's arch serial figure, and re-oriented it towards the Baudelairean *flâneurs* from whose ranks Le Fanu's Marston was an impetuous defector. In retrospect, those particularly lurid stories for which a Lévi-Straussean scheme was devised now appear by their serial exclusion of here this, and there that, to have a recurring element which can be seen to highlight and postpone the final assault on character as such. The catatonic hyper-consciousness of Beckett in 'The Room in the Dragon Volant' and of Borrhomeo, in which continuity of identity is parodied by a ghastly extension, is balanced by the syphoning away of energy and resistance to the other in 'Carmilla'. Whether within a single text, or within a collective volume, or within the larger multi-authored and (to a degree) unauthored body of work which becomes tradition, these balances and acts of mediation are at least as crucial as the notion of intimate and exclusive identity.

Such themes have a certain air of fashion about them at the end of the twentieth century. It is tempting to associate the pervasive patterns observed in Le Fanu with – say – the regular occurrence of certain kinds of accident in the novels of Iris Murdoch, or with the self-citing intertextuality of Thomas Kinsella's poetry. The support of a tradition would be reassuring when one is dealing with work of such uneven quality and unpredictable behaviour. In this might lie also a way of linking the several isolated 'here is hell' texts mentioned in an earlier chapter to a definition of Anglo-Irish literature sufficiently broad to accommodate *Under the Net* and *A Technical Supplement*. Such a definition might manage to illuminate the problematic colonial aspects of nineteenth-century Anglo-Irish relations and, simultaneously, to address the persistent suspicion that something fundamentally unreal characterises Irish experience. However, it is not so easy to accommodate such a tradition with its emphasis on succession and its contempt for the disinherited. In Le Fanu's day 'Anglo-Irish' did not name a specific ethnic group; it was only gradually coming to identify an area of tense social change emerging between – so to speak – the Establishment and the people. Tradition, which seeks to establish rules of exclusivity, is none the less dependent on a definition of its own ambit – the Anglo-Irish – which is patently conglomerate.

If too much has been said about tradition and ascendancy, perhaps the fault lies in a neglect of the Protestant component in these powerful formulations. Within Le Fanu's lifetime, drastic alterations in Irish demographic patterns were taking place. In consequence of these larger movements, a kind of internal migration commenced, sometimes taking the form of religious separatism, sometimes by a merger of local custom and lore with evangelical fervour. The latter attitude characterised many in the generation of O'Grady, Hyde and Yeats; Synge's background was uncompromisingly predicated on the former. The process did not simply involve changes of allegiance or orientation; the very basis of individual identity was altered. As if in response to the injunction that Christians should be in but not *of* the world, there emerged an insistent but uncommitted fraction of Irish society which, while appearing dog-in-the-manger and reactionary, in practice anticipated psychic dislocations thought characteristic of the modernist period. This was a significant fraction among the gradually coalescing Anglo-Irish. Le Fanu was its laureate, unsalaried. If he can still be called a novelist of the Protestant Ascendancy, he holds that title not by descent but by virtue of a prophetic element in his presentation of the house-and-master.

Yeats's account of his great contemporaries has little to say about religious belief, yet repeatedly casts them as figures approaching the Last Judgement. The case of Synge has already been noted. Writing of Douglas Hyde, he encapsulated the life-and-death balance of the writer's condition:

> He had given up verse writing because it affected his lungs or his heart. Lady Gregory kept watch, to draw him from his table after so many hours; the gamekeeper had the boat and the guns ready; there were ducks upon the lake. He wrote in joy and at great speed because emotion brought the appropriate word. Nothing in that language of his was abstract, nothing worn-out; he need not, as must the writer of some language exhausted by modern civilization, reject word after word, cadence after cadence; he had escaped our perpetual, painful purification.[13]

This is admiring, this enacts the transfer of bodily exhaustion into the language over which the writer has preferred another – 'that dying chose the living world for text.' Even when Yeats is not entirely approving, a similar notion of the perpetualness of the artist's repose is invoked. Shaw is famously compared to a sewing machine 'that clicked and shone ... but the incredible thing was that the machine smiled, smiled perpetually'. And again, within a few pages:

> Shaw, as I understand him, has no true quarrel with his time, its moon and his almost exactly coincide. He is quite content to exchange Narcissus and his Pool for the signal-box at a railway junction, where goods and travellers pass perpetually upon their logical glittering road.[14]

The perilous moment of Hyde's creative joy, and the mechanical continuum of Shaw's world, require the same word – perpetual – as the artist's counterpoint. Its implications are most clearly given in the meditation on Synge's death, for his life had been a perpetual Last Day, a perpetual trumpeting and coming up for the Last Judgement. This perpetuality, despite its serial character, also implicates an absolute termination. Recalling his student days, Yeats recalls specifically an unhappy village genius who painted on sheets and nailed his *Last Judgement* to the wall of his bedroom. Recording Wilde's tribute to Pater's *Renaissance* – 'it is the very flower of decadence: the last trumpet should have sounded the moment it was written' – Yeats takes the opportunity again to link artistic achievement with terminality. Similarly in politics: 'Nobody was the better or worse for Lord Salisbury's new Commission. Protestant Ireland could not have done otherwise; it lacked hereditary passion. Parnell, its last great leader ...'[15]

But, as we have seen, Parnell is never a last leader. He is constantly recycled as a demonic figure, more efficacious in the 1930s than fifty years earlier. The demonic 'hero' of Thomas Mann's *Doktor Faustus* remarks wittily before his very terrible end, 'The time we last, a little shorter, a little longer, we call immortality.'[16] One has some responsibility to the broader context of Yeats's authoritarianism, and Mann had witnessed the devillish consequences of gothic politics. The comparative approach illuminates much that admirers of the poet wish to have treated as merely speculative, without consequence. But there are revealing comparisons closer to home also. Yeats's strong preference for the Few over the Many should be compared with Bowen's tacit recommendation that we may grow, or at least learn, by a reduction of our faculties, by perhaps acknowledging that our identity is not one of 'those things which cannot be shaken'. Not arrogance but humility informs her underlying beliefs. Assessing *The Demon Lover*, she committed a sentence which commits a venial sin lengthily commented upon in *The Heat of the Day*: 'though I criticize these stories now, afterwards, intellectually, I cannot criticize their content. They are the particular. But through the particular, in wartime, I felt the high-voltage current of the general pass.'[17]

The positioning of commas, as in Cousin Francie's will, is crucial. Does 'intellectually' lean backwards or forwards? The religious aspect – it would be too much to say religious *nature* – of her work has already been noted. This might be considered locally as a Protestant aspect, especially if a remark of André Gide's be admissible: 'I have a horror of falsehood ... That is perhaps just where my Protestantism lurks.'[18]

It would be scandalous to end on this sectarian note, scandalous in my own terms because I have striven to eliminate from discussion of contemporary Irish culture a terminology which is husk only. Yet it may serve a purpose or two. If the generation of Bowen, Beckett and MacNeice can be described as post-Protestant in that their thought is still coloured and shaped by what is no longer actively believed, then one must emphasise that their great predecessor had never been affected by the same pressure. If – and this is a large if, especially in contemporary Irish debate – there is a close link between ethical acuity and Protestantism then Yeats's non-Protestantism is proven, for again and again a romantic (or heroic–cynical) sovereignty of the imagination is declared over and above other obligations or duties. This is most painfully evident in the 1930s, but has been argued by James Logenbach (and in terms of politics) for a much earlier phase of Yeats's life. Keeping to the 1930s, one finds then that Yeats's gothic politics merge with his enunciation of a distinctly un-Protestant Protestant Ascendancy. Perhaps Bowen discreetly points to the shallowness of this affectation when, in *Bowen's Court*, she finally adopts the terminology of Protestant Ascendancy long after recounting her family's fortunes during the period of its alleged hegemony. Writing of the very late nineteenth century, she summarises her father's resolution: 'The Ascendancy, if it were to remain an ascendancy, must now take its stand on morals and discipline.'[19] It is always too late for profligate élites to take such a stand, not least when they come into existence – like Le Fanu's anti-heroes – by a kind of self-invention in their proflicacy.

To end on such local recriminations would also be scandalous, this time in terms of the Weetabix Theorists and their appetite for homogenised fibre. Fortunately, it is possible to generalise on the procedures of literary history itself as attempted in the preceding pages. Jerome McGann had warned that 'if one is interested in *critical* knowledge, one has to be wary of this impulse to generate continuities – either in the texts we produce or in the social structures which those texts ... replicate'.[20] Now the argument that Le Fanu mediates between Yeats and Bowen with the effect of disclosing the politics she opposes to Yeats's cannot be accused of inattention in this regard. Literary history can develop methods and forms which are not excessively narrative, and do this without lapsing back into allusion hunting, image dissection, and passive contemplation. Our concentration on biblical quotation here and painterly metaphor there may suggest models for other inquiries. But while the distinction between chronicle and history should be pressed home methodologically, there remains a need to examine continuity. Just as a dialectical relationship between 'England' and 'Ireland' in Bowen's novel is made possible by consideration of altered setting in Le Fanu's fiction, so past and present require mediation. In a culture still riven by nationalist isolationism and the self-congratulation of what is now termed Unionism, a need persists to show that the extreme and hardly imaginable horrors of the century – the ovens of some great ogre – did not occur in a fantastical elsewhere. There is no document of civilisation, not even an Anglo-Irish one, which is not also a document of barbarism.[21]

Notes

1 For this obscure detail, further obscured by more recent biographers, see Joseph Hone *W. B. Yeats 1865–1939* (2nd ed.) London: Macmillan, 1962 p. 403 note 1.

2 Elizabeth Bowen *Collected Stories* London: Cape, 1980 p. 388.

3 Lecture to the Yeats Summer School, August 1992, unpublished.

4 *Collected Stories* pp. 406–7.

5 Ibid. p. 392.

6 Idem.

7 Ibid. p. 397.

8 Ibid. p. 398.

9 Ibid. p. 607.

10 Bowen *The Heat of the Day* London: Cape, 1949 pp. 51, 48.

11 See W. J. Mc Cormack *Ascendancy and Tradition in Anglo-Irish Literary History from 1789 to 1939* Oxford: Clarendon Press, 1985 pp. 364–6.

12 Back in the 1840s Charles Lever had been roundly condemned by Charles Gavan Duffy in the pages of *The Nation*, and the extent of his plagiarism in the early picaresque novels demonstrated in parallel columns of evidence. The effect was to drive the novelist out of Ireland and into – eventually – a different kind of fiction where (arguably) humour was replaced by solemn admissions of national self-righteousness. The historian R. R. Madden made something of a special study of plagiarism, acknowledging a kind of non-guilty but embarrassed inevitability in many instances. He appears to have contributed the article on the topic which appeared in *The Dublin University Magazine* towards the end of Le Fanu's editorship.

13 W. B. Yeats *Autobiographies* London: Macmillan, 1955 pp. 439–40. It is important to recall that Hyde outlived both Yeats and Gregory, despite the obituarist

tone of this passage.

14 Ibid. p. 294.
15 Ibid. p. 419.
16 Thomas Mann *Doctor Faustus; the Life of the German Composer Adrian Leverkühn as Told by a Friend* (trans. H. T. Lowe-Porter) Harmondsworth: Penguin, 1968 p. 437.
17 Bowen *Collected Impressions* London: Longmans, 1950 p. 000.
18 André Gide entry for 21 December 1923 *Journals* vol. 2 p. 339.
19 Elizabeth Bowen *Bowen's Court* London: Longmans, 1942 p. 295.
20 Jerome McGann *Social Values and Poetic Acts; the Historical Judgment of Literary Work* Cambridge, Mass.: Harvard University Press, 1988 pp. 132–3.
21 See Walter Benjamin 'Theses on History' in *Illuminations* London: Cape, 1970 p. 258.

INDEX

Index

Index

Index

Index

Index

Index

Index